BYRON: THE ITALIAN LITERARY INFLUENCE

Byron
The Italian Literary Influence

Peter Vassallo

MACMILLAN PRESS
LONDON

First published 1984 by
THE MACMILLAN PRESS LTD
London and Basingstoke
Companies and representatives
throughout the world

ISBN 0 333 33993 2

Typeset by Wessex Typesetters Ltd,
Frome, Somerset

Printed in Hong Kong

To my Father and Mother
and to Madeleine

Contents

Acknowledgements

My thanks are due to the following: the staffs of the English Faculty Library, the Taylorian Institute, the British Library, the Bodleian Library, the Nottingham Public Library and the Keats–Shelley Memorial House in Rome. In particular I wish to thank Mrs Mary Clapinson of the Bodleian Library for kindly allowing me to make use of her draft Catalogue of the Noel, Byron and Lovelace papers deposited there. I also have to thank Signora dottoressa Volpe of the Biblioteca Alessandrina in the University of Rome for kindly supplying me with photocopy material, and Mrs Helen Dunlap of the Humanities Research Center at the University of Texas. I am also indebted to Mr John Murray for his kind permission to consult material in the Murray Archives.

I should like to record my sincere gratitude to my former supervisor, Mr John Buxton of New College, for his kind guidance and for his valuable comments.

My thanks are also due to the Association of Commonwealth Universities for granting me an Academic Staff Fellowship in order to undertake advanced research at Oxford, and to the Marquis Scicluna Trust Fund for a Senior Research Fellowship to consult valuable material in various libraries in Italy. I am indebted to the late Professor Richard Beck, formerly Head of the English Department at the Royal University of Malta, for his constant support and for providing me with the opportunity of a sabbatical at Oxford.

For their permission to incorporate previously published material I should like to thank Professor Erwin Sturzl and Dr James Hogg, editors of *Salzburg Studies in English and American Literature*.

I am also indebted to Dr Stephen Gill of Lincoln College for his interest and encouragement and to the Very Rev. Cassian Reel, Warden of Greyfriars, Oxford, for his advice and support. My thanks are due to Ms Claire Samut for the patience and care with which she prepared the typescript and to my wife for her constant advice and encouragement.

P.V.

Preface

The biographical aspect of Byron's life in Italy has been extensively surveyed by a number of eminent Byron scholars, notably by Doris Langley Moore, Iris Origo and Leslie Marchand. On the literary side, however, there has been no extended treatment of the Italian influence since Claude Fuess's[1] competent but inadequate dissertation written more than fifty years ago. C. P. Brand's[2] fine survey of the Italianate fashion in early nineteenth-century England is too general in its scope to afford a detailed analysis of the Italian literary influence on Byron's poetry. R. D. Waller's[3] introduction to his edition of *The Monks and the Giants*, illuminating though it is on the nature of Italian burlesque poetry, rather surprisingly fails to assess Byron's indebtedness to Casti. More recent critical commentary on Byron's stylistic development has largely ignored the possibility of cross-cultural literary influences on his poetry. Indeed, most studies of Byron's poetical development over the past decade have tended to deal with the poetry as if it existed in a literary vacuum or as an appendage to the English burlesque tradition. Thus, for example, George Ridenour's[4] discussion of the mode of *Don Juan* treats the style of Byron's major work as the result of a process developed *pari passu* with his mature outlook on life, quite independently of his reading. Jerome McGann's[5] analysis of *Don Juan*, on the other hand, traces the style of Byron's epic to his constantly shifting stance, from the good-natured jesting of Horace to the high style of Juvenal, all but disregarding Byron's Italian models. Another recent study by A. B. England[6] argues that Byron's satirical style owes much to the English burlesque tradition of Butler and Swift and virtually ignores the possibility of the poet's debt to the Italian burlesque writers. In fact Robert Ogle's[7] doctoral dissertation on Byron's debt to the Bernesque satire is the only study of the poet's Italian models to appear recently, but it remains too inconclusive to be of any real value to the Byron scholar.

The question of literary influence is a difficult one, particularly for the scholar who seeks to establish a literary relationship between one poet and another. A literary affinity between authors may be due to a variety of factors which tend to complicate the issue. It may, for instance, be the result of a similarity in temperament and disposition, or the affinity in their works may have been induced by a common theme or it may even be due, as Shelley observed, to 'the endowment of the age in which they live'. Byron, in this respect, presents an especially hard problem. It is obvious from his letters and journals that he read widely, if not deeply, in the Italian authors who most appealed to him. His letters to Teresa Guiccioli show a good command of Italian and he himself expressed the desire to write his greatest work in that language. He took great pains over a verse translation of an excerpt from Dante's *Inferno* and another of the first Canto of Pulci's *Morgante*. Literary influence, as far as Byron was concerned, sometimes took the form of a direct borrowing of a few lines which caught his fancy, but more often it was the gradual process of an assimilation of a style which particularly appealed to him. In moments when inspiration seemed to flag, Byron, as Moore shrewdly observed, tended to look for stimulation in the authors he happened to be reading at the time. He had a remarkably retentive memory, as Lady Blessington noted, and he was quick to appropriate what he had read. This probably accounts for his eclectic borrowing from his favourite authors. Byron also wrote much of his later poetry with Murray's literary coterie in mind and he expected the Italian scholars Merivale and Rose to recognise the literary allusions he deliberately interspersed among his verses.

The aim of this study is to discover the extent of Byron's reading in Italian literature and *belles-lettres* and to illustrate how his reading helped to shape his poetry. This book is not so much an exercise in literary detection as an attempt to show the poet in dialogue with his sources, the divergencies being often as illuminating as the poet's actual imitation.

The study concentrates largely but not exclusively on Byron's debt to Casti and Pulci for the satirical mode of *Beppo*, *Don Juan* and *The Vision of Judgement*. It is hoped that this book will afford fresh insights into the nature of Byron's significant debt to the Italian authors he read and enjoyed.

1 Byron's Early Italian Interest

Byron was able to read Italian long before he set foot in Italy. By the time he was eighteen he had dipped into Ariosto's *Orlando Furioso* and had some knowledge of Dante's *Inferno* and felt confident enough to display his little learning in a humorous letter to John Pigot expressing his gratitude for his 'kind connivance' at rescuing him from 'Mrs Byron Furiosa' in one of her tantrums:

> Oh! for the pen of Ariosto to rehearse in *Epic* the *scolding* of that *momentous Eve*, or rather let me invoke the Shade of Dante to inspire me, for none but the author of the 'Inferno' could properly preside over such an attempt.[1]

Towards the end of 1813 Byron was thinking in terms of settling in Italy or the East and he hoped thereby to drink 'deep of the languages and literature of both'.[2] His first acquaintance with the Italian language, interestingly enough, seems to have taken place at a Capuchin monastery during his sojourn in Athens where he accidentally came across a work in thirty volumes on the history of Italy in old and not 'very choice Italian'[3] which he read through with the help of a Capuchin friar. Byron subsequently developed an abiding interest in Italian history and literature – an interest which, as we shall see, was to have an appreciable influence on the manner and method of composition. Byron's ability to read the Italian authors was achieved with considerable effort and application on his part. The Catalogue[4] of his books for auction in 1816 indicated that he had acquired quite a few dictionaries and grammars of the Italian language in order to assist him in his self-imposed task. These included Baretti's *Italian Dictionary* (the 1813 edition), Veneroni's *Italian Grammar* (1806), Graglia's *Guide to Italian* (1803) and Zotti's *Vocabolario Italiano* (1801) in four volumes. The path to the Italian pastures was arduous but not without its rewards. His Italian reading continued to flourish even though he was fully engrossed in his amatory affairs. He scoffed at James Wedderburn Webster's ignorance of and insensitivity to the great Italian authors. To Lady Melbourne, his confidante, he remarked facetiously:

> W[ebster] grows rather intolerable too – he is out of humour with my *Italian* books – (Dante & Alfieri & Some others as harmless as ever wrote) and requests that sa femme may not see them – because forsooth it is a language which doth infinite damage!![5]

In a serious vein, a month later, he recorded in his journal that Ariosto, Dante and Tasso were among the great authors he had read. His familiarity with the language enabled him to carry on a flirtation with an Italian Opera singer at Cheltenham. 'I always strive to repair ye inroads want of practice make in my memory of that dearest of all languages'[6] – he jokingly confessed to Lady Melbourne. Very probably he discussed the Italian authors with Annabella Milbanke who at the time had also developed an interest in Italian literature, especially Ariosto.[7] In his letter of 25 August 1814 he sought to guide Annabella's reading on the subject and enthusiastically recommended Sismondi's *De la littérature du Midi de l'Europe* as the best available introduction to the Italian authors.[8] An entry in his journal for 1813 is of particular interest because it shows the poet's first attempt to write a few exclamatory verses in Italian.[9]

Byron's reading of the Italian authors was at this time unsystematic and desultory. He read Petrarch, excerpts from Machiavelli and Bandello 'by starts'. The sonnets of Petrarch stimulated him to imitation and emulation but the result was none too felicitous, as he himself felt obliged to admit:

> Redde some Italian and wrote two sonnets . . . I never wrote but one sonnet before, and that was not in earnest, and many years ago, as an exercise – and I will never write another. They are the most puling, petrifying stupidly platonic compositions. I detest the Petrarch so much that I would not have been the man, even to have obtained his Laura, which the metaphysical whining dotard never could.[10]

The sonnets in question were those entitled 'To Genevra' and were first published in the second edition of *The Corsair*. Charles Du Bos ascribed the sonnet to 'the Lady Frances Cycle' maintaining that they were written with Lady Frances Wedderburn Webster in mind. It is very likely, however, that the sonnets, as their title implies, were written to express Byron's sublimated feelings for Augusta at a time when his relationship with his half-sister had become intimate. The poems were actually composed on 17 and 18 December 1813 during which time Byron came to realise that:

> ... no woman was so comforting and satisfying to his self-esteem as Augusta, so yielding to his every wish, so sensuous and undemanding, and so motherly and protective at the same time.[11]

The actual title of the sonnets was a clear hint to the public at large that Augusta was the subject of these platonic compositions. Genevra, in Ariosto's *Orlando Furioso* was the daughter of the King of Scotland and beloved sister of the dashing Prince Zerbino with whom Byron felt a strong affinity. Those members of the reading public who were acquainted with the *Furioso* would be reasonably expected to take the hint. Byron's dissatisfaction with the sonnets presumably stemmed from his realisation that the complexity of his feelings for Augusta could not be convincingly expressed in an outmoded literary form.

Machiavelli's *Storie Fiorentine* and Bandello's *Novelle* helped to foster an interest in the colourful historical personages of the turbulent Renaissance. 'I am mightily taken with Braccio di Montone, Giovanni Galeazzo and Eccelino. But the last is *not* Bracciaferro (of the same name), Count of Ravenna, whose history I want to trace', he recorded in his journal.[12] Impressed by Henry Fuseli's painting of Ezzelin, he wrote to the artist enquiring after the subject of the painting:

> I have been looking in vain. Mr. Fuseli, for some months, in the poets and historians of Italy for the subject of your picture of Ezzelin – pray where is it to be found?[13]

This concern with literary authenticity and the urge to trace the subject to the ascertainable facts are characteristic of Byron's cast of mind. The character of Conrad in *The Corsair* was partly based on Sismondi's account of Ezzelin in his history of the Italian republics as Byron himself acknowledged in a note to the poem.[14]

Bandello's *Novelle* attracted the poet mainly because of their literary recasting of well-known historical anecdotes. He requested Murray to secure for him at an auction sale an Italian edition in nine volumes of Bandello's works. Indeed, Bandello was one of his main sources for his *Parisina* in which he sympathetically treated the tragedy of the hapless Parisina Malatesta, second wife of Niccolo d'Este, fated to fall in love with her stepson Hugo. Gibbon had adumbrated the tragic event in his *Antiquities of the House of Brunswick*[15] but in Bandello's account Byron found a fuller treatment of the tragedy in all its psychological complexity,[16] which corroborated and sometimes contradicted the facts in his other source – Antonio Frizzi's *Memorie per la Storia di Ferrara*. The moral ambivalence of Bandello's version which was the result of the Italian author's attempt to exculpate Parisina's love while at the same time condemning her crime ('la commessa scelleraggine'),[17] must have had a particular appeal to Byron who was at the time both fascinated and repelled by his incestuous relationship with Augusta. Indeed, *Parisina* was the outcome of Byron's inward convulsions which perforce had to end in rhyme.[18] Bandello's version, then, must have afforded the poet interesting fresh insights into the delicate theme of incest, thus enabling him to re-enact his own predicament in terms of the plight of Hugo and Parisina. In Frizzi's account of the story of the House of Este which was originally appended to Byron's poem, the Marquis Niccolo is portrayed as the outraged father and husband who is relentless in his obsession with strict justice while Parisina is the victim of her inordinate passion. Bandello's version, however, focuses on the sad plight of Parisina and she is presented in a more favourable light as the tragic victim of deception and adverse circumstance. Her love for the young Hugo (they are both of the same age) is far from wanton and she is given adequate psychological motivation. She claims that she has been neglected by her husband who was, in Bandello's words, 'si diede di si fatta maniera dietro a le femine che in Ferrara e per il contado non ci è cantone ove egli non abbia alcun figliuolo bastardo'.[19] Moreover, she laments the fact that she is the victim of a cruel deception in that although she had been promised in marriage to the handsome Hugo, her father and the Marquis had determined otherwise:

> Avesse pur voluto Iddio che di me quello fosse avvenuto che io già sperai, imperció che quando primieramente il signor mio padre mi ragionó di maritarmi in Ferrara, egli mi disse ch'io dovevo sposarmi con voi e non con vostro padre; ne so io come poi il fatto si mutasse. Che Dio perdoni a chi di cotal baratto fu cagione![20]

> (If only God had wished that what I hoped for might happen, the reason being that when his Lordship my father persuaded me to marry in Ferrara, he told me that I was to marry you and not your father; and I do not really know how things changed. May God forgive the person responsible for that deal!)

In Byron's *Parisina* the focus has been shifted from Parisina's pathetic complaint to Hugo's dignified stance in the presence of his irate father but the reasons behind Hugo's self-justification remain basically the same as those given by Parisina in the Bandello version. Hugo, too, complains that the Marquis his father had selfishly neglected his first wife ('thou work'dst my mother's ill') and deprived him of the woman he loved ('And made thy own my destined bride').[21] Following Bandello, Byron heightens the dramatic import of his story by attributing the tragedy which befalls the Este family to a kind of Nemesis which afflicts the Marquis for his past wrongs.

> 'Tis true that I have done the wrong –
> But wrong for wrong; – this, – deem'd thy bride,
> The other victim of thy pride, –
> Thou know'st for me was destined long;
> Thou saw'st, and coveted'st her charms
>
> (xiii, 252–6)

The conclusion of *Parisina* with its 'controlled pathos' shows a striking affinity with Bandello's treatment of the tragic end of Parisina and her lover. Despite his defiant stand, Hugo is contrite and resigned in the end, with the poet uncharacteristically preserving the Christian 'moralitas' of timely repentance:

As his last confession pouring
To the monk, his doom deploring
In penitential holiness.
He bends to hear his accents bless
With absolution such as may
Wipe our mortal stains away.

(xvi, 413–18)

In Bandello's novella, Hugo spends his last day in the company of two friars:

Il contrito giovane perseverò tre continovi giorni in compagnia dei due frati, sempre di bene in meglio disponendosi a la vicina morte e ragionando di cose sacre.[22]

(The repentent youth remained three whole days in the company of the two friars, gradually reconciling himself to his approaching death, and discussing sacred matters.)

Parisina, however, remains unrepentant and inconsolable. Regardless of her own fate she cannot be reconciled to the death of her lover:

nulla o poco de la sua morte incresceva ma che di quella del Conte Ugo non poteva aver pazienza.[23]

(She was hardly concerned about her impending death, but she could not resign herself to that of Count Hugo.)

In frenzied despair she calls the name of Hugo:

Ella altro giorno e notte mai non faceva che chiamar il suo Ugo, di modo che per tre continovi giorni che in pregione dimorò sempre nomando il Conte Ugo se ne stette.[24]

(Day and night she called her Hugo, so that throughout the three days she spent in prison she repeatedly called the name of Count Hugo.)

Byron's Parisina behaves in a similar manner. She is silent throughout and her only concern is for Hugo ('Less for her own despair than him'). Her inexpressible anguish has its outlet in a demented shriek of despair. It is evident from what has been said above that Byron had Bandello's novella in mind when he composed *Parisina* during his honeymoon at Halnaby in the autumn of 1815 and he skilfully remoulded the source to his own desire by concentrating largely on the dignified bearing of Parisina and Hugo.

Parisina also owes something to Scott's *Marmion*. As Byron reluctantly acknowledged to Murray, he might have borrowed inadvertently from Scott's poem and he accordingly sent for a copy of the original for, as he admitted, 'it comes upon me not very comfortably'.[25] The passage in question was that which described Constance de Beverley's fearless appearance before the Conclave in Canto II of *Marmion* in which the judges are struck by her noble and spirited defence.[26] Although there are no direct verbal echoes, Byron's treatment of the same scene is strikingly similar and it would seem to justify Byron's uncomfortable feeling. It is also possible to suggest, however, that both Byron and Scott may have been influenced by a common source. It is indeed highly probable that they were both acquainted with Boccaccio's celebrated account of Ghismunda's dignified stand on behalf of her lover Guiscardo when she was arraigned before her stern father Tancredi. Here is Boccaccio's account of the scene:

> Per che, non come dolente femina o ripresa del suo fallo, ma come noncurante e valorosa, con asciutto viso e aperto e da niuna parte turbato, così al padre disse: 'Tancredi, nè a negare nè a pregare son disposta, per ciò che nè l'un mi varebbe nè l'altra voglio che mi vaglia; e oltre a ciò in niuno atto intendo di rendermi benivola la tua mansuetudine e 'l tuo amore: ma, il ver confessando, prima con ver ragioni difender la fama mia e poi con fatti fortissimamente seguire la grandezza dello animo mio. Egli è vero che io ho amato e amo Guiscardo, e quanto io viverò, che sarà poco, l'amerò, e se appresso la morte s'ama, non mi rimarrò d'amarlo . . .'[27]

> (Therefore, she thus spoke to her father, not as a repentant woman conscious of her wrongdoing, but regardless and brave, by no means perturbed: 'Tancredi, I am not disposed to deny or beg, since the first would not help my case and the second I am disinclined to do, besides in no way do I wish to rely on your

benevolence and love; but by confessing the truth first I would with true reasons defend my honour and then with strong deeds follow the nobility of my sentiments. It is true that I love and have loved Giuscardo, and so far as I live, which will not be for long, I will love him and being the closer to death I will not cease to love him.')

The passage is indeed one of the finest in the *Decameron*: Ghismunda courageously asserts her love for the low-born Guiscardo against her father's intransigence even though she is fully aware of the terrible consequences. She refuses to plead with her father but calmly maintains that she will follow her ruling passion with true nobility of spirit ('seguire la grandezza dello animo mio').[28] Her defence is both a justification of her love for Guiscardo and a rebuke of her father's wilful prejudice. Tancredi, for his part, wavers between admiration for his daughter's spirit and a relentless will to impose his own kind of justice:

> Conobbe il prenze la grandezza dell'animo della sua figliuola, ma non credette per ciò in tutto lei si fortemente disposta a quello che le parole sue suonavano, come diceva ... e commandò a'due che Guiscardo guardavano che senza alcun romore lui la seguente notte strangolassono ...[29]

(The Prince recognised the nobility of his daughter's spirit but did not however believe that she was so strongly disposed to the drift of her words ... and ordered the two who guarded Guiscardo to strangle him on the quiet the following night.)

The parallel with Parisina is, I think, inescapable.

II

The first stage of Byron's self-imposed journey of exile was from a literary point of view the most productive of his poetical career. In the short space of three months he composed four poems including the stanzas of Canto III of *Childe Harold* and the poetical drama *Manfred*. He also came into contact with Shelley, Monk Lewis and the voluble but brilliant Madame de Staël, all of whom helped to stimulate Byron's literary interests. Shelley, we are told, fed the poet large doses of Wordsworth and aroused his interest in Dante and Tasso.[30] According to Medwin, Madame de Staël and Monk Lewis helped foster an interest in Goethe's *Faust* which in turn considerably influenced the composition of *Manfred*. Byron's indebtedness to Goethe's *Faust* in *Manfred* has been acknowledged by scholars. Goethe himself later confirmed the influence of the Faustian theme on *Manfred* and made the interesting point that:

> This singular intellectual poet has taken my Faustus to himself, and extracted from it the strongest nourishment for his hypochondriac humour. He has made use of the impelling principles in his own way, for his own purposes, so that no one of them remains the same; and it is particularly on this account that I cannot enough admire his genius. The whole is in this way so completely forged anew, that it would be an interesting task for the critic to point out not only the alterations he has made, but their degree of resemblance with, or dissimilarity to, the original.[31]

Besides reinforcing the critic's notion of the pervasive debt to the German poet, the passage throws interesting light on the workings of Byron's creative faculties. The sources of *Manfred* are many and varied. Although *Faust* is the most obvious influence scholars have noted certain affinities with other possible sources such as Joshua Pickersgill's *The Three Brothers*.[32]

There is, however, a passage in *Manfred* which seems to point to the fact that Byron may have been strongly influenced by yet another source. In Act I, Scene ii of *Manfred*, Byron dramatises the situation in which Manfred, stricken by remorse for an unmentioned crime committed in the past, contemplates suicide from a mountain crag:

> And you, ye crags, upon whose extreme edge
> I stand, and on the torrents brink beneath
> Behold the tall pines dwindled as to shrubs
> In dizziness of distance when a leap,
> A stir, a motion, even a breath would bring
> My breast upon its rocky bosom's bed
> To rest for ever – wherefore do I pause?
> I feel the impulse – yet I do not plunge;

I see the peril – yet do not recede;
And my brain reels – and yet my foot is firm:
There is a power upon me which withholds,
And makes it my fatality to live, –
If it be life . . .
                    . . . and to be
My own soul's sepulchre . . .

                                                    (13–27)

There is a remarkable similarity between this passage and part of
an Italian poem by Vincenzo Monti entitled *A Sua Eccelenza il
Signor Don Sigismondo Chigi* which was written in 1783 and
published in 1787. The title is misleading for Monti's poem is not
an occasional poem written in honour of a patron but an
expression of the poet's passionate love for the beautiful young
Carlotta Stewart whom Monti first met in Florence at the house of
his friend Fortunata Sulgher Fantastici in 1782. In a letter to
Signora Fantastici, Monti confessed that he loved Carlotta
beyond belief ('amo Carlotta sopra ogni credere')[33] and the poem
deals with Monti's inability to resign himself to the hopelessness
of his love.[34] Half way through the poem Monti describes how in a
fit of despair he was sorely tempted to hurl himself over a cliff:

                              . . . all'orlo
D'un abisso mi spingo. A riguardarlo
Si rizzano le chiome, e il piè s'arretra . . .
E un pensiero sottentra ed un desio
Disperatio desio. Ritto su i piedi
Stommi, ed allargo le tremanti braccia
Inclinandomi verso la vorago,
L'occhio guardo laggiuso, e il cor respira;
E immaginando, nel piacer mi perdo
Di gittarmi la-dentro, onde a'miei mali
Por termine, e nei vortici travolto
Romoreggiar del profondo torrente.
Codardo: ancora non osai dall'alto
Staccar l'incerto piede, e coraggioso
Ingiù col capo rovesciarmi. Ancora
Al suo fin non è giunta la mia polve,
E un altro istante mi condanna il Fato
Di questo sole a contemplar l'aspetto.

O perché non poss'io . . .
Prigionero mortal.

(*A Don Sigismondo Chigi*, 180–225)

(I move towards the brink of an abyss/ As I look down my hair stands on end and my feet falter/ and a thought strikes me and an urge/ a desperate urge. I stand upright/ and stretch out my trembling arms/ leaning towards the abyss/ my eyes look down and my heart pants/ and in my fantasy I lose myself in ecstasy/ in the urge to fling myself down there to put an end/ to my woes and plunging into the abyss and the rumbling of the swirling torrent./ Coward that I am I cannot from above/ move my uncertain feet and bravely/ plunge headlong. But still/ my clay has not reached its appointed end/ in another moment I am compelled by fate/ to contemplate the aspect of this sun/ O why cannot I . . . O mortal prisoner.)

The general similarity in the treatment of the theme of suicide and the interesting correspondence in some of the particular details would seem to suggest that there may be another explanation other than pure literary coincidence. Admittedly, the notion of a man vacillating on the edge of a precipice would tend to follow a similar pattern when treated by different poets. What is present in both the above passages is the idea of a dichotomy between the spirit which impels a person to seek an end to misery in death and the body which stands firmly rooted to the spot. The spiritual impulse to suicide is thus counteracted, in both these extracts, by the sheer physical urge of self-preservation. More important, perhaps, is the fact that both poets seem to acknowledge that there is some mysterious force of fate or destiny which holds them back and somehow neutralises their yearning for self-annihilation. With Manfred (Byron) it is 'a power upon me which withholds,/ And makes it my fatality to live'.[35] Monti on the other hand complains that 'Ancora al suo fin non è giunta la mia polve/ E un altro istante mi condanna il Fato . . .'.[36] Life, to Manfred, becomes 'my own Soul's Sepulchre' whereas the unhappy lover in Monti's poem refers to himself as being imprisoned in mortality – 'Prigioner mortal'. Earlier on in Monti's *A Don Sigismondo Chigi* we are told that in his desperation the poet rushes out into the countryside calling the name of his beloved until the very caverns echo his lament:

> . . . Io m'alzo e corro
> Forsennato pe'campi, e di lamenti
> Le caverne riempio, che d'intorno
> Risponder sento con pietade.
>
> (*A Don Sigismondo Chigi*, 166–9)

(. . . I arise and run/ demented through the fields and my laments/ resound through the caverns, which all around/ answer back in compassion.)

Manfred, it will be recalled, behaves in the same manner:

> For I have called on thee in the still night,
>   and made the caves
> Acquainted with thy vainly echoed name.
>
> (Act II, Sc. iv, 136–9)

It is also significant that both poems are an expression of the hopelessness of attaining love which is somehow linked to the suggestion of an illicit relationship. Manfred, for instance, hints that there is something unnatural in his love for Astarte:

> though it were
> The deadliest sin to love as I have loved
>
> (Act II, Sc. iv, 122–3)

lines which are taken by the critics to be the poet's oblique proclamation of his love for Augusta. In Monti's poem there is a suggestion that his love for Carlotta is not wholly licit, apart from the realisation that she has married another. The relevant lines are:

> Io dunque
> Suo sposo! ella mia sposa! Eterno Iddio . . .
> . . . perdona al cieco
> Desio che m'arde
>
> (IV, 2–9)

(Indeed her lover! and my wife! Eternal God . . .
. . . forgive this blind desire that burns inside me)

and, again, in the fifth section – *Pensieri d'Amore* – the poet exclaims:

> O se lontano delle ree cittadi
> In solitario lido i giorni miei
> Teco mi fosse trapassar concesso!
> O se mei fosse! Tu sorella e sposa!

(v, 1–4)

(O if far away from the wicked cities/ in quiet pleasure I could spend the days/ and be allowed to while the time with you/ O if you were mine! Sister and wife as well!)

The last line with its curious blending of Platonic love and physical consummation would have attracted Byron's notice and he would have related them to his own feelings for Augusta after his departure from England. It is possible that Byron may have been tempted to endow his hero Manfred with similar emotions.

It may be objected at this stage that when Byron composed his poetical drama he had not as yet set foot in Italy and therefore it is unlikely that he should have been already acquainted with Monti's poetical works. Admittedly, it was after he left Switzerland that he met the celebrated Italian poet. It should be remembered, however, that during his stay in Switzerland in the summer of 1816, Byron was a frequent visitor to Madame de Staël's literary salon in Coppet. Madame de Staël herself was a fervent admirer of Vincenzo Monti whom she first met on a visit to Italy in 1804 and with whom she later corresponded.[37] Monti's works featured prominently in her library, and it seems likely that her unbounded enthusiasm for Monti may have stimulated Byron's interest in his works.

It will also be remembered that as early as February 1814 Byron recorded his liking for Monti's tragedy *Aristodemo* and he went so far as to rate Monti as a more accomplished dramatist than either Schiller or Alfieri. In fact Monti's drama may have had a direct bearing on Byron's literary treatment of the theme of incest in *Manfred*. In *Aristodemo*, Monti dramatises the predicament of an ambitious king who has sacrificed his daughter in order to achieve a lasting peace with his hostile neighbours. He is striken by remorse and afflicted with a 'mortal melancholia' which is partly assuaged by his love for a beautiful Spartan slave

Cesira who, unknown to him, is none other than his second daughter Argia, who he believes was killed in an ambush as she was being carried away to safety. The spirit of his first daughter Dirce appears to him at night and tries to embrace him. Aristodemo shrinks back in horror and he feels that he is a doomed man:

> S'eterna l'esistenza fosse,
> Io sento che del par sarebbe eterno
> Il mio martiro
>
> (Act III, Sc. i)

(If existence were eternal/ I feel that my suffering would be equally eternal . . .)

But what is even more perturbing to his spirit is the profound, inexpressible feeling that his affection for the slave Cesira is unnatural. He hints at this to his faithful retainer Gonippo:

> Un orrendo pensiero, e quanto è truce
> Tu non lo sai. Lo sguardo tuo non passa
> Dentro il mio cor, ne mira la tempesta,
>
> Che lo sconvolge tutto. Ah mio fedele,
> Credimi, io sono sventurato assai,
> Senza misura sventurato! un empio,
> Un maledetto nel furor del cielo,
> E l'orror di natura, e di me stesso.
>
> (Act I, Sc. iv)

(Horrible thought, and how terrible/ you cannot imagine. Your glance does not penetrate my heart, nor does it gaze upon the tempest within/ without causing turmoil. O my loyal one/ believe me, I am so unfortunate/ so utterly unfortunate! Impious,/ Accursed amid the fury of heaven/ the horror of nature and of myself.)

Later, in the act of embracing Cesira he is convinced that he is urged by a demon from the infernal regions. ('Fu d'Averno una furia, che mi spinse ad abbracciarti').[38] It is not difficult to realise the impact Monti's tragic drama must have had on Byron's sensibility during the period of his liaison with his half-sister. Alarmed at the social repercussions of such a relationship, Lady Melbourne had warned the young poet:

> You are on the brink of a precipice, and if you do not retreat, you are lost for ever – it is a crime for which there is no salvation in this world, whatever there may be in the next.[39]

In *Aristodèmo* Monti had dramatically explored the tragic possibility of a man caught on the brink of just such a precipice. Like Manfred, Aristodemo was responsible for the death of a woman he loved; he too feels the relentless pangs of remorse and is absorbed in his feelings of guilt. He is haunted by the spirit of Dirce who appears to him from the grave and is tormented by his presentiment that his love for Cesira is incestuous. Unable to dispel his guilt feelings he eventually commits suicide. There can be no doubt that Byron was profoundly influenced by this tragedy especially in its dramatisation of the theme of incestuous love, which is decidedly the impelling force of *Manfred*.

III

Byron seems to have discovered Italy through Madame de Staël's *Corinne or Italy*, which appeared in an English translation in 1807.[40] Its interest as far as Byron was concerned was twofold. In the first place Byron must have identified with the hero, Lord Nelvil, a young Scottish nobleman who leaves his native land for reasons of health to visit Italy. He carries with him an inexpressible sense of gloom and despondency partly occasioned by the death of his father. His narrow puritanical outlook on life is somewhat broadened by his travels in Italy and especially by his coming into contact with the beautiful, 'Improvisatrice' Corinne – in many respects an idealised picture of the author herself – who enlightens him on the manners and customs of the Italians. More important from Byron's point of view was the fact that in this novel Madame de Staël recorded, under the guise of fiction, her own impressions of a sentimental journey to Italy. As Corinne or her creator guided the reader through the treasures of Rome, she awakened the spirit of the past and recorded her feelings and impressions about the ancient monuments. *Corinne*, in fact, provided the young poet with a scenario of the heart in the presence of the past glory of an ancient civilisation. The novel also combined romance with a sort of travelogue based on personal experience of an actual journey which would certainly have appealed to Byron's penchant for fact.

The fourth Canto of *Childe Harold* was composed during the first year of Byron's stay in Italy and it is commonly assumed that this part of the poem is a record of Byron's own personal observations on the Italian scene and his response to Italian life and culture. This assumption, however, is far from the truth. It was Byron's reading rather than the physical actuality of being in a foreign country which was the primary source of his inspiration. The opening stanzas of Canto IV with its attempt to capture the enchantment of Venice are for the most part a literary reminiscence stemming from Byron's reading of Schiller and Mrs Radcliffe. Moreover, it would not be an exaggeration to say that Byron's response to the monuments of the Eternal City in the middle stanzas of Canto IV is largely conditioned by his reading of *Corinne* and in particular the impact of the sights of Rome on a man of Lord Nelvil's disposition and sensibility. The fine stanzas on Rome and St Peter's Basilica contain distinct echoes of Lord Nelvil's response to the same building in the early chapters of *Corinne*. As Corinne guides Oswald around St Peter's she confesses that the architectural design gives her a sense of composure and that:

La vue d'un tel monument est comme une musique continuelle et fixée, qui vous attend pour vous faire du bien quand vous vous en approchez . . .[41]

The 'gigantic elegance' of St Peter's produces much the same effect on Byron of a

Vastness which grows, but grows to harmonise – All musical in its immensities

Following Madame de Staël, Byron equates architectural symmetry with musical harmony. The overall impact on Corinne of this grandiose architectural achievement was that of the insignificance of man when confronted with the immortality of art. She thus exclaims that:

L'homme se sont tellement passager, qu'il a toujours de l'émotion en présence de ce qui est immuable.[42]

a sentiment which is echoed by Byron in:

> . . . even so this
> Outshining and o'erwhelming edifice
> Fools our fond gaze, and greatest of the great
> Defies at first our Nature's littleness . . .
>
> (*CH*, IV, clviii, 4–7)

Another interesting detail is afforded by Corinne's surmise at the tomb of Cecilia Metella. In Corinne's view, Cecilia is to be compared with the chaste Roman matron Cornelia who could claim 'the noble pride of a blameless life'. Byron, who also visits the tomb, speculates in the same vein:

> Was she as those who love their lords, or they
> Who love the lords of others? such have been
> Even in the olden time, Rome's annals say
> Was she a matron in Cornelia's mien.
>
> (*CH*, IV, ci, 2–5)

It is obvious that Byron is here following the same thought processes.

Perhaps the most interesting confirmation of how profoundly Madame de Staël influenced Byron's response to the Italian scene in the fourth Canto of *Childe Harold* is provided by a passage in *Corinne* which describes in terms of religious symbolism the mysterious attraction of Rome for a man of Lord Nelvil's temperament. The passage in question occurs in Chapter 4 of the first book of *Corinne* where the author describes the impact of the Eternal City on this northern visitor as he surveys the scene from a distance:

L'église catholique est haut de la montagne, et domine à pic sur la mer; le bruit des flots se mêle souvent aux chants des prêtres: l'église est surchargée dans l'intérieur d'une foule d'ornements d'assez mauvais goût, mais, quand on s'arrête sous le portique du temple, on aime à rapprocher les plus purs des sentiments de l'âme, la religion, avec le spectacle de cette superbe mer, sur laquelle l'homme jamais ne peut imprimer sa trace. La terre est travaillée par lui, les montagnes sont coupées par ses routes, les rivières se resserent en canaux, pour porter ses marchandises; mais si les vaisseaux sillonent un moment les ondes, la vague vient effacer aussitôt cette légère marque de servitude, et la mer reparaît telle qu'elle fut au premier jour de la création.[43]

This is surely one of the purple passages in *Corinne* and a good example of Madame de Staël's occasional metaphysical flights. The blending of the ocean's roar with the chant of priests is no doubt a suggestion of the perennial triumph of the church which resists the forces of change and is resilient to the vicissitudes of history. That this passage strongly appealed to Byron's imagination is evident from even a cursory reading of the climactic stanzas of the fourth Canto. The stanzas themselves with their rousing crescendo deserve to be quoted in full:

> Roll on, thou deep and dark blue Ocean – roll!
> Ten thousand fleets sweep over thee in vain;
> Man marks the earth with ruin – his control
> Stops with the shore; upon the watery plain
> The wrecks are all thy deed, nor doth remain
> A shadow of man's ravage, save his own,
> When for a moment, like a drop of rain,
> He sinks into thy depths with bubbling groan
> Without a grave, unknell'd, uncoffin'd, and unknown.
>
> His steps are not upon thy paths, – thy fields
> Are not a spoil for him, – thou dost arise
> And shake him from thee; the vile strength he wields
> For earth's destruction thou dost all despise,
> Spurning him from thy bosom to the skies,
> And send'st him, shivering in thy playful spray
> And howling, to his Gods, where haply lies
> His petty hope in some near port or bay,
> And dashest him again to earth: – there let him lay.
>
> The armaments which thunderstrike the walls
> Of rock-built cities, bidding nations quake,
> And monarchs tremble in their capitals,
> The oak leviathans, whose huge ribs make

Their clay creator the vain title take
Of lord of thee and arbiter of war –
These are thy toys, and as the snowy flake
They melt into thy yeast of waves, which mar
Alike the Armada's pride or spoils of Trafalgar.

Thy shores are empires, changed in all save thee
Assyria, Greece, Rome, Carthage what are they?
Thy waters wash'd them power while they were free,
And many a tyrant since; their shores obey
The stranger, slave, or savage; their decay
Has dried up realms to deserts: – not so thou; –
Unchangeable, save to thy wild waves' play,
Time writes no wrinkle on thy azure brow:
Such as creation's dawn beheld, thou rollest now.

Thou glorious mirror, where the Almighty's form
Glasses itself in tempests; in all time, –
Calm or convulsed, in breeze or gale or storm,
Icing the pole, or in the torrid clime
Dark-heaving-boundless, endless, and sublime,
The image of eternity, the throne
Of the Invisible; even from out thy slime
The monsters of the deep are made; each zone
Obeys thee; thou goest forth, dread, fathomless, alone.

(*CH*, clxxix–clxxxiii)

What we have here is a toning down of the metaphysical aspect of
the original passage and an elaboration in four stanzas of the point
made by Madame de Staël that man in all his pride and glory has
never succeeded in leaving his trace on the ocean. This shift in
focus from the metaphysical to the historical perspective is
characteristic of Byron's attempt to heighten the contrast between
the intractability of the ocean and the transitoriness of all
civilisations. The reference to the recent battle of Trafalgar and
the grim humour of the sea tossing man 'howling, to his Gods' are
a clear indication of the poet's temperamental inability to sustain
the solemnity of tone in the original. In the fifth stanza, however,
Byron elaborates on Madame de Staël's notion that the sea is an
image of the lasting bond between man and his creator.

IV

In the third chapter of Book I of Madame de Staël's novel set in Italy, the heroine Corinne, responding to the acclaim of the crowd at the Capitol extemporises a song about 'the glory and welfare of Italy'. In declaiming her improvised verses Corinne, we are told, is animated by the love of her country and she 'breathes forth thoughts to which prose or another language can do but imperfect justice'. The general drift of her *chanson* is that the genius of ancient Rome which was temporarily suppressed by the barbarian hordes is revived again in the spirit of Italy's great poets. Corinne pays tribute to Dante, Ariosto, Petrarch and Tasso in turn and celebrates the power of poetry to transcend human misery. It seems likely that Byron actually modelled his poem structurally on the drift of Corinne's *chanson* with its blending of patriotic sentiments and brief biographical comments on the famous Italian poets. But whereas Corinne could express the inner feelings of her fellow countrymen, Byron as a pilgrim in an alien land relied heavily upon the patriotic utterances of an Italian poet. It is interesting to note that two of the finest stanzas in Canto IV of *Childe Harold* are a versified rendering of Filicaia's rousing sonnet to Italy.[44] Here is the original:

> Italia, Italia o tu, cui feo la sorte
> Dono infelice di bellezza, ond'hai
> Funesta dote d'infiniti guai,
> Che in fronte scritti per gran doglia porte:
> Deh! fossi tu men bella, o almen più forte
> Onde assai più ti paventasse, o assai
> T'amasse men, chi del tuo bello ai rai
> Par che si strugga, e pur ti sfida a morte.
> Che giù dall'Alpi non vedrei torrenti
> Scender d'armati, nè di sangue tinta
> Bever l'onda del Po Gallici armenti:
> Nè ti vedrei del non tuo ferro cinta
> Pugnar col braccio di straniere genti,
> Per servir sempre, o vincitrice, o vinta.

This sonnet with its curious blending of rhetoric and sincere feeling was one of five sonnets written by Filicaia in protest against the devastations of the French and German armies in Italy at the end of the seventeenth century. It seems likely that Byron first read the poem in Sismondi's *De la littérature* where the sonnet is quoted in full as 'the most celebrated specimen which the Italian literature of the seventeenth century affords'.[45] Byron had no hesitation in incorporating his verse translation into *Childe Harold* where they appear as stanzas xlii and xliii:

> Italia! oh Italia! thou who hast
> The fatal gift of beauty, which became
> A funeral dower of present woes and past,
> On thy sweet brow is sorrow plough'd by shame
> And annals graved in characters of flame.
> Oh God! that thou wert in thy nakedness
> Less lovely or more powerful, and couldst claim
> Thy right, and awe the robbers back, who press
> To shed thy blood, and drink the tears of thy distress;
>
> Then mightest thou more appal; or, less desired,
> Be homely and be peaceful, undeplored
> For thy destructive charms; then still untired,
> Would not be seen the armed torrents pour'd
> Down the deep Alps; nor would the hostile horde
> Of many-nationed spoilers from the Po
> Quaff blood and water; nor the stranger's sword
> Be thy sad weapon of defence, and so,
> Victor or vanquished, thou the slave of friend or foe.

Byron's version is for the most part a close rendering of the original. There is, however, one interesting change where Byron deliberately tones down Filicaia's specific reference to the 'Gallici armenti' and substitutes the 'many-nationed spoilers' mostly because he felt the need to generalise such patriotic utterances in the light of Italy's turbulent history. This method of borrowing the sentiments and expression of an Italian poet who was outraged at the rape of Italy by barbarian hordes was Byron's way of identifying with contemporary nationalistic movements in Italy and making the Italians aware of their own illustrious past. When he composed the fourth Canto, he certainly achieved his purpose. Indeed, Michaele Leoni attested to the fact that his translation of this Canto of *Childe Harold* was considered subversive by the Austrians:

> Non ignorerà forse, che la mia versione del 4° Canto del Childe Harold fu confiscata in ogni parte: ed io stesso ho dovuto soffrir vessazioni oltrettanto ridicole quanto illiberali, ad onta che alcuni versi fossero esclusi dalla censura.[46]

> (You will not perhaps ignore the fact that my version of the fourth Canto of Childe Harold was confiscated in every place, and I myself had to suffer harassment, ridiculous and illiberal though this was, beside the fact that some verses were expunged by the censors.)

V

In *Childe Harold*, Byron used poetry as a medium for projecting a public image of himself and in so doing he became a prisoner of this image. The image of himself that Byron put forward was, I believe, largely conditioned by his reading. The *Weltschmerz* of *Childe Harold*, for instance, is largely compounded of the wretchedness of Lord Nelvil and the melancholic soul-searching of Jacopo Ortis or Werther. It seems likely that Byron had read *Le Ultime Lettere di Jacopo Ortis*, Ugo Foscolo's Wertheresque novel, for he came close to uttering the very sentiments of the love-tormented Jacopo when he claimed in the *Epistle to Augusta* that he had been 'the careful pilot' of my proper woe (iii, 8) – a close echo indeed of Jacopo's reflection that 'pare che gli uomini sieno fabbri delle proprie sciagure'.[47] It also seems probable that the Childe's melancholy musing on the 'universal pall' enshrouding the world was directly influenced by Jacopo's introverted brooding on man's insignificance in an alien universe. Jacopo Ortis, in his misery, had reflected on the darkness which pervaded the universe and mirrored his soul:

> M'affaccio al balcone ora che l'immenso luce del sole si va spegnendo, e le tenebre rapiscono all'universo qu'raggi languidi che balenano su l'orizonte; e nella opacità del mondo malinconico e taciturno contemplo la immagine della Destruzione divoratrice di tutte le cose.[48]

Likewise the Childe's shadow 'fades away into Destruction's mass' as he contemplates a twilight scene:

> Which gathers shadow, substance, life and all
> That we inherit in its mortal shroud,
> And spreads the dim and universal pall
> Through which all things grow phantoms; and the cloud
> Between us sinks and all which ever glowed,
> Till Glory's self is twilight, and displays
> A melancholy halo scarce allow'd
> To hover on the verge of darkness . . .
>
> (*CH*, IV, clxv, 1–7)

From Foscolo, too, Byron may have derived the idea of making use of Santa Croce as a focal point for his reflections on the Italian writers – 'the spirits that soar from ruins'. In his *Dei Sepolcri*, Ugo Foscolo had argued that the tomb strengthened the bond of affection between the living and the dead – a kind of spiritual bond between the mourner and the mourned which he called a celestial 'corrispondenza di amorosi sensi'. In the central part of the poem Foscolo alludes to Santa Croce as a symbol of hope for all patriotic Italians and the church itself is 'elevated to a position it never previously held in Italian tradition – that of a national Valhalla'.[49] Byron may have had Foscolo's poem in mind in focusing on the apotheosis of the great Italian poets of the past and, especially, in exalting Santa Croce as the hope and salvation of the Italy of his day.

2 Byron, Dante and Italy

I

L'Italie, au temps de sa puissance, revit tout entière dans le Dante. Animé par l'esprit des républiques, guerrier aussi bien que poète, il souffle la flamme des actions parmi les mortes et ses ombres ont une vie plus forte que les vivants d'aujourd'hui.

(Madame de Staël, *Corinne*)

Like Shelley, Byron came under the spell of the greatest of Italian poets when he first read the *Divine Comedy* in the translations of Henry Boyd and Henry Cary.[1] His reading of the *Divina Commedia* was at first almost entirely restricted to the better known Cantos of the *Inferno*, in particular Dante's moving account of the tragic love of Paolo and Francesca and the terrible fate of Count Ugolino da Gherardesca. Byron responded temperamentally to Dante's sensitive portrayal of human anguish in the *Inferno* but, unlike Shelley, he showed little enthusiasm for the transcendental and mystical flights of the *Purgatorio* and the *Paradiso*. While Shelley characteristically chose to translate the Matilda passage in the *Purgatorio* for its 'exquisite tenderness and sensibility and ideal beauty',[2] Byron was attracted to the episode of Francesca's tragic plight and applied himself to the task of a versified rendering of the passage into an English equivalent of *terza rima*.

The mottoes from Dante heading each Canto of *The Corsair* are a clear indication that Byron's reading of Dante at the time was almost entirely limited to the Francesca episode in the *Inferno* from which these were taken. Although the epigraphs themselves bore no direct relation to the theme and events of *The Corsair*, they probably served the purpose of displaying the poet's knowledge of Italian literature while enabling him to refer obliquely to the 'dubbiosi desiri' of his relationship with Augusta. For Byron the episode of Francesca da Rimini in the fifth Canto of the *Inferno* was a literary objective correlative with his affair with his half-sister. Indeed, he must have been struck by Dante's sensitive treatment of Francesca's plight, the sympathetic portrayal of adultery with its overtones of incest, the ineluctability of love and Francesca's aquiescence in the nature of God's justice. At about the same time he read Hunt's poetical adaptation of the story with much interest and made a number of helpful suggestions during its stages of composition.[3] On hearing that Tom Moore and his wife were planning to go to France in 1814, Byron suggested to Moore that he join them adding facetiously 'I will connubiate and join you; and we will write a new *Inferno* in our Paradise'.[4] Even after he settled in Italy he still considered his relationship with Augusta in Dantean terms:

> It is heart-breaking to think of our long Separation – and I am sure more than punishment enough for all our sins – Dante is more humane in his 'Hell' for he places his unfortunate lovers (Francesca of Rimini & Paolo whose case fell a good deal short of *ours* – though sufficiently naughty) in company – and though they suffer it is at least together.[5]

At the same time, when he was about to transfer his affections to the Countess Guiccioli he described his love for her in terms of Paolo's love for Francesca:

> Quella storia di amor funesto, che sempre m'interessava, adesso mi interessa doppiamente dove che Ravenna rinchiude il mio cuore.[6]

Byron was pleased to note that Ravenna, where Dante breathed his last after fifteen years of exile, also happened to be the birthplace of his mistress.

After reading Dante in the original, Byron felt that contemporary English translations had for the most part misrepresented the text of the *Divina Commedia*. Dante, he was convinced, was 'non tradotto, ma tradito',[7] and he accordingly tried his hand at an experimental rendering of his favourite Canto. Byron was also convinced that the *terza rima* measure, even though it was unfamiliar to the British reader, was the only appropriate form for a proper translation and he persisted in using it despite the fact that previous translators had discarded it as unwieldy. The actual translation of the Dante excerpt was to prove more laborious than he had imagined. As the different versions show,[8] Byron wavered

between an over-familiar and colloquial tone which was strictly
rigid in its verbal correspondence with the original and a freer
version which somehow produced a stilted effect as in the
following lines first published by Moore:[9]

> Love, who to none beloved to love again
> Remits, seized me with wish to please so strong,
> That, as thou seest, yet, yet it doth remain.
> Love to one death conducted us along,
> But Caina waits for him our life who ended.
>
> (Ll. 7–11)

Byron's interest in Dante was probably reawakened by Shelley
during the summer of 1816 which the poets spent in close
companionship near Lake Geneva. *The Prisoner of Chillon* was
occasioned by an actual visit to the Castle of Chillon, but the
literary treatment of the anguish of physical and mental incarcer-
ation was in all probability inspired by Dante's awe-inspiring
account of the horrible fate of Count Ugolino. There is undoubtedly a parallel between Ugolino's helpless witnessing of the slow
death of his sons and the prisoner of Chillon's ordeal in outliving
the gradual death of his brothers. The terrible realisation of a
living grave has the effect of petrifying Ugolino's emotions to the
extent that he is unable to weep at his misfortune. As he in fact
says, 'Io non piangea, si dentro impietrai'.[10] This is directly
echoed by Byron in the prisoner's confession that:

> I had no thought, no feeling – none –
> Among the stones I stood a stone.
>
> (ix, 235–6)

Again, in the Ugolino episode, the idea of a living death is
conveyed by the mention of the staleness of the Tower and the
striking contrast with the flow of life outside which Ugolino can
only perceive through a 'pertugio' or chink in the wall. Byron's
prisoner, likewise, is condemned to an existence:

> Which neither was of life nor death;
> A sea of stagnant idleness,
> Blind, boundless, mute and motionless
>
> (ix, 248–50)

and his only glimpse of life outside is by means of a crevice in the prison wall. The Gothic horror of the fate of Ugolino captivated Byron's imagination. Medwin records that Shelley and Byron discussed the death of Ugolino and that Shelley for his part was horrified by his friend's interpretation of the line 'Più che dolor potè il digiuno' to mean that Ugolino in his frenzy actually fed on his children after their deaths. Medwin's comment is of particular interest since it also throws light on the element of Dantean influence:

> 'The story,' observed Shelley, 'is horrible enough without such a comment,' – and he added, 'that Byron had deeply studied this death of Ugolino, and perhaps but for it, would never have written the *Prisoner of Chillon*.[11]

Yet despite these correspondences the tragic pathos of Dante's account seems to elude Byron, for where Dante achieves a dignified poignancy by succinct utterance, Byron's narrative method is incorrigibly discursive.

The extent of Dante's influence is also apparent in *Mazeppa* which Byron composed during the summer of 1818. Despite Mazeppa's lively and spirited account of his youthful, hair-raising adventure, there are distinct Dantean overtones in Byron's treatment of the theme of guilt and love in this poem. To begin with, the adulterous love of the Countess for the young page must have been associated in Byron's mind with his own affair with the Countess Guiccioli. Moore was undoubtedly right in remarking that the poem had its basis in fact:

> It is impossible not to suspect that the poet had circumstances of his own personal history in his mind, when he portrayed the fair Polish Theresa, her youthful lover and the jealous rage of the old Count Palatine.[12]

Like *Manfred*, *Mazeppa* had its origin in the poet's desire to project the 'veracious myth'[13] to an English audience. However, the adulterous situation at the core of the poem must have recalled to the poet's mind the similar predicament of Paolo and Francesca. Indeed, the whole conception of the guilt of the young Mazeppa and the punishment meted out to him was very probably affected by Byron's reading of Dante's *Inferno*. There is, for instance, a

· remarkable correlation between the actual offence and the punishment, which operates throughout the *Inferno*.[14] This process is again at work in Byron's practical treatment of the wild horse to which Mazeppa is bound. In the poem the horse becomes a symbol of Mazeppa's uncontrollable passion and self-indulgence. As the mature Mazeppa observed in retrospect he was chastened by his ghastly experience:

> But could not o'er myself evince
> The like control . . .   (vii, 293–4)

In failing to curb his youthful passion Mazeppa allowed his reason to become subservient to his lust. The Ukrainian wild steed that carries the helpless Mazeppa into the depths of the black forest is Byron's poetical elaboration of the Dantean concept of the eternal correspondence between guilt and punishment. Mazeppa, in Graham Hough's words is 'delivered over to a force more wild and tameless than himself'.[15] There is a striking parallel here with the 'bufera infernal' in the fifth Canto of the *Inferno* which relentlessly lashes and torments the lustful sinners who, as Dante remarks, subjected their reason to the yoke of their carnal desires:

> Intesi ch'a così fatto tormento enno dannati i peccator carnali, che la ragion sommettono al talento.[16]

> (Into this torment/ were the carnal sinners damned/ who make their reason servant to their lust.)

Mazeppa, like Dante's sinful lovers, is not punished for his sin but by his sin. The similarity with Dante ends here, however, for Mazeppa survives his ordeal and becomes a powerful king among his own people.

Although Byron found it difficult to respond to the complex allegorical structure of Dante's *Divine Comedy*,[17] he nonetheless appreciated Dante's treatment of human passions and emotions in this poem. He was in fact outraged when he read Friedrich Schlegel's criticism of Dante in the *Lectures on the History of Literature* in January 1821. Schlegel had taken Dante to task for his lack of gentle feelings – a rash assertion which aroused Byron's indignation:

He says also that Dante's chief defect is a want of gentle
feelings! – of gentle feelings! – and Francesca of Rimini and the
father's feelings in Ugolino – and Beatrice – and 'La Pia'! Why
there is gentleness in Dante beyond all gentleness, when he is
tender. It is true that, treating of the Christian Hades or Hell,
there is not much scope or site for gentleness – but who but
Dante could have introduced any 'gentleness' at all into *Hell*?
Is there any in Milton's? No – and Dante's Heaven is all
love, and glory and majesty.[18]

II

It was the romance attached to Dante's life and the veneration of
Dante by his fellow countrymen that seemed to appeal most to
Byron's imagination. According to Medwin, Byron was most
impressed by the genuine admiration of the Italians for the author
of the *Divina Commedia*:

> There is no Italian gentleman, scarcely any well-educated girl,
> that has not all the finer passages of Dante at the fingers' ends, –
> particularly the Ravennese. The Guiccioli for instance could
> almost repeat any part of the 'Divine Comedy' . . .[19]

In Byron's view, however, Dante's claim to greatness rested not so
much on his poetical achievement as on the fact that he was a
martyr to his high principles. An exile himself, he readily
identified with Dante's prolonged suffering in the cause of liberty,
and admired the Italian poet for his unwavering adherence to his
beliefs. As he remarked to Medwin:

> Persecution, exile, the dread of a foreign grave could not shake
> his principles.[20]

Tasso and Dante were in fact heroes whom Byron readily
associated with the nascent spirit of Italian nationalism. *The
Prophecy of Dante* was written, as Byron acknowledged in the
Preface, at the suggestion of Teresa Guiccioli during his stay in
Ravenna in the summer of 1819. The temptation to equate
Dante's suffering with his own predicament was irresistible and
the poem, as critics have pointed out, is another instance of

Byron's use of poetry as disguised analytic autobiography. Byron himself was aware of this and confessed to Medwin that:

> The place of Dante's fifteen years' exile, where he so pathetically prayed for his country, and deprecated the thought of being buried out of it; and the sight of his tomb, which I passed in my almost daily rides, – inspired me. Besides, there was somewhat of a resemblance in our destinies – he had a wife, and I have the same feeling about leaving my bones in a strange land.[21]

There is no doubt a correlation in the *Prophecy of Dante* between Dante's feelings for Florence and Byron's own situation. The bitterness of Dante's exile must have struck a responsive chord in Byron. He indeed went so far as to project himself into his persona and contrary to historical fact attributed to the Italian poet the wretchedness of an unhappy marriage.[22] Quite apart from using Dante and Tasso as vehicles for his Romantic ventriloquism, Byron had another, perhaps more important reason for choosing to write a poem about Dante. Dante, in the eyes of most Italians at the time, was a symbol of the indomitable spirit of Italy which survived the oppression of foreign powers. To Alfieri, for instance, Dante was a patriarchal figure and a seer ('vate nostro') who penetrated far into the mystery of existence. He was also a moral philosopher and a patriot who refused to bow to the petty tyranny of scheming men. Although this view of Dante was shared by most educated Italians in the early nineteenth century, there was some measure of dissent in literary circles as to the real nature of Dante's patriotism.

An interesting side-issue of the literary controversy raging at the time of the composition of the *Prophecy of Dante* between the Classicists who sought inspiration from the old masters and the new-fangled Romantics who turned to contemporary foreign models, was the question of Dante's *saeva indignatio*.[23] The *Divina Commedia*, to be sure, was generally regarded as the finest poem in the Italian language but Dante's patriotism was impugned by the more avant-garde of the moderns who claimed that the poet's outbursts against his fellow-countrymen stemmed from his bitter hatred of the Florentines who had banished him from his native city. It seems that Byron's interest in this literary polemic was aroused by Teresa Guiccioli who, as an ardent worshipper at the shrine of Dante, must have resented the allegation that Dante's fine patriotic sentiments emanated in reality from deep feelings of animosity. Although there is no record of any discussion between Byron and La Guiccioli on this subject, it is likely from the evidence of their correspondence that the topic was raised. In a letter to Teresa written during the actual composition of the 'canticles' Byron claimed that he was reading Perticari's treatise on the subject: 'il secondo volume della proposta di quel' becco classico Perticari'.[24] This statement is significant because the second volume to which Byron refers constituted the continuation of Count Perticari's scholarly vindication of Dante entitled *Dell' Amor Patrio di Dante*, and is an indication that Byron was sufficiently interested in the Dante controversy to read Count Perticari's *Apologia* of the Italian poet. More important still, is the fact that this work seems to have exerted a considerable influence on Byron's *Prophecy of Dante*. Before attempting an analysis of this particular influence it is necessary, I believe, to examine the basis of Perticari's actual defence of Dante.

Giulio Perticari's treatise in two volumes[25] was written in reply to the accusation put forward by Dante's detractors that he lacked the fine feelings of a patriot. The drift of Perticari's argument is that Dante's vehemence in condemning the Florentines of his day – his 'parole acerbissime' – were aimed at those he considered traitors to his country. His *saeva indignatio* stemmed not so much from an implacable hatred of his political opponents as from an affectionate regard for his country. Perticari's main case for the defence rests on the argument that when Dante denounced his fellow countrymen, as in the famous outburst against the Florentines which he puts in the mouth of Brunetto Latini,[26] he was motivated by an intense love of his country prompted by the disdain of noble minds – 'lo sdegno de'forti animi'.

Ma Dante, per lo contrario, dette quelle cose che fruttassero infamia ai soli traditori dipinge il buon tempo eroico della sua patria con un amore ed una reverenza che quasi accostasi a religione. La quale poscia di continuo traspare, e specialmente da que' luoghi, ove gl'incontra di nominare Firenze secondo quel modo che i retori chiamano della *circumlocuzione*. Perciocchè nel decimo dell'Inferno per bocca di Farinata ei l'appella *la patria nobile*; nel ventesimo terzo la *gran villa sul bel fiume d'Arno* . . .[27]

(But Dante on the contrary said those things that bespeak infamy only in the case of traitors. He depicts the good heroic times of his country with love and reverence which almost amount to a religion. This becomes evident thereafter in places where he mentions Florence according to the rhetorician's manner of using circumlocutions. Thus in the tenth Canto of the *Inferno* he makes Farinata refer to it as the noble country; and in the twenty-fifth, the great villa on the lovely river Arno.)

In a central passage of his *Apologia*, Perticari attempts to justify the severity of Dante's condemnation of Italy:

Perchè cacciato egli dal nido, sfolgorato dalla fortuna, solo, inerme, diviso da ogni cosa più caramente diletta, non puo ascoltare il danno della ingiusta patria, senza che sparga lacrime.[28]

(Because banished from his nest, blasted by fortune, alone and helpless, separated from everything dear to him, he could not hear about the wrongs of his unjust country without shedding a tear.)

The second treatise by Perticari besides being a scholarly defence of Dante's decision to use the vernacular ('il volgare') is also an impassioned re-statement of the argument of the first volume. The conclusion of *Della Difesa di Dante: e del suo Libro intorno il Volgare Eloquio* which is the most memorable part of the *Apologia*, is both an eloquent eulogy of Dante and an attempt to exonerate the poet from the imputation of unpatriotic sentiment. It is an impressive piece of writing and worth quoting:

egli non fu mai vile e falso: che fu sempre fidato all bontà del vero; che al prezzo di comparire colpevole gli era stato di nuovo offerto e il retaggio paterno e la patria tanto di lui lacrimata; ma che a pregio si reo non volle nè retaggio, nè patria: che tutto sostenne fuorche il titolo della colpa, perchè cosi volle la rigida sua virtù amando più tosto di girare pellegrino per Italia e gridare:
    'L'esilio che m'è dato a onor mi tegno:
    Che se giudicio o forza di destino

Vuol pur che il mondo versi
I bianchi fiori in persi,
Cader tra i buoni e pur di laude degno.'[29]

(he was never base or a traitor; he was always committed to the virtue of the truth; and that for the price of appearing guilty he was newly offered both his paternal inheritance and his country so often bewailed by him. But he refused both inheritance and country at such a vile price; that he endured all except the attribution of blame, because his unswerving virtue compelled him rather to wander as pilgrim throughout Italy and exclaim:

> The exile to which I was condemned is an honour for me/ for if men's judgment or fate obliged me to lose the world/ the white flowers in verses/ will fall among the good and make me worthy of praise.)

By focusing on Dante's dignified refusal to humiliate himself by accepting a conditional pardon, Perticari stresses Dante's nobility of spirit in preferring exile to a life of servility.

Byron's attitude to the subject suggested by Teresa Guiccioli was influenced by his reading of Giulio Perticari's work on Dante. Although it is true that *The Prophecy of Dante* does express Byron's misgivings about leaving his bones in another country as well as his deep-seated feelings of revenge, *The Prophecy of Dante* is not merely disguised autobiography. The poem also relates in its own way to the recent Dante controversy and is an interesting example of how Byron's previous reading tended to interlock with his original work. Byron's method of procedure in *The Prophecy of Dante* is to portray Dante from the classicist point of view and indeed in very much the same light as he is presented by Perticari. It is evident from the Preface that he had the Italian as well as the English readers in mind when he referred to 'the present bitterness of the classic and romantic war'. Following Perticari's defence of Dante, Byron in this extended monologue makes Dante proclaim his genuine love for his country:

> Alas! how bitter is his country's curse
> To him who *for* that country would expire
> But did not merit to expire by her
> And loves her, loves her even in her ire!

(I, 69–72)

The repetition of 'loves her' seems to me to be Byron's emphatic refutation of the charge of Dante's lack of patriotism and his own indirect contribution to the Dante controversy. In fact, the same sentiment is echoed again in the third Canto when Dante exclaims:

> To thee my country! whom before, as now,
> I loved and love.
>
> (25–6)

The concluding lines of the first Canto of *The Prophecy* are a versified synthesis of Perticari's concluding passage extolling the dignity of Dante's preference for a life of freedom in exile:

> . . . but it leaves me free:
> I have not vilely found, nor basely sought,
> They made an exile – not a slave of me.
>
> (76–8)

The general drift of Perticari's argument, as we have seen, was to present Dante as the victim of petty malice and as a patriot more sinned against than sinning. In the course of *Dell'Amor Patrio di Dante*, Perticari resorts to the device of quoting Dante's own words in his favour, or indeed the words attributed to Dante by Lionardo Bruno, such as Dante's exclamation to the Florentine potentates when he decided not to accept their humiliating conditions – 'Popolo mio che feci a te?'.[30] Byron's attitude to Dante is interestingly similar, and in the climactic lines of the fourth Canto of *The Prophecy* he actually quotes the same line from Dante:

> 'What have I done to thee, my people?'
> Stern are all thy dealings, but in this they pass
> The limits of man's common malice, for
> All that a citizen could be I was.
>
> (141–4)

The Prophecy of Dante is also Byron's attempt to appeal directly to the nationalistic sentiments of the Italians through the medium of poetry at a time when Byron himself had become increasingly involved in the Carbonari movement. *The Prophecy*, in fact, endorsed political revolution by urging the Italians to forget their 'petty strife' and organise themselves against Austrian domination:

> Are ye not brave? Yes, yet the Ausonian soil
> Hath hearts, and hands, and arms, and hosts to bring
> Against Oppression; but how vain the toil,
> While still Division sows the seeds of woe
> And weakness, till the stranger reaps the spoil!
>
> (II, 131–5)

It is worth observing here that Byron very probably responded directly to a personal plea from a contemporary Italian poet to use his poetical talent in the service of Italy's struggle against oppression. In his book of verse written under the pseudonym of Albo Crisso, Count Giuseppe Bossi, a patriot, had urged Byron earlier in 1817 to take up the cause of Italian liberty. In a poem dedicated to Byron, *Al Lord Byron, celebre poeta inglese*,[31] Bossi appealed to Byron to enter the lists on behalf of those countries oppressed by the 'smemorate e pazze Reggie Europee':

> Animoso Byron, d'Italia oppressa
> Odi 'l nobil lamento e le severe
> Voci che pel mio labbro a questa manda
> Ch'ammirare ed amar vorria pur solo
> Congenial terra . . .
> Questi, o dotto Byron, d'Italia i sensi,
> Son, d'Italia che alfin co prischi marmi
> Disotterar la virtù prisca anela . . .[32]

(Valiant Byron, listen to the noble lament and grave voices/ concerning oppressed Italy which my lips utter/ for I wish to admire and love this congenial land . . . Such are the feelings of Italy, O learned Byron/ which in the end desire to exhume ancient virtue with old monuments . . .)

Bossi's poems on the whole are inferior imitations of Alfieri's odes and as such are monotonous variations on the themes of Tyranny and Liberty. Bossi's patriotic sincerity, however, occasionally comes to the fore despite the plangent rhetoric of most of his verse. In an important note appended to his poem addressed to Byron, Bossi attempted a diagnosis of the political malaise of his country as he saw it and drew Byron's attention to the fact that internal disputes among the potentates of the states constituted the main obstacle to Italian unification:

> . . . questa politica antinazionale fu onorata da alcuni statisti di collegio dello specioso titolo d'Indipendenza Italiana; come se l'indipendenza di dieci o dodici signorotti impotenti a far rispettare nell'estero i loro vassali ma potentissimi per angustiarli e apogliarli nell'interno altro fosse che una dipendentissima tirannia, un vero flagello di questa nobilissima parte del mondo . . .[33]

> (. . . this anti-national movement was honoured by certain statesmen of the old school with the title of Italian Independence; as if the independence of ten or twelve lordlings impotent in earning the respect of their subjects abroad, but potent in afflicting and despoiling them at home was something more than a most dependent tyranny, a real scourge in this most noble part of the world . . .)

The second Canto of *The Prophecy* may well have been Byron's attempt to write a poem on the lines suggested here by Count Bossi.

III

Critics have rightly assumed that in this poem Byron projected himself into the character of Dante and at times made the Italian poet a mouthpiece for his own real or imagined wrongs. It also seems likely, however, that Byron's poetical conception of the character of Dante in this poem was somewhat influenced by his high regard for the Italian patriot Vittorio Alfieri, who indeed shared with Dante a deep love of his country and an abiding hatred of tyranny. Alfieri, in the view of most Italians of Byron's time, was regarded as a national poet who articulated his people's desire for national consciousness. He was also exalted as the champion of Italian liberty. In *Corinne* Madame de Staël had quoted a line from one of his sonnets on liberty as a rallying call for the Italians to regain their self-respect. Byron himself felt a kindred spirit with the Italian aristocrat which he admitted in his

journal, was 'related merely to our apparent personal disposi-
tions'.[34] The topic of Italian patriotism was firmly associated in
the minds of most Italians with Alfieri's fiery spirit. Indeed, Byron
confirmed this when he recorded in his diary that at the Countess
Guiccioli's 'Talked of Italy, patriotism, Alfieri, Madame Albany
and other branches of learning'.[35] It is significant that in the
Preface to *The Prophecy*, Byron refers to Alfieri's fine sonnet on
Dante[36] and it is not surprising that in a poem urging the Italians
to awake from their spiritual lethargy Byron should have been
influenced by the Italian poet's ideas on a similar theme.

In his autobiographical *La Vita*, Alfieri had analysed his
feelings on paying his respects to Vittorio Amedeo ii when he
passed through Turin upon his return from France in 1784.
Although he had nothing personal against the monarch of
Piedmont who seemed favourably disposed towards him, Alfieri
recalls that he was suddenly seized with an intense longing to
leave Turin, the reason being, as he put it, that 'chi entra in casa
del tiranno si fa schiavo'.[37] Rather than enter the house of a
despot, however benevolent, the Italian patriot decided to leave
Piedmont. In the third Canto of *The Prophecy of Dante* Byron
expresses his distrust of tyrants in much the same words and he
goes on to elaborate on the Alfierian notion of the subtle processes
of tyranny:

> He who once enters in a tyrant's hall
> As guest is slave, his thoughts become a booty,
> And the first day which sees the chain enthrall
> A captive, sees his half of manhood gone –
>
> (80–3)

The lines immediately following seem to be inspired by Alfieri's
account of his indignant refusal to be introduced to Metastasio
who was then imperial poet at the Court of Vienna. Alfieri records
that he felt a revulsion for the Italian poet's cringing attitude to his
Austrian patrons and on no account would he have sought
acquaintance of a poet who had prostituted his Muse:

> ... non avrei consentito mai di contrarre nè amicizia nè
> familiarita con una Musa appigionata o venduta all'autorità
> despotica da me si caldamenta abborita.[38]

(. . . I would never have accepted to contract friendship or
familiarity with a Muse which was hired or sold to a despotic
authority so bitterly abhorred by me.)

Byron's lines on the abject subjection of poets to their patrons
have a similar resonance:

> . . . thus the Bard too near the throne
> Quails from his inspiration, bound to *please*, –
> How servile is the task to please alone!
> To smooth the verse to suit his sovereign's ease
> And royal leisure, nor too much prolong
> Aught save his eulogy, and find, and seize,
> Or force, or forge fit argument of song!
>
> (III, 85–91)

Very probably the lines are also a dig at Monti's political
unreliability and his readiness to temper his verse to suit those in
authority.[39] At any rate, in his *Del Principe e delle Lettere* Alfieri
developed the notion of the prostitution of art for purposes of
propaganda and the poets' self-abasing dependence on royal
patronage. Alfieri's main argument in this treatise is based on the
fact that the potentates of his times kept writers and artists in their
pay in order to suppress the truth and the conclusion he comes to
is that the arts cannot thrive under a despot:

> Gli scrittori a vicenda contra-cambierranno i principi con le
> smaccate lodi, con le deificazioni, co'falsi poemi, storie alterate,
> libri di diletto senz'utile, false massime in politica, falso
> filosofia.[40]

(The writers in turn will reciprocate their prince with exagger-
ated praise, with deifications, with false poems, with distorted
stories, with useless books of amusement, with false political
maxims and false philosophy.)

The Italianism of *The Prophecy* was a literary mood which Byron
conveniently assumed for the purpose of arousing the Italians to
an awareness of their cultural heritage at a moment he considered
to be opportune. It was not so much a pose as a genuine attempt
to write in a manner which would strike a responsive note in most

cultured Italians. Shelley was right in surmising that the subject was addressed to the select few and would 'only be *fully* appreciated by the select readers of many generations'.[41] There were signs in Ravenna of a clandestine uprising against the Austrians and Byron sincerely hoped that Italian patriotism would find expression in action. *The Prophecy*, then, resonant with echoes from Dante and Alfieri, would serve as a trumpet call to freedom from foreign oppression. As his letter to Murray shows, the poem was inspired by a deep feeling for Italy and a genuine sympathy for the cause of the Italians:

> . . . for I shall think it by far the most interesting spectacle and moment in existence – to see the Italians send the Barbarians of all nations back to their own dens – I have lived long enough among them – to feel more for them as a nation than for any other people in existence.[42]

Ravenna with its inescapable memories of Dante was a constant source of inspiration to Byron. A ride in the Pineta forest outside Ravenna occasioned the conscious imitation of the opening stanza of the eighth Canto of *Il Purgatorio*[43] with its fine evocation of a serene Italian sunset:

> Soft hour! which wakes the wish and melts the heart
> Of those who sail the seas, on the first day
> When they from their sweet friends are torn apart;
> Or fills with love the pilgrim on his way
> As the far bell of vesper make him start,
> Seeming to weep the dying day's decay;
>
> > (*DJ*, III, cviii, 1–6)

The Italian landscape aroused literary associations in Byron's mind. As he admitted to Medwin:

> I was never tired of my rides in the pine forest: it breathes of the Decameron; it is poetical ground. Francesca lived, and Dante was exiled and died at Ravenna. There is something inspiring in such an air.[44]

Byron's attachment to the Guiccioli had its effect on his assimilation of the Italian language. He was confident of his ability to write and speak the language. In a letter to Tom Moore he announced that he intended to write his best work in Italian, though he added self-critically that it would take him at least nine years to master the language. His letters to Teresa at the time show he wrote fluent Italian even though he occasionally translated the English idiom.[45] The remarkable thing about these letters is that Byron allowed himself to be influenced by the native effusiveness of the Italian amatory style. It should be remembered, however, that Byron may have been all too conscious of the effect such letters would have on Teresa's romantic disposition. Indeed, Byron's fondness for La Guiccioli led him to share her literary taste. Although as we have seen he much preferred Dante to Petrarch, Teresa recalls that he was delighted to hear her recite some of Petrarch's sonnets and *canzoni*. Strangely enough, despite his disparaging remarks about Petrarch in his journal and later in *Don Juan*, Byron chose to imitate the Italian poet. During a temporary separation from Teresa Guiccioli when she followed her husband to the Guiccioli estate to the north of the Po, Byron found solace in writing a poem to his new 'amica'. *The Stanzas to the Po*, as he admitted to Hobhouse, were written 'in red-hot Earnest'[46] and I would suggest that in composing this poem Byron deliberately imitated a sonnet by Petrarch. The reason is, I believe, that Byron felt obliged to write in a manner which would appeal to the sentimental Teresa who was herself an ardent admirer of Petrarch. A comparison between Byron's poem and Petrarch's sonnet will demonstrate that Byron very probably had this particular poem in mind when he wrote his *Stanzas to the Po*. Here is Petrarch's original sonnet:

> Rapido fiume, che d'alpestra vena
> rodendo intorno, onde l'tuo nome prendi,
> notte e di meco disioso scendi
> ov'Amor me, te sol natura mena,
>
> Vattene innanzi: il tuo corso non frena
> nè stanchezza nè sonno: e pria che rendi
> suo dritto al mar, fiso i' si mostri attendi
> l'erba più verde e l'aria più serena.
>
> Ivi a quel nostro vivo e dolce sole
> ch'addorna e infiora la tua riva manca
> forse (o che spero) e l'mio tardar le dole.

Basciale'l piede, o la man bella e bianca;
dille, e 'l basciar sie'n vece di parole;
'Lo spirito è pronto ma la carne è stanca.'[47]

(Swift river, which from its alpine source/ winds around the place and whence you derive your name/ night and day you descend to me/ where love solely possesses me while nature nourishes you./ Go before me, for weariness and sleep do not stop your course/ and before you flow direct to the sea/ you pass by a greener grass and a more serene sky./ For there the bright and sweet sun which adorns and fills your banks with flowers is lacking/ perhaps (what do I hope for) my lingering upsets her./ Kiss her feet, or her lovely white hand/ tell her, and let your kisses be a substitute for words/ 'the spirit is willing but the flesh is weak'.)

Byron's poem preserves the Petrarchan notion of an address to the river which both separates the lovers and affords a medium of communication:

> River, that rollest by the ancient walls,
> Where dwells the lady of my love, when she
> Walks by thy brink, and there perchance recalls
> A faint and fleeting memory of me.   (1–4)

The river, as Petrarch conceives it, is a go-between carrying an urgent message of love which the poet expresses in quasi-blasphemous terms in the last line. The Po, on the other hand, becomes a mirror of Byron's passionate feelings:

> A mirror of my heart, where she may read
> The thousand thoughts I now betray to thee,
> Wild as they wave, and headlong as they speed!
>   (6–8)

The Po for Byron is a symbol of an inescapable destiny and gives rise to an ambivalent attitude to his love as expressed in:

> But left long wrecks behind, and now again
> Borne on our old unchanged career, we move:

Thou tendest wildly onwards to the main,
And I – to loving *one* I should not love.

(17–20)

The variant of the last stanza which, as Leslie Marchand noted,[48] differed considerably from that first published by Medwin, transcends Byron's Petrarchan model and expresses the complexity of his feelings about falling deeply in love again. At the time of the composition of these stanzas, Byron was wary of his newly-formed relationship with the Countess for as Marchand says 'he would not be made a fool of – or a *cicesbeo*; yet he lingered, hoping for a letter from Teresa which did not come'.[49] The Petrarchan notion of the indifferent mistress impervious to her lover's plea is discarded, for it is the poet's own heart which 'pants to be unmoved'.

3 The Libertine as Artist: Giambattista Casti's *Novelle Galanti* and *Beppo*

. . . I have lived among the natives – and in parts of the country – where Englishmen never resided before (I speak of Romagna and this place particularly) – I have lived in their houses and in the heart of their families – sometimes merely as 'amico di casa' and sometimes as 'amico di cuore' of the Dama – and in neither case do I feel authorized in making a book of them. – Their moral is not your moral – their life is not your life – you will not understand it – it is not English nor French – nor German – which you would all understand – the Conventual educational – the Cavalier Servitude – the habits of thought and living are so entirely different – and the difference becomes so much more striking the more you live intimately with them – that I know not how to make you comprehend a people who are at once temperate and profligate – serious in their character and buffoons in their amusements – capable of impressions and passions which are at once sudden and durable . . .

(Byron: Letter to John Murray
Ravenna, 21 February 1820)

Count Fries's arrival, however, gave me fresh incentive to lead a more social life. With him was the Abbé Casti, who gave me great pleasure by reading his unpublished *Novelle Galanti*. His clear and natural style of recitation brought his witty, if very risqué, stories vividly to life.

(Goethe: *Italian Journey*,
trans. W. H. Auden and Elizabeth Mayer)

John Hookham Frere's *Whistlecraft* has long been recognised by

43

Byron scholars as the immediate precursor of *Beppo*. *The Prospectus and Specimen of an Intended National Work, by William and Robert Whistlecraft, of Stow-market, in Suffolk, Harness and Collar-Makers. Intended to Comprise the most Interesting Particulars Relating to King Arthur and his Round Table*,[1] as Frere's poem was facetiously entitled, was sent to Byron by John Murray and carried to Venice by William Stewart Rose in the summer of 1817. Byron was much taken with Frere's ingenious adaptation of the Pulcian burlesque style and felt inspired to emulate Frere. The result of this attempt was *Beppo*, which Byron hastily composed in the short space of five weeks, from 6 September to 10 October 1817, adding five more stanzas to the original eighty-four of the first draft by 23 October.[2]

Frere's clever *jeu d'esprit*, capturing the very essence of Pulci's genial humour and flair for the grotesque, while at the same time skilfully preserving an English flavour and topicality, immediately suggested to Byron the satirical potential of this manner of writing. Frere followed his Italian models, Pulci and Berni, quite closely, but allowed himself a greater freedom of authorial digression and intrusion which enabled him to make veiled comments on the contemporary scene. In writing *Beppo*, Byron acknowledged his debt to Frere in a letter to Murray dated 12 October 1817, announcing that he had written a poem of eighty-four octave stanzas 'in or after the excellent manner of Mr Whistlecraft (whom I take to be Frere), on a Venetian anecdote – which amused me'.[3] Byron was quick to realise that acclimatisation of the *ottava rima* used by the Italian burlesque writers was a complete success and he wrote enthusiastically to Murray declaring that '*Berni* is the father of that kind of writing – which I think suits our language too very well'.[4] Frere, himself, gives an interesting account in a letter to the expatriate Italian writer Ugo Foscolo of his first attraction to Pulci. He had read a critical commentary on Pulci's *Morgante Maggiore* in a volume of Ginguené's *Histoire littéraire d'Italie* and it seemed to him that Pulci's 'ingenious and humorous assumption of the vulgar character and vernacular phrase and rude popular attempts at poetry among his countrymen were capable of being transferred *mutatis mutandis* to the English nation and the present times'.[5] This transference to English soil was brilliantly contrived by the introduction of a loquacious pseudo-author as Frere's persona, and the retention of the essential comic details in the bizarre story of the conversion of the giant Morgante, interspersed with carefully veiled satirical allusions to prominent generals and politicians of the moment. But Frere's satire was too vague and mild to be effective. As John Gibson Lockhart pointed out in his pseudonymous review of *Don Juan* published in 1821, 'Mr Frere writes elegantly, playfully, very like a gentleman, and a scholar, and a respectable man, and his poems never sold nor ever will sell', and though the measure was the same, Lockhart perceived that 'the spirit of the two poets is as different as can be'.[6]

Taking his cue from Frere, Byron developed the art of improvised digression and *par parenthese* chatting and the knack of picking up the thread of the story with remarkable virtuosity. Indeed, in Byron's poem, as R. D. Waller remarks:

The shadows of chivalry give place to the living world. For King Arthur's feast we have the Venetian carnival; for fabulous knights and giants, amorous men and women.[7]

The spirit of Venetian life with its gay frivolity and dissipation undoubtedly contributed much to the composition of *Beppo*. In fact Byron's immediate source for the plot of *Beppo* was an anecdote, supposedly based on a real incident, which was related by Pietro Segati (Marianna's husband) in the presence of Byron and his mistress, and recorded by John Cam Hobhouse in his diary.[8] It concerned a 'Turk' who, arriving at an inn in Venice, demanded to see the mistress of the place and eventually revealed his identity as her former husband presumed lost at sea many years before. Byron, with his obsessive concern with 'some foundation of fact', immediately perceived the opportunity of harnessing poetry to life itself for he was constantly striving to 'exact from life itself the qualities of great poetry'.[9] This strange anecdote, stranger indeed than fiction, provided the brittle framework for *Beppo* and, in its own way, must have reminded Byron of the Abbate Casti's delightful *Novelle Galanti* with their humorous treatment of the motif of the husband's unexpected return. Byron was well acquainted with Casti's work. He had in fact read Casti's *Novelle* in the original a year earlier, in June 1816, in a copy given to him by Major Pryse Gordon in Brussels. So delighted was he with the *Novelle*, that he immediately wrote to thank Pryse Gordon for:

. . . the treat your gift of Casti has been to me; I have almost got him by heart. I have read his *Animali Parlanti*, but I think these 'Novelle' much better.[10]

It is my purpose in this chapter to demonstrate that it was mainly Casti's style in the *Novelle Galanti* which was responsible for Byron's new satirical technique in *Beppo* and not, as is commonly supposed, that of *Mr Whistlecraft* or Frere's Italian models, Pulci and Berni.

Giambattista Casti's somewhat lascivious *Novelle* in *ottava rima* were first published in 1790 and achieved instant popularity. This edition contained eighteen of Casti's *Novelle* but a subsequent edition, published in Paris in 1804, included all the forty-eight *novelle* which Casti wrote before his death in 1803. Casti's lifetime experience as poet of the Court – in Florence, Venice, St Petersburg and Vienna, gave him a unique insight into the courtly life of political intrigue and scandal of the times, and accounts for the knowing, cynical, man-of-the-world tone in his licentious *Novelle*,[11] which he unashamedly addressed to the women of the court. Most of these *ottava rima* satires are *rifacimenti* of earlier stories told by Casti's more famous literary predecessors: seven of these – *Il Rusignolo, Il Purgatorio, Il Diavolo nell'inferno, L'Arcangelo Gabriello, La Communanza, L'Incantesimo* and *La Celia* – are adaptations of stories told by Boccaccio.[12] Bandello's thirty-sixth *novella* was the source of one of Casti's satires – *L'Apoteosi* – and for the theme of *La Sposa Cucita*, Casti was indebted to Firenzuola. Voltaire, of whom Casti was a great admirer, inspired two of the *novelle, Geltrude ed Isabella* and *La Fata Urgella*. A few, such as *L'Arcivescovo di Praga* (which was Goethe's favourite), *La Scommessa, Monsignor Fabrizio* and *Il Cavalier Servente*, are Casti's own invention and derive their inspiration from the poet's detached and cynical observation of the sexual mores of the times.

Casti's *Novelle Galanti* are characterised by a certain gusto in the actual telling of the story, a penchant on the author's part for the unusual or even bizarre situation, and the narrator's interruption of the tale to comment facetiously on the naïveté of the characters concerned or on the intractability of the story itself. There is an obsessive concern with fact in Casti's satires, to the exclusion of any form of speculative reasoning or moralising:

Ma L'astratto lasciam tuon metafisico,
Poichè non è di nostra competenza;
E d'altra parte non vo'correr risico
Di stancar la gentil vostra indulgenza.
Un fatto narrerò reale e fisico . . .
(*L'Ossessa*, xxx, ii, 1–5)

(But let us set aside the metaphysical tone/ since it is not within our competence/ and besides I don't wish to run the risk/ of tiring your gentle indulgence./ I shall narrate a real and physical fact . . .)

This matter-of-fact approach with its Voltairian scorn of ignorance and superstition pervades most of the *Novelle*. Time and again Casti will digress, with his customary mock-seriousness, to dilate upon the hypocrisy of a society bent on deceiving itself or to underline the folly of belief in meaningless and effete traditions and customs. The tone, however, is not that of an outraged Juvenal castigating a corrupt and decadent society, but rather that of a tolerant and detached old cleric, who, in his worldly wisdom, has grown indulgent of human frailty and amused by it.

A certain coarseness and indelicacy in a number of the *Novelle* mar their artistic quality. Foscolo, in his learned dissertation on the *Narrative and Romantic Poems of the Italians*, takes Casti to task for his lack of 'urbanity, propriety and variety of harmony in his verse' and goes on to censure the poet for 'spitting his venom at virtue and religion'.[13] In all fairness to Casti, it must be said that Foscolo's heightened sensibility was shocked by the poet's obscenity and disregard for subtleties of style. However, Casti's manner *is* devoid of that artistic refinement with which Boccaccio and Ariosto charmed their audiences even in the more profane passages, and his satire is not tempered by any moral purpose or by a zest to stir the imagination of men to nobler ideals. His world is the world of gallantry and intrigue of Italian and indeed European decadent society in the late eighteenth century. It is a world of *cavalieri serventi* and *cicisbei*, of resourceful women outwitting old and jealous husbands, of farcical bedroom scenes and of roguish friars seducing naïve virgins. Time-honoured institutions and customs are often the butt of Casti's mordant irony, and one can at times detect a hint of sneaking admiration for the libertine's knack of making a virtue out of vice, as in:

Spesso il vizio per lei divien virtù
E ciò 'ch'era virtù vizio diviene.

(For him vice often becomes a virtue/ and what was a virtue
becomes a vice.)

The cardinal sins, in Casti's *Novelle*, are ignorance and indiscretion, while ingenuity, 'spirit' (Casti's 'spirito' eludes translation) and native shrewdness are extolled as virtues. Moral scruples and religious fervour are often equated with gullibility, for the society depicted in the *Novelle* is both materialistic and hedonistic. Casti's propensity to scoff at all things human – 'giullare di tutto e di tutti' (as Carducci put it) – earned him the unqualified censure of most nineteenth-century critics, and his virulent attacks on the clergy caused his books to be placed on the *Index Librorum Prohibitorum*.[14]

Benedetto Croce, in his survey of Italian literature of the eighteenth century, makes the interesting point that Casti's satires were more often appreciated by foreigners than by the Italians themselves, mostly because Casti perversely cultivated a deliberately unpoetic language and showed little regard for form. According to Croce the Italians:

. . . non danno il loro cuore a quel che è floscio e banale nella forma, senza forte nerbo e senza delicata fantasia.[15]

(. . . do not pay heed to what is flabby and banal in form, and lacking in nerve and delicate fantasy.)

Croce's main criticism was that Casti was too dispassionate and detached and lacked the warmth of Ariosto, commenting:

Ma il Casti sta in quel piano nel quale la tepidezza e l'indifferenza tengono il luogo della passione, e l'osservazione degli errori e delle malefatte dei governanti tengono quella della scienza.[16]

(But Casti is on that level where lukewarmness and indifference take over from passion, and observations on the errors and misdeeds of rulers take the place of knowledge.)

This criticism is valid: there is no appeal whatsoever in the *Novelle* to man's better nature or any awareness on the poet's part of the gap between the actual and the ideal. Society is utterly corrupt and Casti acutely describes this degradation with cynical detachment and amusement. Despite their shortcomings, the *Novelle* possess an engaging humour and vitality which Byron found most attractive. 'I long to go to Venice to see the manners so admirably described',[17] he wrote to Pryse Gordon, probably meaning that he hoped to see in Venice the manners described by Casti of Italian life in general, since only two of the *Novelle* are actually set in Venice.[18]

I would suggest that it was Casti – not Frere – who taught Byron the satirical mode he was to assume throughout *Beppo* and *Don Juan*; Piero Segati's strange and amusing anecdote of the 'Turk' who returned to claim his former mistress, his odd behaviour and his absurd request, caught Byron's fancy and suggested to him an outline for a light-hearted satire on Italian life and morals which would appeal to Murray and the 'knowing ones'. This strange anecdote, in its own way, showed remarkable affinities with the plots of Casti's satires, especially those *novelle* based on the theme of Italian *serventismo* with their focus on the return of the lover or husband and the subsequent absurd *ménage à trois*. It is more than likely that the *Novelle* were still fresh in Byron's retentive mind and that they consciously or otherwise influenced his treatment of a similar theme. *Whistlecraft*, it is true, had come as a revelation, and Byron had admired Frere's skill in assimilating the *ottava rima* to the vernacular. But in *Beppo*, undoubtedly a 'breakaway from his literary past', Byron was greatly indebted to Casti for the technique of his new satirical style.

Before proceeding to examine the extent of the influence of the *Novelle Galanti* on Byron's *Beppo*, I should like to consider the wider perspective of Byron's literary development in relation to his search for a form which would best express his complex poetic self. When Byron read Casti's *Novelle* during the summer of 1816, he had written about thirty stanzas of the fourth Canto of *Childe Harold* dealing with the historical and political vicissitudes of Italy. The themes of death, fame and the human condition provided Byron with a convenient opportunity to indulge his tendency to dramatic posturing with its consequent 'sonorous affirmations of the commonplace'.[19] The stanzas on Ferrara and Santa Croce, with their solemn stress on the value rather than the vanity of human achievement, are strongly redolent in tone of the patriotic sonnets of Alfieri (especially the latter's fine sonnet to Florence).[20] The intense outbursts of self-justification and self-pity which are interspersed were, as we have seen, influenced by the sufferings of the sentimental Jacopo in Foscolo's *Le Ultime Lettere di Jacopo Ortis*. It is remarkable that particularly in this Canto, Byron owed more to his wide but desultory reading than to his personal observation of Italian life and the Italian landscape. Nor is this the only instance where Byron was heavily indebted to foreign authors for their observations on the Italian scene. It was his reading of Corinne's reflections on Rome in Madame de Staël's *Corinne* which furnished Byron with material for his observations on the former grandeur of Rome and on the intractability of the Ocean as 'an image of eternity'. It is likely, in view of this, that in the more deeply reflective or 'metaphysical' passages, Byron as yet self-conscious and unsure of himself, felt the need to lean for support on the authority of those authors of repute whom he himself revered. His natural poetic temperament was strongly inclined towards the factual and the 'real', and as Marchand rightly observes 'he always returned from the most airy speculations to reason and common sense'.[21] Even his Wordsworthian metaphysic – the result of frequent 'doses' patiently administered by Shelley during their stay at Diodati in 1816 – soon wore off, mostly, one imagines, because he must have felt that it was basically alien to his own materialistic conception of the Universe.

The point that I wish to make is that Byron's poetry, written at this stage in his artistic development, failed to accommodate the many facets of his personality. Andrew Rutherford has remarked that the fourth Canto of *Childe Harold* is 'the most loosely organized as well as the longest section of Childe Harold's pilgrimage'[22] partly because Byron added sixty stanzas as afterthoughts to the original one hundred and twenty-six, and partly because in Rutherford's words, he found it 'much more difficult to maintain the personality he had assumed'.[23] This seems to me to be a just view. Certainly in this Canto Byron seems unable to shake off the habitual melancholy and ranting pessimism which he had deemed appropriate to his projected image of himself. William Gifford, whose literary judgment Byron greatly respected, had advised him against persisting in this attitude of gloom and misanthropy. Referring to Harold, Gifford suggested in a letter dated 15 June 1813 that:

His fixed melancholy might be shaken and glimpses of delight break in occasionally over his habitual gloom.[24]

Some of the dramatic posturing of Harold, however, remained, even though the Childe had disappeared from the scene. In a mood of critical self-awareness, Byron confessed to Murray (9 March 1817): 'I certainly am a devil of a mannerist – and must leave off' and a day later, writing to Thomas Moore apropos of Jeffrey's review, he admits:

> . . . I was not, and, indeed, am not even *now*, the misanthropical and gloomy gentleman he takes me for, but a facetious companion, well to do with those with whom I am intimate, and as loquacious and laughing as if I were a much cleverer fellow. I suppose now I shall never be able to shake off my sables in public imagination . . .[25]

It is obvious from these words that there was another side to Byron's personality that had remained hitherto unexpressed in his poetry – Byron as revealed in the letters to Murray, Kinnaird and Moore with their robust satirical humour, facetiousness and ribald comments on the 'incontinent continental system'. Although Byron had originally intended to introduce 'variations' in *Childe Harold* 'of a droll or satirical character' in the manner of Thomson and Ariosto, he felt diffident about the actual blending of the serious and the jocose as can be seen in his letter to R. C. Dallas (21 August 1811):

> . . . of course there are little things I would wish to alter, and perhaps the two Stanzas of a buffooning cast (on London's Sunday) are as well left out.[26]

However, the two stanzas in question (Canto I, lxix, lxx) were allowed to stand and, in Moore's view 'continued to disfigure the poem'.[27] The overall effect is one of dissonance – a gratuitous shifting to a different key – and Byron, one feels, with his ungovernable impulse to flippancy rudely interrupts his own persona's solemn and serious meditations on the 'voluptuousness' of vice in Spain. Besides, the Spenserian measure with the slow and dignified movement of the alexandrine does not easily lend itself here to fitful changes of tone and mood.

This assumption of different styles and changing points of view is prevalent throughout the fourth Canto, though there are no lapses into drollery. The Italian scene in its historical perspective provided the stimulus for self-assertive posturing and facile speculations on fame and liberty. This constant attitudinising has the effect of masking those personal impressions of Italy which he had communicated in his letters to his friends. The stanzas on Santa Croce's 'holy precincts' afford an interesting example of Byron's rather ambivalent reaction to the monuments of Italy. The church itself which he visited in April 1817 provided Byron with a starting point for his solemn reflections – in the manner of Alfieri and Foscolo – on the immortality of Italy's men of genius ('the spirits which soar from ruin'). About the same time he composed these stanzas he confessed to Murray, in a letter dated 26 April 1817, that 'the church of "Santa Croce" contains much illustrious nothing' and expressed his indignation at the fact that the Medici Chapel with its 'fine frippery in great slabs of various expensive stones' was there to 'commemorate fifty rotten and forgotten carcases'.[28] It is obvious that, especially in this final Canto, the image of himself that Byron had projected in his poetry was dictating the shape of his poem at the expense of suppressing his deeper emotions. Byron, with his usual self-awareness, gives a hint of this in the dedicatory letter to Hobhouse prefaced to Canto IV; the 'labyrinth of external objects' conditioned his subsequent reflections and prevented his touching 'upon the present state of Italian literature and perhaps of manners'.[29]

It is not difficult to prove why Casti's *Novelle Galanti* had such an impact on Byron, coming as they did at a time when he was most conscious of being trapped in the 'mannerist' style he could not easily discard. In the course of this chapter I should like to demonstrate that in composing *Beppo* Byron was considerably influenced by Casti and in particular by four of the *Novelle Galanti*; namely, *Il Cavalier Servente*, *Il Ritorno Inaspettato*, *La Scommessa* and *Il Rosignuolo*. Broadly speaking, the raw materials of *Beppo* were the Segati anecdote of the 'Turk', the episode of Colonel Fitzgerald – the 'unshaken Abdiel of absence'[30] – and Byron's own observations on Venice in 'the *estro* of her Carnival'.[31] The opening stanzas of *Beppo* are for the most part a clever versification of the substance of his letters to Hobhouse and Moore. The actual unfolding of the story of Laura, Beppo and the Count is, however, strongly reminiscent of the manner employed by Casti in the

Novelle – that man-of-the-world attitude with its carefully modulated tone and its delicate equipoise between approval and condemnation:

> And then, God knows, what mischief may arise,
> When love links two young people in one fetter,
> Vile assignations, and adulterous beds,
> Elopements, broken vows, and hearts and heads.
>
> (*Beppo*, xvi, 5–8)

The *Novelle* mentioned above deal exclusively with the theme of *serventismo* and are in themselves a vehicle for Casti's clever display of wit; they also contain some of Casti's most cynical observations on the subject. In *La Scommessa* for instance, Casti comments wryly on the changes of fashion in society which, he sardonically maintains, are to be welcomed because they brighten up the tiresome tediousness of life ('la nojosa servil monotonia'). The overriding concern for honour, which in the past made the outraged husband take the law into his own hands had now, according to the poet, given place to a convenient acquiescence in adultery. This is in fact what Casti says:

> Tempo già fu che col ferro omicida
> Fiero marito vendicò l'oltraggio,
> Che all'onor suo facea la moglie infida.
> Più mansueto or divenuto e saggio,
> Sovente avvien, che sen diverta e rida,
> E applauda al conjugal libertinaggio;
>
> (*La Scommessa*, xlv, iv, 1–6)

(Time was when with a murderous sword/ the proud husband would avenge the outrage/ with which the unfaithful wife stained his honour./ He is meeker now and wiser/ and it often happens that this amuses him and he laughs/ and applauds this conjugal profligacy.)

It is interesting to notice how closely Byron echoes this line of thought using the same mock-serious tone in the first part of his poem:

> And to this day from Venice to Verona
> Such matters may be probably the same,

> Except that since those times was never known a
> Husband whom mere suspicion could inflame
> To suffocate a wife no more than twenty,
> Because she had a 'cavalier servente'.
>
> (*Beppo*, xvii, 2–8)

The pleasure-loving, sensual Donna Maddalena in *La Scommessa*, who spends long evenings in the company of *damerini* and *cicisbei*, was Byron's prototype for Laura though, of course, Byron drew on his own experience of Venetian women. Laura, like Donna Maddalena, is a flirt and a coquette and particularly fond of appearing in society. The charming picture of Laura as the 'cynosure of neighbouring eyes' at the Ridotto:

> Now Laura moves along the joyous crowd,
> Smiles in her eyes, and simpers on her lips;
> To some she whispers, others speaks aloud;
> To some she curtsies, and to some she dips,
> Complains of warmth, and this complaint avow'd,
> Her lover brings the lemonade, she sips . . .
>
> (*Beppo*, lxv, 1–6)

owes much to Casti's description of Donna Maddalena surrounded by her circle of admiring friends as is evident in the following lines taken from Casti's *La Scommessa*:

> Ella a tutti facea viso benigno,
> E ora a questi una dolce parolina,
> Ed ora a quegli un lusinghier sogghigno
> O un vezzo dispensava o un'occhiatina;
> Nulla curando di censor maligno . . .
>
> (*La Scommessa*, xlv, ix, 1–5)

(She looked benignly at every one/ and now to one a sweet word/ and to another a flattering smile/ dispensing either charms or glances/ not caring about the malign censor.)

The similarity ends here, for whereas Laura is true to her *cavalier servente*, Donna Maddalena as the story progresses degenerates into a promiscuous and dissolute woman who takes a number of lovers in succession.

The *Novelle*, however, were still uppermost in Byron's mind in the process of the composition of *Beppo*. The parting scene of Laura and Beppo and Laura's subsequent languishing are reminiscent of the scene in Casti's *Il Ritorno Inaspettato* (*Novella* XXXIII) in which the happily married Lindoro suddenly decides to enlist in the army to defend his country in war and takes leave of his attractive young wife Climene who is left utterly disconsolate at their parting. In Casti's story Climene, in the long absence of her husband, consoles herself by taking a lover and, true to type, shows remarkable resourcefulness when her husband unexpectedly returns. Commenting on Lindoro's sudden departure, Casti refers to the classical story of the desertion of Ariadne by Theseus:

> E Climene in lasciar non mica feo,
> Siccome fe con Arianna in Nasso
> Più gran birbon, che grand'eroe Teseo,
>   (*Il Ritorno Inaspettato*, XXXIII, xxiv, 1–2)

(And in leaving Climene he did not do/ what was done to Ariadne in Nasso/ by that great rascal, rather than hero, Theseus himself.)

This reference to Ariadne is taken up in Byron's description of Beppo's parting from his 'Adriatic Ariadne', but the sarcastic allusion to the 'grand hero' Theseus is dropped. There is, besides, a similarity in the behaviour of the two women Laura and Climene: they are both inconsolable, for a short time they both lose their appetite and feel lonely and insecure.

Byron's first-hand knowledge of the Venetian way of life as well as his own role as *servente* in his liaison with Marianna Segati, no doubt provided him with the material for his humorous comments on the duties of the *cavalier servente* or 'vice husband'. However, some of the more cynical observations in *Beppo* may well be due to the influence of Casti and, in particular, to the Italian poet's treatment of this 'occupation' as a rather boring pastime for a man of wealth. The 'moral' of Casti's *Il Cavalier Servente* (*Novella* XVI) is that *serventismo* can become a very tedious affair if the woman concerned is possessive and domineering. The duties of the *cavaliere servente* are almost sacrosanct and the relationship between the gallant and his lady is, ironically, more binding than matrimony. As Casti facetiously remarks:

> Servì per tutto e accompagnò la dama;
> E così a quel mestier bel bel s'inizia,
> Che di servente cavalier si chiama:
> E un galantuom, se in certi impegni entrò,
> A grado suo disciorsene no può.
>
> (*Il Cavalier Servente*, XVI, xvii, 4–8)

(He served the lady in all and accompanied her,/ and thus one gradually is accustomed to the trade/ which is called that of a servant cavalier/ and if a gentleman subscribes to certain commitments/ he cannot disengage himself freely.)

Casti goes on to comment cynically on the ways in which the lover's ardour is gradually stultified by custom and the force of habit:

> Si commincia talor per complimento
> Per gentilezza o per convenienza,
> E si continua poi per sentimento
> D'amicizia, e talor per compiacenza;
> E di natura alfine un andamento
> Divien d'un atto stesso la frequenza,
> Passa in necessità la consuetudine,
> E sempre in noi gran forza ha l'abitudine.
>
> (*Il Cavalier Servente*, XVI, xviii, 1–8)

(It all begins with a compliment/ out of gallantry or convenience/ and it then continues out of sentiment/ of friendship, and sometimes out of complacency/ and in the course of things a way of life/ sanctioned by frequency/ and habit soon makes it a necessity/ and the force of custom is very strong with us.)

These lines may have actually suggested to Byron the tone he was to adopt in describing the function of the *cavalier servente* in *Beppo*:

> But 'Cavalier Servente' is the phrase
> Used in polite circles to express
> This supernumerary slave, who stays
> Close to the lady as a part of dress,
> Her word the only law which he obeys,
> His is no sinecure as you may guess . . .
>
> (xi, 1–5)

Casti was also probably the source of Byron's witty comment on the constancy of the dutiful *servente* in stanza xxxiv of *Beppo*:

> His heart was one of those which most enamour us,
> Wax to receive and marble to retain:
> He was a lover of the good old school,
> Who still become more constant as they cool.
>
> (4–8)

The recognised duties of *serventismo* are scrupulously performed by Alceste in *Il Cavalier Servente*, and these include accompanying his mistress in public to shows and social gatherings ('adunanze'). Byron's Count is even more accomplished in that he is also an art connoisseur, a raconteur and formidable music critic. It is interesting to observe how Byron improved on his source in the creation of the character of the Count. In the original versions of the story (that is, in the account of Segati's anecdote in Hobhouse's diary and that recorded by Cicogna),[32] the lady had married the innkeeper of the *Regina di Ungaria* after the 'death' of her first husband. Byron deliberately altered this 'fact' and introduced the character of the Count as the woman's *cavalier servente* mostly because it gave him wider scope for his humorous observations on the Venetian way of life. Another reason – that suggested by Meneghetti in his *Lord Byron a Venezia*, and which seems to me to be most likely – is that Byron wished to caricature his Venetian friend Count Francesco Rizzo-Patarol, a *bon viveur* and man-about-town and a close acquaintance of Hoppner, the British Consul in Venice.[33] Indeed, Count Rizzo-Patarol with his love of intrigue and gossip might have been a character in one of Casti's *novelle*.

The influence of Casti, however, is most obvious in Byron's effusion on the joys of youthful love half way through the poem. The passage in question occurs in Byron's description of the 'new arrangement' of the Count and Laura and their subsequent happiness. The stanza reads as follows:

> But they were young: Oh! what without our youth
> Would love be! What would youth be without love!
> Youth lends it joy, and sweetness, vigour, truth,
> Heart, soul, and all that seems as from above;
> But, languishing with years, it grows uncouth –

One of few things experience don't improve,
Which is, perhaps, the reason why old fellows
Are always so preposterously jealous.

(*Beppo*, lv, 1–8)

The lines are a close rendering of the passage in *Il Rosignuolo* (*Novella* xi) in which Casti comments on the passion of the young and innocent Irene for her cousin Sempronio. The latter succeeds in eluding the surveillance of Irene's strict parents and the young lovers consummate their love on the terrace near Irene's bedroom. This is Casti's comment on the bliss of the young couple:

Che vale senza amor la giovinezza,
Che vale senza giovinezza amore?
Gioventù con amor gioja e dolcezza
Spirito vigor diletto infonde in core;
Ma se insipida langue e amor non prezza
Fatuo foco divien, che passa e muore.
E se amor non si accende in giovin petto,
E sol di scherno e di dispregio oggetto.

(*Il Rosignuolo*, xi, xxxv, 1–8)

(What is youth worth without love/ what is love worth without youth?/ Youth with love instils joy and sweetness/ and infuses into the heart a pleasing vigour;/ but if it languishes away unfulfilled by love/ it becomes an *ignis fatuus* which fades and dies/ and if love is not kindled in a youthful heart/ it becomes the object of scorn and ridicule.)

This wistful, passionate outburst is indeed most untypical of Casti who is usually detached in his attitude throughout the *Novelle*. Nor are the sentiments expressed here to be found in the original version in Boccaccio.[34] Casti's own feelings intrude into the poem in spite of himself, and his habitual cynicism gives place to a momentary nostalgic yearning for the vitality of youth. This is more understandable if we bear in mind that Casti was in his late sixties when he composed this *novella*.

The stanza referred to above is certain evidence of Byron's direct borrowing from the *Novelle Galanti* and is of particular interest in that it throws light on Byron's method of composition. The lines themselves appear to be incongruous in their context in

Beppo, for Laura, unlike Casti's Irene, is not a 'vergin fanciuletta' in the flower of her youth but rather as Byron says:

> She was not old, nor young, nor at the years
> Which certain people call a 'certain age',
> Which yet the most uncertain age appears.
>
> (xxii, 1–3)

and later, that 'several years elapsed since they had met'. Nor in effect can the dutiful and refined Count be taken for an impetuous young lover in the prime of life. 'His heart', says Byron facetiously, was 'wax to receive and marble to retain' – constancy being his great virtue. I would suggest here that the passage in *Il Rosignuolo* quoted above first appealed to Byron partly because of the unexpected sincerity of Casti's utterance (it is perhaps the only instance in the *Novelle* where Casti momentarily discards his cynical pose) and partly, one feels, because the lines reflected Byron's own increasing awareness of the waning of passion with age. It is reasonable to suppose that the lines were inserted in the poem in the actual heat of composition since they form part of the matrix stanzas of the first draft and, interestingly enough, they assume a different tone in their new context, as Byron was undoubtedly aware. For here, as applied to Laura and the Count, the verses become pointedly ironical since it is plain throughout the poem that the lovers are neither young nor intemperate. Byron also altered the concluding couplet in his original because it expressed an idea which was at variance with his satirical purpose. In this couplet which Byron rejected, Casti maintains that love 'not kindled in a young heart' soon becomes the object of derision. But it is obvious that in *Beppo* it is the 'Blues' and the 'bustling Botherbys' rather than Laura and her Count who become the butt of Byron's ridicule and he accordingly altered the lines by inserting his frivolous comment on the jealousy of 'old fellows'.

The influence of Casti's *Novelle Galanti* was, in my view, crucial to the development of Byron's new satirical style after 1816. Indeed, under the spell of Casti, Byron's verse acquired a particular incisiveness and 'mobility' which are not to be found in his earlier satires modelled on Gifford and Pope. It was the *Novelle* Byron had 'almost got by heart' which provided him with a new model for his versified story of Venetian life and manners. The

banter, frivolity and equivocal tone of Casti's *Novelle* – 'the licence
of this kind of writing' – had left their mark on *Beppo*. Byron's
direct borrowing from Casti was eclectic: Casti's ideas and actual
turn of phrase, on the whole suggested themselves to the poet
when there tended to be some correspondence between the plot of
Beppo and a similar situation described by Casti in the *Novelle*. But
this is not to suggest that 'Lord Byron was an authorised spoliator
of other men's goods' as Alaric Watts attempted to demonstrate
during Byron's lifetime.[35] Byron characteristically went further
than Casti in introducing random and desultory digressions
which were an expression of his own dominant and self-centred
personality. Furthermore, Byron eschewed the sudden lapses into
coarseness and downright obscenity which spoil the overall effect
of some of Casti's best work. In Casti, however, Byron found the
poetic form which was most congenial to him chiefly because it
echoed 'the diffuse and sprawling pattern of human existence'.[36]
It was the nearest poetry could come to mirroring the reality of life
itself – the stuff of life out of which, as Byron firmly believed, great
poetry is made.

One further point could be made in relation to the influence of
Casti on the composition of *Beppo*. There seems to me to be a trace
of Casti in Byron's humorous comments in his digression on the
fate of the 'poor dear Mussulwomen' who have little means of
entertainment in the seraglio – unlike the ladies of the northern
nations who are constantly courted by their gallants. On this
Byron says:

> They lock them up, and veil, and guard them daily,
> They scarcely can behold their male relations,
> So that their moments do not pass so gaily
> As is supposed the case with northern nations.
> Confinement, too must make them look quite paley;
> And as the Turks abhor long conversations
> Their days are either pass'd in doing nothing,
> Or bathing, nursing, making love and clothing.
>
> (*Beppo*, lxxi, 1–8)

In his digression on Turkish customs Byron, of course, relied on
his own impressions of his visit to Constantinople in 1810, but the
stanza curiously echoes a passage in Casti's *Relazione di un Viaggio
a Costantinòpoli* in which the Italian poet recorded his observations

of his journey to Turkey in 1788. Although there is no definite record in his letters and journals that he had read this book, it is not unlikely that Byron, addicted as he was to travel books, should have read Casti's description of his visit to this city. The passage I refer to occurs in the first part of Casti's account where the Italian poet reflects on the monotony of life of women in Turkey at the time:

> Le donne gelosamente chiuse e custodite nei loro *harem*, altra compagnia non hanno che dei loro mariti o padroni, delle more schiave e degli schifosi eunuchi: e solo il vedere sarebbe delitto non meno grave di quello del favoloso Atteone. Dite pure alle nostre belle, che sian contente delle costumanze europee che procuran loro ammiratori e adoratori ... I Turchi non hanno spettacoli, teatri, ridotti, passeggi, divertimenti pubblici, se per tali non si vogliono prendere le loro solennità religiose.[37]

> (The women who are jealously locked and guarded in their *harem*, do not enjoy other company except that of their husbands or masters, or that of the moorish slaves or the despicable eunuchs; and to gaze on them would be a crime no less serious than that of mythical Acteon. Let our beauties know that they should be content with our European customs which provide for them admirers and adulators . . . The Turks do not have theatres, spectacles *ridotti*, promenades, public amusement places, unless you mean their solemn religious occasions.)

This passage contrasting the boredom of the women confined within the seraglio with the gaiety and freedom of European women in society may have suggested to Byron the notion of the humorous comparison of the 'poor Mussulwomen' with the bluestockings in English society harassed by the 'antique gentleman of rhyme'.

It is indeed surprising that in view of his indebtedness to Casti in *Beppo* and in *Don Juan* no mention is made of the Italian poet in Byron's letters to Murray concerning the origin and development of the Italian burlesque style, nor in the Preface to his translation of Pulci's *Morgante Maggiore* where he traces the descent of the 'new style of poetry very lately sprung up in England' to the mock-serious poetry of Berni and Pulci. Byron himself was

inconsistent in his opinions as to the precursor of this style of
writing and tended to depreciate the immediate source of his style.
This, I think, was mainly due to the fact that he was well aware of
his debt to the Italians, and to Casti in particular, and had
become increasingly sensitive to the charges of plagiarism.
Captain Medwin's account of Byron's conversation with him on
the subject of Casti is of particular interest in this connection.
Medwin had asked Byron to lend him his own personal copy of
Casti:

> 'I mean,' said I one day, 'to translate the *Novelle*.' Byron seemed
> rather alarmed at the idea. 'Casti' said he, 'why you could not
> have a notion of such a thing. There are not ten Englishmen
> who could have read the *Novelle*. They are a sealed book to
> women. The Italians think nothing of it.' 'What do you think
> of it, Byron?' – 'I sha'nt tell you,' he replied laughing.[38]

Medwin seems to imply that Byron made light of Casti because he
was wary of disclosing his debt to the Italian satirical poet. The
remark that the Italians thought nothing of the *Novelle* was far
from the truth: Casti's *Novelle* were enormously popular in his own
day and went through many editions on the Continent.

However, in the context of the literary influence of one author
on another – an influence which may not be solely attributed to a
similarity in temperament, or to the 'endowment of the age in
which they live' – it would be interesting to cite Byron's own
words on the subject as recorded by Lady Blessington. The
Countess of Blessington had asked Byron for his opinion apropos
of the controversial question of Montaigne's literary plagiarisms.
Byron's reply is most illuminating especially if we relate it to his
own poetry:

> Who is the author that is not intentionally or unintentionally, a
> plagiarist . . . for if one has read much, it is difficult, if not
> impossible, to avoid adopting, not only the thoughts, but the
> expressions of others, which, after they have been some time
> stored in our minds, appear to us to come forth ready formed,
> like Minerva from the brain of Jupiter and we fancy them our
> own progeny, instead of being those of adoption . . .[39]

These words, I think may well epitomise the nature of Casti's influence on Byron's poetry. Byron, of course, improved on his original, but the Italian poet was instrumental in showing Byron the ways in which poetry and life tended to coalesce.

4 'The Style of Volubility': *The Novelle Galanti* and the First Cantos of *Don Juan*

A fashion of poetry has been imported which has had a great run, and is in a fair way of being worn out. It is of Italian growth, – an adaptation of the manner of Pulci, Berni and Ariosto in his sportive mood. Frere began it. What he produced was too good in itself and too inoffensive to become popular; for it attacked nothing and nobody; and it had the fault of his Italian models, that the transition from what is serious to what is burlesque was capricious. Lord Byron immediately followed; first with *Beppo*, which implied the profligacy of the writer, and lastly, with his *Don Juan*, which is a foul blot on the literature of his country, an act of high treason on English poetry.

(Letter from Robert Southey to Walter Savage Landor, February 1820)

Shelley recorded his impressions of the first Canto of *Don Juan*, which Byron actually read out to him, in a letter to Peacock dated 8 October 1818. He was quick to discern that it was written 'in the style of *Beppo*, but infinitely better'[1] but he was not too enthusiastic about the dedicatory stanzas which seemed to him 'more like a mixture of wormwood and verdigrease than satire'.[2] Byron himself had previously acknowledged to Moore in September that he had completed about a hundred and eighty octaves 'in the style and manner of *Beppo*' which were meant to be 'a little quietly facetious upon everything'.[3] This tone of mocking irreverence which he had borrowed from Casti and which Byron found congenial to his satirical temperament was now to pervade the opening Canto of *Don Juan*.

In his detailed analysis of the composition of the first Canto of

Don Juan, T. G. Steffan has endeavoured to account for the ever-shifting variety of *Don Juan* by relating the poem to Byron's experience of Venetian life, his daily conversations with his friends, and situations and attitudes taken from life.[4] Indeed, Steffan's article is largely concerned with reconstructing analytically 'an emotional and environmental biography' which he believes to be the 'psychological reservoir for the first Canto'.[5] This attempt at a minute recording of the poet's physical and emotional life at Venice during the composition of the first Canto is doubtless illuminating, but one is left with the feeling that if life in Venice were the inspiration of the first Canto, Byron's verse would have reflected in some measure his sense of isolation, his dissatisfaction with himself, and his hopelessness about the future'.[6] As it happens, the spirited rollicking farce of the bedroom scene interspersed with the poet's facetious comments belie the feelings of despondency and loneliness with which Byron was periodically afflicted. This is not to argue that the exuberance and gusto of the first Canto presuppose a cheeful and genial disposition on Byron's part which found its way into the poem. The point I would like to make is that Venetian life and the poet's emotional and psychological condition, however carefully scrutinised, cannot solely be made to account for the main material out of which the first Canto took shape. Certain factors, I believe, should also be taken into consideration, such as Byron's extensive reading and the process by which Byron, as Lady Blessington observed,[7] assimilated what he read and the manner in which, identifying with some of the characters, he retold the story in terms of the life he experienced around him. In the course of this chapter I propose to demonstrate that the influence of Casti's *Novelle Galanti* extended beyond *Beppo* and was largely operative in the opening Cantos of *Don Juan*.

The Julia–Juan episode, as Byron himself stated in a letter to Hobhouse, was grounded on fact – an entertaining piece of gossip he had picked up in Venice. 'The *Julian* adventure,' he wrote, 'was none of mine; but one of an acquaintance of mine (*Parolini* by name), which happened some years ago at Bassano, with the Prefect's wife when he was a boy – and was the Subject of a long cause, ending in a divorce or separation of the parties during the Italian Vice-royalty.'[8] The actual facts of the case, however, remain vague. Hobhouse's diary is none too revealing and his entry for 5 December 1817 merely confirms that Parolini or Parilini dined with him and Byron on that day.[9]

The adulterous amour of the Prefect's wife with a youth half her age suggested to Byron the thin fabric of a plot which he proposed to expand in the manner of *Beppo*. For the actual development of the narrative and the psychological complexity of the affair leading to the bedroom farce, Byron, I would suggest, depended less on his own experience of the life of amorous intrigue and 'vile assignations' in Venice and more on his own capacity to absorb and assimilate what he had read and obviously enjoyed. Casti's *Novelle* with their waggish description of the *mores* of a degenerate society had appealed to Byron because they endorsed the reality of life in Venice and confirmed in verse his own experience of Italian women. It is with the effect of Byron's reading of Casti on the early Cantos of *Don Juan* that I am mainly concerned in this chapter – that gradual process whereby Byron, the stronger poet, absorbed and transformed the narrative stylistic features in his original.[10]

The similarity which Shelley perceived between *Beppo* and *Don Juan* was by no means fortuitous but was derived from Byron's partial adherence to the *Novelle*, which at this time were firmly imprinted in his retentive memory. The Juan–Donna Julia episode was occasioned by Parolini's reminiscences of his youthful amour with the Prefect's wife and these in turn suggested to Byron the outline of a *novella* in the manner of Casti and the development of the familiar Castian motif of the old jealous husband who is eventually cuckolded by a pretty and scheming young wife. Byron, it will be recalled, had expressed his intention earlier in the year to write 'some work of fancy in prose, descriptive of Italian manners and of human passions'.[11] Murray's suggestion (in July 1818) that he should compose 'another lively tale like "Beppo", or some prose relating all the adventures that you have undergone, seen, heard of, or imagined with your reflections on life and manners',[12] confirmed the success of the experiment with the *ottava rima* and encouraged him to persevere in that same style. It is most likely that, in responding to Murray's request for 'a lively tale', Byron, inspired by the Parolini anecdote, conceived the idea of writing a humorous verse tale about the handsome young Don Juan with whom he identified, and the seductive Donna Julia.

A close look at the manuscripts of *Don Juan* as analysed by T. G.

Steffan and W. Pratt in their valuable Variorum edition, and in particular at their detailed recording of Byron's cross-margin insertions and additions,[13] will show that the Julia–Juan episode, beginning with the stanzas on Don Alfonso and ending with the affray in Julia's bedroom, belongs to the original matrix and is an entirely self-contained passage. The stanzas containing a catalogue of forgotten heroes, the expansion of Inez's character, the popularity of the word 'fifty', were almost certainly inserted into the matrix at some later stage in composition as were the stanzas on the mixed blessings of inventions and discoveries, Byron's own half-hearted resolutions to reform Julia's letter, the epic content of the Canto and Byron's sneering at Southey. If we for a moment isolate the accretive stanzas and focus on the original matrix stanzas it will become apparent that Byron's first draft of *Don Juan* comprised the following: the characterisation of Don Jose and Donna Inez and their marital relationship, Juan's education, the description of Julia and her growing concern and love for Juan, Juan's reciprocal love, the fatal day of June, the bedroom scene and Julia's tirade against Don Alfonso, the discovery of the shoes, the brawl and Juan's subsequent escape. Byron's original draft, therefore, was a *novella* in the manner of Casti on a theme which is all too familiar in the *Novelle*. In his letter to Murray (dated 10 July) he referred to it as a story 'ludicrous (à la *Beppo*) not yet finished . . .'[14] and later in replying to Hobhouse's misgivings concerning the publication of the Donna Inez stanzas, he alluded to Juan's mother as 'a ludicrous character of a tiresome woman in a burlesque poem'.[15] It is certainly likely that while Byron was in the process of writing the matrix stanzas of the burlesque episode of Juan's love affair the idea occurred to him that he could superimpose an 'epic' framework on to a burlesque tale in the Castian style.

There is a parallel between the first Canto of *Don Juan* and Casti's *Il Ritorno Inaspettato* which indicates that the *Novelle Galanti* still continued to exert considerable influence on Byron at this stage. *Il Ritorno Inaspettato*, a *novella* of seventy-eight *ottava rima* stanzas on the theme of a young wife's infidelity, is one of Casti's better-known tales.[16] Climene, the pretty young wife of Lindoro, in the absence of her husband who has gone to war, falls in love with a young boy of the village who lives nearby and she eventually seduces him. After a while Lindoro, her husband, unexpectedly returns and Climene manages to extricate herself from a compromising situation by keeping her wits about her. The husband is cleverly deceived and marital bliss eventually restored. The plot is simple enough and the charm of this *novella* lies mainly in Casti's skilful delineation of character and deception. *Il Ritorno Inaspettato* is indeed one of the finest of the *Novelle Galanti* for it depicts with remarkable subtlety the insidious corruption of innocence by experience and guile.

Four distinct phases are discernible in the actual plot of this *novella*. The first is the pastoral-idyllic scene in which the young married couple Lindoro and Climene declare their love for each other which is as yet uncorrupted (says Casti) 'by distant society'. The second phase is the disruption of this paradise on earth by man's uncontrollable urge to wage war against his kind. Lindoro feels that he must take leave of his beloved wife and enlist in the navy in order to gain glory. The loneliness of Climene and her gradual seduction of the young village lad Rosmin constitute the third phase and the fourth relates Lindoro's sudden and unexpected return from the war and his reunion with his unfaithful wife. Phases three and four in this *novella* are of particular interest in that they afford a striking parallel with Byron's treatment of the similar theme of Juan's seduction by Donna Julia. Climene's growing concern and love for the shy young Rosmin in *Il Ritorno Inaspettato* must have provided Byron with a convenient model for his fine portrayal of the seduction of Juan in *Don Juan*, not only in the details of the situation itself but also in the psychological study of the heroine's innate inability to stem the tide of her passions. Casti's philosophical outlook in the *Novelle Galanti* is not so much pessimistic as deterministic: the mysterious force which Casti considers to be the ruling amorous instinct is so overwhelmingly powerful that education, religion and even conscience are woefully ineffectual when pitted against it. This is why Casti assures his readers half way through this *novella* that they need not be shocked by the married Climene's passion for a young boy of thirteen:

> Che stupir? giovin'egli e giovin'ella,
> Accadde ad essi ciò che accade in noi
> O giovintù, io mi appello a voi.
>
> (XXXIII, xxxii)

(Why wonder? Young she was and so was he,/ what happened to them happens to us/ O Youth, I appeal to you.)

Nor, in Casti's dubious morality, is a beautiful woman to be censured for breaking her marriage vows especially when it has been her fate to be linked with an old and jealous husband or when cruel destiny has separated her from a loving young husband. No pretty woman, in Casti's view, can be expected to resist the overpowering force of her passionate instincts and cannot therefore be blamed for giving in to them so long as she is discreet about it and quick-witted in an unexpected crisis.

But to return to the actual influence of *Il Ritorno Inaspettato* on the 'Julian adventure' in *Don Juan*. In the absence of her husband who has left for the war, Climene seeks the company of nearby country-folk to console herself. She is gradually attracted to a fine-looking schoolboy in his early teens called Rosmin who coyly admires her from a distance. Casti's description of Climene's awakening passion for the young Rosmin and Rosmin's awkward and embarrassed first reactions is indeed one of the finest passages in the *Novelle*. Rosmin's confused emotions in the presence of the attractive Climene are aptly described:

> E or sì mesta in vederla ei prova in petto
> Commozion ed inquietudin tale,
> Più che compassion, più che rispetto,
> Qualche timido sguardo trasversale
> Dalle furtivamente il giovinetto
> Poi bassa gli occhi, e un palpito l'assale
> Di pena e di piacer: ma che amor sia
> Neppur di sospettarlo ardito avrìa.
>
> (XXXIII, xxxiii)

(So sad he felt at heart when he beheld her/ so moved and so disturbed/ – more than compassion and more than respect –/ a few timid sidelong looks/ this youth furtively gives/ then he lowers his eyes/ and is assailed by palpitations/ of pleasure and pain; but what love is/ he did not even dare to suspect.)

This idea of the young Rosmin's initiation into the mysteries of love with all its conflicting feelings is taken up by Byron in his portrayal of Juan as being 'tormented with a wound he could not know' and consequently like Rosmin he is unable to communicate his feelings except in 'stolen glances' and 'burning blushes' – the silent language of love. Byron says:

Then there were sighs, the deeper for suppression
And stolen glances, sweeter for the theft,
And burning blushes, though for no transgression,
Tremblings when met, and restlessness when left;
All these are little preludes to possession,
Of which young passion cannot be bereft,
And merely tend to show how greatly love is
Embarrass'd at first starting with a novice.

(DJ, i, lxxiv)

There is no direct borrowing of phraseology here but the stanza is
clearly an adaptation of a similar situation in Casti's *novella*,
almost as if Byron were writing a versified paraphrase of this
relationship. The awkwardness of Climene and Rosmin is such
that they cannot help staring at each other and blushing, relying
as it were on their embarrassed looks to convey their regard for
each other. Casti's description is both subtle and succinct:

Ed ei guardolla, e si fè rosso e tacque.
Eloquente il silenzio ancor diviene,
E quel tacer quell' arrosir non spiaque
A lei, che in quel silenzio in quel rossore
Segni scorgea di mal celato amore.

(xxxiii, xxxix)

(And he beheld her, blushed and was silent,/ and the silence
then became eloquent,/ and that silence and blushing did not
displease her/ who amid the silence and blushing perceived/
signs of ill-concealed love.)

Climene, with her feminine intuition rightly interprets Rosmin's
embarrassment as the signs of nascent love in its first innocence.
Byron's version of this situation is strikingly similar. This is how
he describes the sudden change that came over Julia when it
becomes clear that she has developed more than a passing interest
in the young Juan:

Whate'er the cause might be, they had become
Changed; for the dame grew distant, the youth shy,
Their looks cast down, their greetings almost dumb,
And much embarrassment in either eye;

There surely will be little doubt with some
That Donna Julia knew the reason why,

(*DJ*, I, lxx, 1–6)

This could well have been Byron's commentary on the Climene–Rosmin affair in *Il Ritorno Inaspettato*. Byron, however, develops the situation and improves on it and has the romantic young Juan take to the countryside to find solace in Nature, thus cleverly satirising Wordsworthian doctrine and Coleridgean metaphysics.

There is further evidence in Casti's *novella* to suggest that Byron fashioned Donna Julia with all her psychological complexity on the character of Climene. Certainly, there are interesting parallels which cannot be ascribed to mere coincidence. For instance, Climene in the process of seducing the innocent Rosmin, begins to realise the danger she trifles with and makes a half-hearted effort to curb her passion and rationalise the situation:

> Ella intanto dicea sola e pensosa,
> Bada, Climene, bada ben che fai,
> Se un poco più lasci inoltrar la cosa
> Vorrai forse arrestarla, e non potrai;
> Bada che il villanel già prende ardire,
> E un dì chi sa, come potrai finire.

(XXXIII, xliii)

(Meanwhile, alone and pensive she said to herself/ Take heed, Climene, take heed of what you do/ if you let things go a little further/ you perhaps won't be able to restrain yourself;/ for this young peasant is getting bolder/ and who knows one day how it will end.)

Casti, by making Climene talk to herself, conveys her agitated state of mind and her intuitive sense of the inevitability of her predicament. Casti's use of the stock Petrarchan phrase 'sola e pensosa' in this context is, I think, significant. The cliché is meant to recall the conventional situation of the Platonic lover who roams the countryside afflicted with the bitter-sweet pains of awakening love. The use of the phrase in this context is a deliberate travesty of Petrarchan notions of the refining influence of Platonic love especially since there is nothing ennobling about Climene's illicit passion for a young boy of thirteen.

It is interesting to note that Byron develops the Julia–Juan
affair along similar lines and he goes so far as to assume very much
the same stance adopted by Casti in this phase of the *novella*. Like
Climene, Julia is momentarily perturbed and falters in her
resolution not to give in to her passion:

> Poor Julia's heart was in an awkward state;
> She felt it going, and resolved to make
> The noblest efforts for herself and mate,
> For honour's, pride's, religion's, virtue's sake,
> Her resolutions were most truly great . . .
>
> (*DJ*, i, lxxv)

Whereas Casti had allowed Climene to voice her own misgivings
thereby assimilating the speech of his heroine, Byron quietly
disengages from the proceedings and gives, as it were, a running
commentary on the situation.

Both Climene and Julia become victims of self-delusion.
Climene, flattered by Rosmin's shy response, deceives herself into
thinking that she can restrain her passion within the confines set
by prudence. Casti's worldly comment on the frailty of a woman's
will is typical:

> Ma quando a sormontar taluno è giunto
> Certi fissi confin, come impedire
> Ch' oltre non passi, e debba ivi far punto!
> Che vo' inferir da ciò? Voglio inferire,
> E da provarvi sol l'impegno ho assunto
> Che d'inesperienza egli è un errore
> Volger prefigger limiti all'amore.
>
> (xxxiii, li)

(But when a person has arrived at certain/ fixed confines, how
can he be stopped from going beyond where he should stop!/
What do I infer from this? I must infer/ and I have made it my
task to prove/ that it is an error of inexperience/ to want to
prescribe limits to love.)

Casti attributes Climene's inability to come to terms with her
predicament to inexperience on her part, but a few stanzas later
he proceeds to qualify this statement by ascribing her apparent
lack of resolve to woman's infinite capacity for self-delusion:

Ed in prova di questo io vi dirò
Che anche ad onta di quei proponimenti
Quel loro baciucchiar continuò
Ma sempre con decisa voluntà
Di non andar un briciolin più in là.

(xxxiii, lii)

(But as proof of this I will tell you/ that in spite of those proposals, their kissing went on . . ./ But always with that determined will not to go a little bit beyond.)

Julia is made to follow a similar behavioural pattern in her seduction of Juan. She too, like Climene, resolves to proceed no further or at least to keep her feelings for Juan within the limits of propriety. As Byron says:

Love, then, but love within its proper limits
Was Julia's innocent determination
In young Don Juan's favour, and to him its
Exertion might be useful on occasion . . .

(*DJ*, i, lxxxi)

Byron, indeed echoes Casti's cynical comments on woman's innate hypocrisy:

But, who, alas! can love, and then be wise?
Not that remorse did not oppose temptation;
A little still she strove and much repented,
And whispering 'I will ne'er consent' – consented.

(*DJ*, i, cxvii)

Both Climene and Julia before eventually succumbing to their passion reach a stage where they are firmly resolved to keep their marriage vows at all costs. Climene declares to herself that she will be true to the absent Lindoro:

Ma possibil non è, Lindoro mio,
Possibil finchè avrò quest'alma in petto,
Non fia mai che tal torto a te facc'io;
E che Climene tua l'antico affetto
E le promesse sue ponga in obblìo.

Tu sempre del mio amor l'unico oggetto
Fosti o Lindor, e lo sarai pur sempre:
No, questo cor non cangerà mai tempre.

          (XXXIII, xliv)

(But it is not possible, my Lindoro,/ not while this heart lies
within my breast,/ it can never be that I will do you such wrong/
that your Climene will forget/ her old love and her promises./
You were the only object of my love/ O Lindoro and so you will
be for ever; no, this heart will never change its temper.)

Following Casti, Byron exploits the situational irony of *Il Ritorno
Inaspettato* by making Julia give in to her passion for Juan
immediately after pledging her constancy to Don Alfonso:

Julia had honour, virtue, truth and love
For Don Alfonso; and she inly swore,
By all the vows below to powers above,
She never would disgrace the ring she wore,
Nor leave a wish which wisdom might reprove . . .

          (*DJ*, I, cix)

Byron, however, goes on to develop the idea that Platonic love is
the insidious cause of Julia's self-deception and is at the root of her
'immoral conduct'. The idea, as we have seen, was already
implicit in *Il Ritorno Inaspettato* where Climene's concealed passion
for the bashful Rosmin assumes the guise of an innocent, Platonic
relationship swaying 'the controlless core of human hearts'.
According to Casti, Climene's fault lay in her inability, through
inexperience, to assess the full impact of Love, whom Casti likens
to a cheeky charlatan who takes more than he is offered:

Perocchè Amor è un chiappolino ardito
Che la man prende se gli porge il dito.

          (XXXIII, xlix)

(For love is a cheeky quack/ who takes your whole hand if you
but offer him a finger.)

Casti's attitude to Love throughout this *novella* may have
occasioned Byron's sardonically rhetorical outbursts on the

'confounded fantasies' of the Platonic system, especially in the context of woman's natural tendency to self-deception. It is likely that Byron had Casti's lines in mind when he wrote apropos of Plato and his system:

> . . . You're a bore,
> A charlatan, a coxcomb – and have been,
> At best, no better than a go-between.
>
> (*DJ*, i, cxvi)

It is also probable that Byron's condemnation of Plato's idealised notions of love originated in his reading of another work by Casti entitled *I Tre Giulii* first published in 1762 – a remarkable *tour de force* comprising two hundred sonnets on the theme of a resourceful debtor who succeeds in eluding a persistent and importunate creditor.[17] Within his restricted theme Casti, in the words of an anonymous translator, 'mingles very aptly and agreeably with his *badinage* allusions both classical and scientific'[18] on a number of related themes. As Casti himself claimed in the introduction to this *bravura* piece:

> . . . ond'io procurai in queste mie Poesie
> sparger di tratto in tratto alcune erudizione,
> e riflessioni filosofiche, acciò a me stesso,
> ed a'Leggitor di giocondo ed erudito intrattenimento
> riuscir potessero.[19]

(. . . and therefore I attempted in these poems to sprinkle from time to time a few erudite and philosophical reflections which I hoped would provide jocund and erudite entertainment.)

In the preface dedicated to Abate Giambattista Luciani, Casti defends the apparent frivolity of his theme by alluding to the insipidity of much contemporary imitation of conventional Petrarchan poetry with its prettified pastoral setting:

> . . . sapendo io bene quanto sciocca e ridicolosa sia la persuasione di chi tutto il vezzo di vaga e graziosa Poesia in altro consister non crede, che nel mentovare, sovente anche male a proposito l'erbetta e l'agnelletta, la quadrella, e la Pastorella.[20]

(. . . knowing full well how foolish and ridiculous is the conviction of some that all the charm of vague and gracious Poesie exists in nothing except the mention, often in bad taste, of grass, sheep, a love-quarrel and the shepherdess.)

Two sonnets in *I Tre Giulii* deal in particular with the theme of Platonic love and the poet's cynical disbelief in its ennobling powers. In these sonnets addressed to Crisofilo, his imaginary creditor, Casti contends with his customary facetiousness, that it is as impossible for Platonic love to exist in reality as it is unlikely for a creditor to forget the money owed him. The sonnet reads as follows:

> Crisofilo mio caro, io sò, che tu
> Vuoi sostener la gran bestialità,
> Che l'amore Platonico si dà,
> Cosa che sempre contrastata fu:
>
> E vuoi che se con questa alta virtù,
> Ama talun la feminil beltà,
> In bel volto fissar gli occhi potrà,
> E insiem tener l'Alma rivolta in sù.
>
> Or Crisofilo mio sopra di ciò
> Se vuoi sapere, il mio parere qual'è,
> Sincerissimente io ti dirò,
>
> Chè è difficil così, secondo me,
> Il Platonico amor, com'esser può,
> Difficil, che io ti renda i Giulj tre.[21]

(Crisofilo, my dear, I know that you mean to uphold/ that great bestiality that Platonic love proposes/ – a thing which has always been thwarted./ And you maintain that if anyone/ loves female beauty by this virtue/ he can fix his eyes upon her beautiful face/ and at the same time keep his soul uplifted./ Concerning this, my Crisofilo,/ if you would like to know, what my advice is/ I will candidly tell you/ that this Platonic love is in my view as difficult/ as it would be for me to return the three coins I owe.)

It is not unlikely that *I Tre Giulii* with its virtuoso variations on a theme may have influenced Byron's treatment of the subject of Platonic love in *Don Juan*.

The extent of Casti's influence is also apparent, I believe, in Byron's handling of the bedroom scene itself and the unexpected return of the jealous Don Alfonso. The *novella* in question is Casti's *Le Brache di San Griffone*[22] which treats of the customary subject of marital infidelity. In this *novella*, a jealous old doctor from Benevento by the name of Don Meo is eventually cuckolded by his beautiful young wife Madonna Almerina. Casti exploits the conventional *fabliaux* situation by turning the farcical scenes into a downright condemnation of the abuses of the clergy and the crass stupidity of credulous religious fanatics. There are echoes of *Le Brache di San Griffone* in Byron's description of the bedroom scene in the first Canto of *Don Juan*, which suggest that Byron had this *novella* very much in his thoughts at the time. For instance, Madonna Almerina despite her jealous husband's surveillance secretly takes a lover – a handsome young Franciscan novice – who visits her while her husband is away. The climax of the *novella* is reached when Don Meo suddenly and unexpectedly returns and makes straight for his wife's bedroom where he finds Almerina in the company of Fra Niccolò and Tolla the maid-servant. With amazing sagacity and resourcefulness Almeria manages to allay her husband's suspicions for a while.

It is probable that Byron borrowed some of the details of this *novella* for the bedroom scene sequence in *Don Juan* and appropriated them to his own artistic purposes. The main similarities of incident in the two poems are: the jealous husband's unexpected return in the night, the faithful maidservant who gives the alarm, the crowded bedroom with the wife still in bed protesting her innocence, the husband's temporary mollification, his stammering apology which immediately precedes the fortuitous discovery of 'incriminating' evidence and finally the husband's indignant outburst and loss of self-control.

Byron's refinement on a typical Castian technique inherent in the structure of the narrative is one of the interesting aspects of his debt to the Italian poet. Casti's plots, as we have seen, are simple enough and are in the main borrowed from the works of known authors whom he admired. Casti's main contribution to the *ottava rima* satirical narrative was the psychological development of his quick-witted and resourceful female characters and his acute insight, based on his own worldly experience, into the secret and devious machinations of the female mind. Much of the narrative in *Il Ritorno Inaspettato*, for instance, is devoted to an account of Climene's fluctuating state of mind, her willingness to deceive herself and the subtle way she goes about the seduction of Rosmin who is eventually made to fancy himself as the seducer. Similarly, in *Le Brache di San Griffone*, Casti focuses the reader's attention on the wiliness of Madonna Almerina and the subtlety with which she deceives her husband. A favourite device employed by Casti is that of making the unfaithful wife take the offensive in a moment of crisis when the husband is on the verge of discovering the truth about her infidelity. Indeed, Byron may have had Casti's astute heroines in mind whe he wrote:

> Julia said nought; though all the while there rose
> A ready answer, which at once enables
> A matron, who her husband's foible knows,
> By a few timely words to turn the tables,
> Which, if it does not silence, still must pose, –
> Even if it should comprise a pack of fables;
> 'Tis to retort with firmness, and when he
> Suspects with one, do you reproach with three.
>
> (*DJ*, i, clxxv)

Byron, however, goes a step further and expands Julia's rebuke of her husband's suspicious nature and lack of manners into a humorous list of the suitors she has previously spurned for his sake. Alfonso himself is fashioned on Casti's ludicrous old cuckolds who are made to appear foolish boors in the end. Don Meo and Don Alfonso in fact both apologise at one stage for their rashness. There is, however, one significant alteration of detail which should be considered. In *Le Brache di San Griffone* Don Meo stammers an apology and asks forgiveness of his wife as she lies in bed. Moving closer to arrange her pillow he catches sight of a pair of underbreeches belonging to his wife's lover and flies into a passion. In a similar situation in *Don Juan*, the perplexed Don Alfonso in the moment of beseeching Julia's pardon stumbles over a pair of shoes. This detail was very probably suggested to Byron by his reading of Agnolo Firenzuola's *L'Asino D'Oro*, an elegant *rifacimento* of the original classic by Apuleius. In a particular anecdote in *L'Asino D'Oro* a youth by the name of Filero seduces the attractive wife of an old boor nicknamed Scorpione. The suspicious husband returns unexpectedly during the night and this is how Firenzuola describes the situation:

> E Filero in quel mentre, presa subitamente una sua veste e tutte le altre cose, e per la gran fretta lasciato un paio di pianelle di velluto, calatosi per una finestra della camera, che riusciva in una stradetta dietro, se nè ando a casa sua. Della qual cosa accortosi Mirmece, ritrovata la chiave, e aperta la porta, mise dentro il padrone: il quale, minacciando e borbottando, se ne corse subito in camera della moglie, per vedere se egli vi era alcuno che se la mangiasse; ne avendo ritrovato persona, per quella sera non ne fu altro. Ma venuta poscia la mattina, il buon uomo, che non aveva dormito in tutta quella notte un sonno in pace, come più tosto fu levato, andando guardando per la camera, se e' vedesse segno alcuno che non gli piacesse e gli venne vedute sotto il letto quelle pianelle . . .[23]

(Meanwhile Filero hurriedly gathering his clothes and all his things and leaving behind, because of his haste, a pair of velvet slippers, lowered himself from a window in the room which overlooked a little street at the back and returned to his house. Mirmece, perceiving this, found the key and opening the door, let in her master who entered, threatening and muttering. He rushed straight into his wife's room to see if anyone was about to devour her, but not finding anyone he did nothing else that night. But on the following morning, the good man who did not sleep in peace that night, woke up and pacing about the room searched it looking for something which might not please him and under the bed he caught sight of those slippers.)

The operative details in this extract from *L'Asino D'Oro* are the lover's panic and quick escape from the bedroom window leaving his velvet slippers behind, the husband's aggressive attitude and unsuccessful search, his sleepless night and the discovery under the bed in the morning. Byron substituted a pair of shoes for the slippers, reduced the time gap between the husband's fruitless search and the actual discovery of the shoes and added the farcical brawl in the bedroom, thus quickening the tempo of the narrative.

Another probable source for the treatment of the bedroom

scene of the first Canto is Bandello's tale[24] of the wily Bindoccia who is unhappily married to a suspicious and boorish husband. Byron, as we have seen, read Bandello as early as 1814 and the Italian author's subtle treatment of a literary commonplace – the tirades of a young wife feigning innocence in the presence of an outraged husband – may well have been in his thoughts at the time. Certainly there are striking similarities between the episode in Canto I and the narrative sequence in Bandello. In Bandello's *novella* it is the jealous Angravalle who arouses his neighbours at night to witness his wife's infidelity, accusing the young Bindoccia of being a 'rea femina di mala sorte'.[25] Knowing her lover to be safely disguised as a maidservant, she berates her husband for coming home at so late an hour and coolly rebuts his accusations ('molto meglio che tu ti fossi morsa la lengua').[26] She goes so far as to suggest that he is out of his mind and attributes her husband's behaviour to 'qualche sghiribizzo che in capo ti è nasciuto'.[27] Bandello's treatment of Angravalle's reaction is of particular interest here since the parallel with Don Alfonso's behaviour is remarkably close. After the fruitless search around the room, the shamefaced husband is made to appear a fool in front of the bystanders. In Bandello's words:

> . . . stavasi il misero e scornato Angravalle tutto fuori di se, e non sapeva se desto ero o se si sognava, e di modo gli era morta la parola in bocca che non poteva a modo veruno ragionare . . . [28]

> (. . . the wretched and scorned Angravalle stood there utterly beside himself, not knowing whether he was awake or dreaming and his words stuck in his mouth so that he could not in any way reason . . .)

The passage with its mockery of the cuckolded husband must have appealed to Byron with his penchant for realism and authenticity. There is indeed an obvious similarity between this humorous tale by Bandello and Byron's account of the behaviour of the confounded Don Alfonso:

> But Don Alfonso stood with downcast looks,
> And truth to say, he made a foolish figure
> When after searching in five hundred nooks,

And treating a young wife with so much rigour
He gained no point, except some self-rebukes.
. . .
He cast a rueful look or two, and did
He knew not wherefore, that which he was bid.

(*DJ*, i, clxi, 1–4; clxiii, 7–8)

Although Byron may have borrowed some of the details of the
bedroom scene from Firenzuola and Bandello, it was to Casti that
he was most indebted for the knowing, worldly tone throughout
Beppo and the first Canto of *Don Juan*. I should like to stress here
that Byron's poetic development, especially after 1817, was not a
matter of mere facile imitation. To think of Byron as a plagiarist
quick to appropriate the thoughts of other writers is to miss the
essential features of Byron's development as a poet. Byron was not
slow to recognise a good literary model when he saw it and Casti
and the Italian authors he had read provided a congenial
narrative form which enabled him to express various aspects of his
personality with the conviction and assurance of a man of the
world. Byron's method of borrowing was, as we have seen, eclectic
and this chapter has been largely concerned with demonstrating
how Byron tended to synthesise his favourite authors when he
composed the first Canto of *Don Juan*. Casti, no doubt, presented
him with a convenient model, but it should also be pointed out
that Byron pursued his own way, developing his narrative and
trying out new effects, enriching the texture of his verse with his
own observations, sometimes facile and sometimes penetrating,
on life as he experienced it.

5 *Don Juan, Il Poema Tartaro* and the Italian Burlesque Tradition

The *Marvellous* and the *Wonderful* is the Nerve of the Epic Strain:
But what marvellous things happen in a well-ordered state?
(Thomas Blackwell, *Enquiry into the Life and Writing of Homer*,
1735)

In his dissertation on Byron's verse satire written more than sixty years ago, Claude Fuess first put forward the hypothesis that Casti's *Il Poema Tartaro* may have suggested to Byron the idea of allowing his hero to gravitate towards the East.[1] Most critics of Byron have since accepted Fuess's conclusions that there was little influence of the Italian poem on *Don Juan* except for some minor similarities in the details of the plot and, in particular, the fact that both protagonists in the course of their adventures are taken to the court of the Empress of Russia. Although there is no documentary evidence to corroborate the view that Byron actually read *Il Poema Tartaro* – no mention is made of the poem in his letters and journals, though there is a reference to Casti's more popular *Gli Animali Parlanti* in his letter to Major Pryse Gordon[2] – it is indeed likely that Byron was familiar with Casti's burlesque on the Russian court of the Empress Catherine.

Il Poema Tartaro, an *ottava rima* mock epic in twelve Cantos was first published in 1797 and is totally alien in spirit from his *Relazione di un Viaggio a Costantinopoli* written nine years earlier. Casti's judicious observations on the Russian way of life and his favourable impressions of the buildings, canals and monuments of St Petersburg recorded in the *Relazione* are in striking contrast with the poet's vitriolic indictment of the Court of Catherine II, thinly disguised as a modern epic recording the adventures of his fictitious hero Tommaso Scardassale. It is difficult to account for

Casti's sudden and seemingly inexplicable change of attitude reflected in his scathing satire on the Russian Court of his day, especially in the first six Cantos of *Il Poema Tartaro*. Gabriele Muresu, Casti's most recent biographer, is at pains to find a convincing explanation for Casti's change of heart and attributes it to some slight received by the poet during his sojourn in St Petersburg.[3] At the time Casti was the official poet attached to the Court of the Emperor Joseph of Austria and he may have felt that he was not treated with the deference and honour normally due to a poet of his rank. Whatever the reason, the fact remains that the total effect of *Il Poema Tartaro* is marred by the poet's over-indulgence in personal invective, with the unfortunate result that the poem degenerates into a bizarre and hysterical denunciation of Catherine and her 'ossequiosa nobilità mogolla' in the final Cantos of his 'epic'.

The twelve Cantos of *Il Poema Tartaro* are loosely knit together in the form of episodes recording the vicissitudes of Tommaso Scardassale, 'gentiluom d'Irlanda' after his escape from the seraglio of the Caliph of Babylon. Taken prisoner in a crusade against the Turks, Tommaso, together with twelve other comrades in arms, is sent by Sala Melech, Sultan of Egypt, as a gift to his friend the Caliph of Babylon. Tommaso's demeanour and charm, we are told, eventually win him the favour of the Caliph himself who places him in charge of the enchanting gardens of the seraglio where he catches sight of and falls in love with Zelmira, one of the beautiful odalisques and the Caliph's favourite concubine. Zelmira returns his love and is quick-witted enough to steal the key to the garden-gate and makes plans to escape with her lover. The attempt, however, is thwarted by the sudden death of the old Grand Eunuch, keeper of 'la più distinta carica di corte' – says Casti maliciously, and the Caliph's determination to honour the worthy Tommaso by promoting him to that rank. While the unhappy Tommaso bemoans his fate, Zelmira takes the initiative and coolly devises another plan of escape. At nightfall the lovers let themselves down from the garden wall and they flee from the harem – Zelmira having previously diguised herself as a Saracen warrior. The first Canto ends with the lovers at the tent of the Tartar Prince Battu (Count Souan, the nephew of Peter the Great) who decides to employ Tommaso as his adjutant. Battu and his entourage slowly make their way to the Capital Caracora (St Petersburg).

Cantos II–V deal with Tommaso's rise to favour at the Court of the Empress Cattuna (Catherine the Great) amidst the intrigues of Toctabei (Potemkin) and Caslucco (Prince Orloff). Tommaso is befriended by Siveno, a foreign prince of Greek extraction, who proceeds to enlighten him on the peculiar customs and habits of the Empress and her courtiers. Casti, in effect, uses Siveno as a mouthpiece to voice his utter condemnation of the policies of Catherine and the inane artificiality of her Court. The climax of the first part of this mock epic is reached in the fourth Canto where Tommaso is seduced by the lascivious Empress and becomes her new favourite and protegé. He is forthwith promoted to the rank of general and lavish festivities are held in his honour. The remaining Cantos (VI–XII) are largely concerned with Catherine's ludicrous attempts to educate and civilise her barbarous subjects, her overweening ambition to dominate European politics, her absurd claims to divinity, the disastrous war against Geppano (the Ottoman Empire) and the subsequent waning of her glory. The poem ends with the downfall of Tommaso as a result of a conspiracy led by Orloff and Souvaroff. So much for the plot which in effect consists of slight variations on a theme which tends to border on the monotonous – the sustained satire on Catherine in the second half of *Il Poema Tartaro* is laboured and the poem sags under the excessive weight of Casti's invective. The later Cantos leave little doubt in the reader's mind that malignancy is the deforming animus of this work and that Casti exaggerates and distorts *ad absurdum* the Empress's defects and shortcomings. The overall impression one is left with is that *Il Poema Tartaro* is uneven in execution – the spirited burlesque of the first five Cantos giving way to a coarse and uninspired satire lacking direction and restraint.

Herman Van den Bergh calls *Il Poema Tartaro* 'un poème à clef'[4] and in a sense he is right for Casti made no attempt to conceal his personal animosity or to broaden the narrow scope of his satire. Casti's critics, however, in proclaiming this poem to be inferior to the *Novelle Galanti* and *Animali Parlanti* have tended to disregard its positive aspects of style and purpose.

Il Poema Tartaro, besides being an attack on the Court of the Empress Catherine, is also a burlesque poem and as such it draws on the whole tradition of burlesque poetry – 'la poesia satirico-giocosa' – from Burchiello to Pulci. There is an obvious attempt to parody the long-winded and popular romantic narrative verse of which Casti himself was fond. Tommaso Scardassale, the protagonist, is endowed with all the attributes of the traditional hero of the 'romances':

> Era grande e bel giovane, e dell'aio
> Dalla tutela uscito era di poco,
> Forte, complesso, capel biondo e un paio
> D'occhi di nobiltà pieni e di fuoco,
> Un carattere franco, un umor gaio
> E colle donne avea sempre buon giuoco
>
> (*PT*, i, v)

(He was a big and handsome youth, and had only just/ left the threshold of tutelage,/ strong and well built with yellow hair and a pair/ of eyes resplendent with nobility and fire,/ frank by nature, with a gay disposition/ and sportive with the ladies.)

It is interesting to note how Casti superimposes eighteenth-century bourgeois values – Tommaso's refinement and ease with women – on the more traditional attributes of physical handsomeness. The anticlimax of the concluding couplet with its inconsequential mention of Tommaso's long nose sets the tone of this 'epic' and anticipates some of the author's frivolous comments and digressions.

Although Casti writes in the burlesque tradition – there are echoes of Berni's shrewd jesting and Pulci's mocking irreverence – *Il Poema Tartaro* does not limit itself to a parody of exalted epic values in an outrageously incongruous style. Berni's *rifacimento* of Boiardo's *Orlando Inamorato* was a travesty of the chivalric romances in terms of middle-class affluence and temperament in early sixteenth-century Tuscany. In a sense, what Berni succeeded in doing was to impose his own middle-class outlook on a stilted convention which in his own time had become meaningless and effete. In rewriting Boiardo's gentle version of the romance of Orlando to suit middle-class taste, Berni, perhaps unwittingly, produced a parody not of the romances themselves but of carefree bourgeois life in all its coarseness. As De Sanctis pointed out:

> Ma la materia ordinaria del Berni è la caricatura della borghesia in mezzo a cui viveva. Non è più la coltura che ride dell'ignoranza e della rozzezza; è la coltura che ride di se stessa: la borghesìa fa la sua propria caricatura.[5]

(But Berni's ordinary theme is the caricature of the bourgeoisie in the midst of whom he lived. It is no longer culture that laughs at ignorance and boorishness; but it is culture that now laughs at itself. The bourgeoisie caricatures itself.)

In Pulci's *Morgante*, the spirit of travesty still abides and the heroic material of the Carolingian cycle, already popularised in the 'cantastorie' tradition, sinks to the level of vulgar comedy in a world in which Rinaldo becomes a highwayman and Gano an oaf. Yet in the second part of the *Morgante* there is a seriousness of tone which belies the irreverent buffoonery of the Margutte episodes and dispels the notion that Pulci was primarily a writer of comic verse.

With Casti, however, we are on a different plane. There is, as I have said, an obvious allegiance to the burlesque mode of Berni and Pulci, particularly noticeable in the *Novelle Galanti*, but in the *Poema Tartaro* he adds a new dimension. His method was not to dress a low subject in high style as Tassoni had done in *La Secchia Rapita*, nor was it to encompass lofty ideals within the ambience of plebeian life to show how vacuous they had become, as is the case in the works of Berni and Pulci. Casti's use of epic or mock-epic devices in *Il Poema Tartaro* is not so much a means to debunk the epic itself, as an oblique way of showing how far below the epic ideal and indeed the epic poet's vision of human greatness, contemporary aristocratic ideals had fallen. The imperial Court at St Petersburg in the late eighteenth century becomes, in Casti's clever satire, the very antithesis of the virtuous and the heroic as represented in Ariosto in the Court of Charlemagne.

Casti's worldly experience as court poet and his own cynical cast of mind enabled him to see through these courtiers of his time who sought advancement by virtue of their good looks and personal charm rather than by innate intelligence or valour. Casti's attitude to these upstarts is unobtrusively reflected in his presentation of Scardassale as a good-looking young man who by means of great personal charm, won the affection of those in authority:

> Ma frattanto Tommaso Scardassale
> Per la figura e per le sue maniere
> Acquistossi l'affetto universale,

E 'l favor del calif in breve ottenne:
E in corte uom d'importanza allor divenne.

(*PT*, i, ii, 4–8)

(But in the meantime Tommaso Scardassale/ because of his aspect and his manners/ earned for himself the affection of all/ and soon obtained the favour of the caliph/ and so became a man of importance in the court.)

The bland reference to his 'maniere' quietly underlines the fact that these pleasant manners will ironically become the means of his own undoing for they prevent him from rejecting the Sultan's proposal that he should take the place of the old Grand Eunuch, and furthermore, they also account for his chivalrous inability to decline the advances of the amorous Catherine. Ineffectual and passive, Tommaso relies on his charm and good looks so that he predictably falls easy prey to the seductive Empress.

The fourth Canto relating Tommaso's adventures in the Russian Court and, especially, his experience in Catherine's boudoir is decidedly the finest in the whole poem. Casti is here firmly in control of his material and cleverly sustains the analogy between the excessive opulence and glittering splendour of Catherine's court and the sumptuous palace of the enchantress Armida in Tasso's *Gerusalemme*, or the blissful bower of Alcina in Ariosto's *Furioso*. Catherine's antechamber is no less overwhelmingly sensual:

Nel tranquillo silenzio ivi risplende
Copia d'accese faci, e dilettosa
Sensazion soave al cor discende
In quell'oscurità misteriosa;
Pregno e l'aer d'odori, e tutto spira
Qui il lusso perso e la mollezza assira.

Cristalli nitidissimi e perfetti
Pendon sopra le vasche, e col riflesso
Van raddoppiando del piacer gli oggetti:
Ed in leggiadre camarette appresso
Ergonsi intorno in varie foggie i letti
Ove giacer vorebbe amore istesso:

(*PT*, iv, ix, xi)

(In that peaceful silence where/ resplendent torches shine and/ a pleasing sensation subsides in the heart/ in that mysterious obscurity;/ the atmosphere is impregnated with odours/ and everything breathes Persian luxury and Assyrian softness./ Translucent and beautiful crystals/ hang over the ponds and with their reflection/ intensify the objects of pleasure;/ and in charming little rooms nearby/ the beds are spread around in various fashion/ on which love itself would gladly rest.)

The proverbial luxury of the Orient, so lavishly described in the romances, has been given actuality in this description of Catherine's love-nest, with the implication that the fictions of Ariosto and Tasso had, in Casti's own day, become a reality. Indeed, as Casti implies, truth as represented by the Court of the Empress of Russia had become stranger than the fictions of the romantic narrative poets. Dazzled by the glittering lights and mirrors of Catherine's chamber, Tommaso, like Ruggiero and Rinaldo before him, is unable to see through the deception for he has already been seduced by the appearance of this earthly paradise.

Casti's frequent allusions to the chivalric romances serve to underline the absurdity of all human enterprise and endeavour by deflating and pooh-poohing contemporary notions of heroism and glory in a society dominated by political intrigue and opportunism. To Casti's cynical frame of mind, the Court of Catherine was as far removed from the noble ideals of chivalry as the fantastic world of the romances was divorced from reality. By making the Grand Empress of Russia address her naïve lover in the language of the heroine of the romances, Casti burlesques both the romances themselves and Catherine's grandiose pretensions to fame. Catherine in fact says:

> O cavalier valente,
> Tu il campione sarai di Turrachina,
> Ed io far soglio precedentemente
> Saggio di quei cui suo favor destina,
> Per riconoscer se coll'apparente
> Aspetto il merto radical combina;
> Nè la carica ottien chi da me stato
> Non è prima provato ed approvato.
>
> (*PT*, IV, xxiv)

(O valiant cavalier/ you will become Turrachina's champion/ and in due time I will bestow a throne on whom my favour falls/ and discover if true merit goes with apparent demeanour,/ nor will he obtain the post/ unless he is tried and tried again.)

This is a travesty of the hero's trial or testing of virtue, for it is Tommaso's ability to gratify the lust of the Empress which will be put to the test and not his powers of resistance and abstinence. Unlike Ruggiero or Rinaldo with whom he is implicitly contrasted, Tommaso lacks that inner strength which leads his worthier counterparts to self-redemption.

The world of chivalry, fantastic and unreal as it was often represented in the romances, is used by Casti to reflect the distortion of values in the Court of this Semiramis of the North. This is particularly true of Casti's handling of the love scene in the fourth Canto in which the amorous Catherine, momentarily forgetting her imperial dignity, throws herself upon her timid lover and smothers him with caresses. This is how Casti describes her impulsive action:

> E mostrando il desir avido e caldo
> Nei tremoli occhi, nell'accesa faccia,
> Con trasporto allor fallace e baldo
> Licenziosamente il bacia e abbraccia.
> Egli in postura tal parea Rinaldo
> Quando giacea d'Armida in fra le braccia;
> E somigliato Armida avrebbe anch'ella
> S'era men grassa e vecchia, e un po più bella.
>
> (*PT*, iv, lxxi)

(And revealing her eager and warm desire/ in her trembling eyes and her shining face,/ and with bold and erring abandon/ she lustfully kisses and embraces him./ In posture he seemed like Rinaldo/ when he lay in Armida's arms, and she would have even resembled Armida/ had she been less fat and old and a little more attractive.)

The overall effect produced is that of grotesque comedy. The analogy with Armida serves to underline the fact that the Russian Empress, in Casti's view, is far less beautiful and certainly more promiscuous. Catherine, as it were, is weighed in terms of the fantastic world of the chivalric romances and is found wanting. The enchantress Armida, by comparison, has a splendour and regality which are lacking in the Empress of Russia for all her opulence and magnificence. The point Casti makes obliquely is that the dazzling brilliance of Catherine's Court is shown to be as spurious as the enchanting bower of Armida and that her yearning for fame and glory is nothing more than an empty delusion. The passive, acquiescent Tommaso has neither the will nor the inclination to extricate himself from the clutches of this modern enchantress and, unlike Rinaldo, he is pathetically unable to follow the dictates of reason and duty when these summon him to a worthy cause. Casti's half-serious and half-mocking comment on the situation is worth quoting:

> Appendete o guerrier, l'inutil spada,
> Deponete, o scrittor, piume ed inchiostri;
> Se vuol cader la monarchia, che cada,
> Voi dormite tranquilli i sonni vostri:
> Facil s'apre a gran sorte a ognun la strada,
> Pur ch'uom d'intrigo e damerin si mostri:
> Alla malvagità che in auge siede
> La timida virtude il campo cede.
>
> (*PT*, IV, xliii)

(Hang up your useless sword, O warrior/ lay down, O writer, your quill and inkpot/ if the monarchy will fall let it fall/ you dream your dreams in peace;/ the way is easily open for anyone to make his fortune/ so long as he shows himself to be a man of intrigue and a fop/ in the face of perfidy that sits on high/ timid virtue must abandon the field.)

There is no defence against the corrupting atmosphere of Catherine's 'bower' nor is it worthwhile to resist the inevitable. The warrior may just as well lay down his sword and the poet his pen for nobility and valour must give way to the perfidy ('malvagità') of absolute power. It is not the brave whom Fortune favours (the last four lines seem to imply) but the opportunists who are prepared to masquerade as politicians and fops. The glitter and sensuousness of the Court bring about the emasculation of the noble adventurer and Tommaso, like Ruggiero and Rinaldo, is first seduced by the appearance of the place which leaves him vulnerable to the blandishments and wiles of the 'enchantress' Catherine. Casti's method, as we have seen, is to rewrite the chivalric romance in terms of the political world of which he had considerable experience.

Earlier on in the poem Siveno, Casti's *alter ego* had advocated his homespun opportunist philosophy of 'carpe diem' as the only means of survival in a corrupt world. His advice to his friend Tommaso as a much travelled man of great experience was to stretch out a hand to Fortune:

> Se non mentisce il ben formato busto
> E quell' aria maschil che in te se scorge,
> Esser tu devi un fantocchion robusto;
> L'occasion propizia il crin ti porge,
> Tenta la sorte tua: d'un simil fusto,
> Credi, Cattuna invan mai non s'accorge.
> Di farti a lei veder solo si tratta:
> Piacile sol, la tua fortuna è fatta.
>
> (*PT*, ii, lvi)

(If that robust frame of yours does not give me the lie/ and that manly aspect which shines in you,/ you must be a grand puppet;/ the propitious moment is ahead of you,/ try your fortune; and such a ploy/ Cattuna will never see through, believe me./ Only let yourself be seen by her/ just please her and your fortune is made.)

In all this Tommaso emerges less as a satiric butt than as a kind of naïve youth who, acted upon by circumstance and events, has few inner resources to withstand them.

That *Il Poema Tartaro* may have had considerable influence on the composition and method of the middle Cantos (v–ix) of Byron's epic is highly probable. There are instances in *Don Juan* which seem to point to the fact that Byron adapted Casti's style and manner to his time and to his own frame of thought. One could argue further that the scenes in the Sultan's seraglio and Juan's adventure at the court of Catherine owe their inspiration to the early Cantos of *Il Poema Tartaro*. There is, for instance, an interesting similarity in the delineation of the Sultan in Canto v and Casti's satirical portrait of the Caliph of Babylon in the first Canto of *Il Poema Tartaro*. Of the Caliph, Casti says:

Tenea splendida corte e numeroso
Tren di muli, cavalli e molta gente;
E siccome era assai lussurioso
E portato pel sesso estremamente,
S'era fatto un serraglio sontuoso
Delle più belle donne d'Oriente:
Esercitando il sommo sacerdozio
Con viver sempre infra le donne e l'ozio

Dal mento gli scendea sin sotto al petto
La barba maestosa e veneranda,
Onde a guardarlo impor solea rispetto,
Cosa tanto importante a chi commanda
Rispondea sulla fede ogni domanda
Da interprete fedel di Maeometto,
In pubblico era assai religioso,
E di sua dignità molto geloso.

(I, xvi and xviii)

(He held a splendid court and numerous trains/ of mules, horses and many people./ And since he was very lascivious/ and extremely inclined towards sex/ he had around him a sumptuous harem/ of the most beautiful women in the Orient/ exercising his sacerdotal rite/ of living between women and idleness . . . From his chin to his breast there flowed/ a majestic and venerable beard/ and his very aspect commanded respect/ – an important thing for those in power –/ He answered every question about religion/ deeming himself a faithful interpreter of Mahomet./ In public he was very religious/ and very jealous of his dignity.)

Much of the point of the satire is achieved through Casti's ironic interplay between the Caliph's seeming dignity and his total ignorance of the world outside; his religiosity is shrewdly equated with his amorous propensities and his inclination to idleness. Byron's description of the Sultan, though based in part on the poet's memories of Ali Pasha, is tinged with Castian humour. The Lord of the seraglio is 'shawled to the nose and bearded to the eyes'; he says his prayers with 'more than Oriental scrupulosity' and superbly dominates his 'four wives and twice five hundred maids'. Like the Caliph, Byron's Sultan is smugly and blissfully ignorant of the world outside his domain:

He saw with his own eyes the moon was round,
Was also certain that the earth was square,
Because he had journey'd fifty miles and found
No sign that it was circular anywhere:

(*DJ*, v, cl, 1–4)

This passage is strongly reminiscent of Casti's account of the young lion's education under the tutelage of the ass in Casti's *Gli Animali Parlanti* and is in itself an instance of Byron's thorough assimilation of the Castian spirit. Byron's own experience of Oriental rulers and his notion of their civilised barbarity displayed here as the Sultan's ruthless settling of all crimes by 'sack and sea', are modified by his reading of Casti. The result is pure burlesque, for the Sultan, in T. G. Steffan's words, is 'too absurd an autocrat to be other than a harmless nincompoop'.[6]

Besides, Casti's subtle juxtaposition of callow youth and worldly experience in the persons of the naïve Tommaso and his sagacious friend Siveno, may have suggested the analogous situation in *Don Juan* where the downhearted and unfortunate Juan is befriended by that middle-aged stoic named Johnson. There are echoes of Siveno's pragmatic cynicism in Johnson's lecture about vanishing rainbows and time's casting off its slough of illusions. Indeed, Siveno's words of encouragement and advice to his crestfallen friend show striking affinities with the similar form of consolation given by Johnson to his friend at their acquaintance in the Court of Catherine:

But droop not: Fortune at your time of life,
Although a female moderately fickle,
Will hardly leave you (for she's not your wife)
For any length of days in such a pickle.
To strive, too, with our fate were such a strife
As if the corn-sheaf should oppose the sickle.
Men are the sport of circumstances, when
The circumstances seem the sport of men.

(*DJ*, v, xvii)

Acquiescence in one's fortune or misfortune and making a virtue of necessity in a ruthlessly egoistic society were the basis of the practical philosophy of life advocated by the much travelled Siveno, who in many respects is Casti's mouthpiece. Johnson goes a step further and rationalises this vacuum in men's hearts as the price they must pay for sophistication:

> Society itself, which should create
> Kindness, destroys what little we had got:
> To feel for none is the true social art
> Of the world's stoics – men without a heart.
>
> (*DJ*, v, xxv, 5–8)

The lines are not, as Professor Steffan suggests, a nihilistic conclusion which comes pat.[7] They evoke, rather, a feeling of satiety and world-weariness which momentarily rises to the surface in spite of the poet. Byron the libertine, sated with a life of dissipation in decadent Venice, warns his young hero – in many ways an idealised version of himself – against the soul-destroying perils which he must inevitably encounter in his progress through life:

> This skin must go the way, too, of all flesh,
> Or sometimes only wear a week or two: –
> Love's the first net which spreads its deadly mesh;
> Ambition, Avarice, Vengeance, Glory, glue
> The glittering lime-twigs of our latter days,
>
> (*DJ*, v, xxii, 3–7)

The context is important for Juan, banished from a natural state of happiness and innocent love on Haidée's idyllic isle, is about to be ensnared by a debased form of love symbolised by Gulbeyaz in all her Oriental splendour.

Don Juan has much in common with the Italian tradition of narrative romance as exemplified in Ariosto and Berni and as parodied by Casti and Forteguerri. Miss Boyd has drawn our attention to the fact that the shipwreck in Canto II matches that of Ariosto in his description of Ruggiero's passage from Marseilles to North Africa in Canto XLI of the *Furioso*. Byron himself was fond of Ariosto and there are several references to the Italian poet in his letters. Moreover, in the Catalogue of his books drawn up in 1816, Byron possessed two Italian editions of the *Furioso*. As Giorgio Melchiori pointed out, Byron admired Ariosto's loose, sprawling method of composition and occasionally imitated it implicitly in *Don Juan*.[8]

The structure of *Don Juan* is loosely based on the sense of quest and pilgrimage common to most chivalric romances. Although Byron's hero is less a hero than a man, he is nonetheless subjected to the same trials and ordeals which beset a Ruggiero or Rinaldo in both their amorous and military adventures. Juan's progress through life involves an enrichment of experience at the expense of innocence, if by innocence we mean that simple-minded, code-bound limiting frame of vision which tends to mistake illusion for reality. In Ariosto, Boiardo, Tasso and even in Casti, we are constantly aware of the hero's ineffectual attempts to come to terms with the reality of everyday life and to see through the dazzling attraction of all that is artificial and false. The arts of civilisation and sophistication lure unsuspecting man away from his original paradisal state and his better nature is tainted by contact with beautiful enchantresses and apparently blissful bowers which in fact become more treacherous the more attractive they appear.

The scenes with Gulbeyaz in Cantos v and vi and those set in the Court of Catherine afford an interesting parallel with the corresponding seduction scenes in Ariosto and Tasso. I refer in particular to the sojourn of Ruggiero in the realm of Alcina and that of Rinaldo in the Bower of Armida. These scenes in both the *Furioso* and the *Gerusalemme* are allegorical representations of the triumph of the sensuous over the rational, of illusion over reality. The island of Alcina and the garden of Armida are more than conventionally lineal descendents of Homer's palace of Circe: they are spurious and dangerous imitations of the earthly paradise – that desirable place of bliss and repose that man has perennially sought in his yearning to recover his lost innocence.

The episode on Haidée's idyllic isle symbolised for Byron the purity of young innocent love as yet uncorrupted by worldly experience. They were, in Byron's own words, 'children still' who, in their youthful innocence, 'never knew the weight of human hours'. Yet life and the world, as Byron suggests, will not admit of perpetual childhood and innocence and Lambro's homecoming signifies for the poet, as Robert Gleckner has observed, Byron's 'vision of the archetypal loss of love and the ruins of paradise' for the world is so ordered that 'soon or late love is his own avenger'.[9] The selfless and spiritual love of Juan and Haidée is shattered by the sudden arrival of Lambro, that much travelled man of harsh experiences: the bitter reality of life, as it were, impinges on the

innocence of the lovers and shatters their blissful dream with the
full force of an incubus.

It was Byron's intention in the subsequent Cantos of *Don Juan*
to show the vicissitudes of his hero in his quest for his earlier state
of innocence and bliss in the form of another perfect love
relationship which constantly eludes him. In his analysis of the
style of *Don Juan*, George Ridenour has cogently argued that the
metaphors of Byron's epic persistently refer to a fall from a former
state of happiness, that paradisal state lost by the first Adam,
tainted by our 'common clay' or civilisation.[10] In the progress of
the poem and in the course of Juan's amorous adventures, love
strives to recreate for Juan, albeit ineffectually, that irretrievable
state of bliss from which he has been expelled.

Juan's adventure in the seraglio is described in images
suggesting the Christian knight's progress through an enchanted
landscape, strongly reminiscent of the treacherous earthly paradise in the 'epics' of Ariosto and Tasso. Led by the eunuch Baba,
Juan and Johnson embark on a 'gilded caïque' until they reach a
'little creek below a wall/ O'ertopped with cypresses, dark-green
and tall'. A small door suddenly opens in front of them, and they
are guided through a large thicket flanked by towering groves
where they 'plod on their winding way/ Through orange bowers,
and jasmine and so forth' until they eventually reach a lighted
'noble palace'. Their senses are assailed by the savour of food,
lavishly displayed, and, momentarily overpowered, they give up
'all notions of resistance'. The alluring magic of the place has
taken hold of them and there are echoes of the trial of the two
knights in the *Gerusalemme* who are sent to fetch the love-sick
Rinaldo from Armida's bower. The sumptuous hall which Juan
and Johnson are led through, leads to a still more splendid
chamber 'full of all things which could be desired'. This very
magnificence calls to mind the opulence of Armida's palace:

> The moveables were prodigally rich:
> Sofas 'twas half a sin to sit upon,
> So costly were they; carpets every stitch
> Of workmanship so rare, they made you wish
> You could glide o'er them like a golden fish.
>
> (v, lxv, 4–8)

The parallel with the bowers of Alcina and Armida becomes all

the more striking in the stanzas where Baba leads the bewildered
Juan through the 'glittering galleries and marble floors'. The
massive portal at one end of the hall towering 'in almost
pyramidic pride' and guarded by misshapen pigmies is almost a
replica of the four-pillared gate on the threshold of Alcina's realm
guarded by grotesque creatures with cat or ape-like heads.
Amidst the array of dazzling gems and gold, Gulbeyaz, an
Oriental version of Alcina or Armida, makes her appearance in all
her Eastern splendour.

The parallel with the Italian poets is further developed in
Byron's description of Gulbeyaz as another Armida or Alcina.
The Sultana's deadly seductive charms and her fatal hypnotic
power are quietly emphasised:

> Her form had all the softness of her sex,
> Her features all the sweetness of the devil,
> When he put on the cherub to perplex
> Eve and paved (God knows how) the road to evil.
>
> (v, cix, 1–4)

and again:

> Something imperial or imperious threw
> A chain o'er all she did; that is, a chain
> Was thrown as 'twere about the neck of you, –
> And rapture's self will seem almost a pain
> With aught which looks like despotism in view
> Our souls at least are free, and 'tis in vain
> We would against them make the flesh obey –
> The spirit in the end will have its way.
>
> (v, cx)

There is, however, an important difference for Juan, unlike
Ruggiero or Rinaldo, resists Gulbeyaz's offer of love with a noble
spirit worthy of Sir Guyon:

> 'I am not dazzled by this splendid roof;
> Whate'er thy power, and great it seems to be,
> Heads bow, knees bend, eyes watch around a throne,
> And hands obey – our hearts are still our own.'
>
> (v, cxxvii, 5–8)

with the result that the frustrated 'enchantress' is reduced to tears. Determined though he is to meet his death rather than succumb to the lure of sensuality, the bewildered Juan is taken aback by Gulbeyaz's sudden display of emotion. Byron's humorous comment underlines the fact that feminine wiles have got the better of man's worthy resistance:

> But all his great preparatives for dying
> Dissolved like snow before a woman crying.
>
> (v, cxli, 7–8)

The impact on Juan is disarming and he comes dangerously close to yielding to temptation. The facetiousness of Byron's comment belies the seriousness of Juan's predicament:

> So Juan's virtue ebb'd, I know not how;
> And first he wonder'd why he had refused;
> And then, if matters could be made up now;
> And next his savage virtue he accused,
> Just as a friar may accuse his vow,
> Or as a dame repents her of her oath,
> Which mostly ends in some small breach of both.
>
> (v, cxlii)

The critical situation is resolved with Baba's timely arrival on the scene with the news that the Sultan is on his way. Juan must live to endure yet another test of his virtue.

This episode, as Miss Boyd pointed out, may have been modelled on Wieland's *Oberon* which Byron must have read in Sotheby's translation.[11] There is a parallel, albeit remote, between Almansaris's attempted seduction of Huon whom she encounters in the seraglio gardens and Gulbeyaz's contriving with Juan. In some details, according to Miss Boyd, Byron's portrayal of Gulbeyaz echoes Sotheby's description of Almansaris. It is indeed likely that Byron thought it fit to 'covet Mr Sotheby's Muse' for a short while. But it is interesting to note, however, that Byron consciously adapted the Oriental setting of the Sultan's seraglio to the conventional landscape of romance, with its notion of the 'paradiso terrestre' and its ambiguous nature suggestive of the conflict between Love and Duty, illusion and reality. Nowhere is this more evident than in this description of Gulbeyaz's bower;

Mother of pearl, and porphyry, and marble,
Vied with each other on this costly spot;
And singing birds without were heard to warble;
And the stain'd glass which lighted this fair grot
Varied each ray;[12]

Gulbeyaz's boudoir is skilfully transmuted into a 'fair grot'
animated by the warbling of birds amidst Oriental splendour –
the exquisite blending of the 'rude' with the 'polish'd', the
juxtaposition of natural and artificial beauty where nature seems
to vie with art with its concomitant implication of moral
ambiguity – all this suggests that Byron translated life into epic
romance thereby achieving very much the same satirical effects as
in Casti's burlesque poem.

The abruptness of the transition from the episode with
Gulbeyaz to Juan's sudden appearance at the Court of the
Russian Empress has been considered to be a flaw in the narrative
structure of the poem attributed to Byron's hasty method of
composition. It is possible to argue, however, that Byron was
consciously following Ariosto's method of a quick shift of scene
from love to war and vice-versa, bridged by a casual and almost
inconsequential digression in which the author-narrator picks up
the thread of the narrative with a humorous appeal to the reader's
powers of imagination. It is left to the perspicacious reader to
suppose what has meanwhile taken place. What Professor Brand
says of Ariosto's style could, I think, with some modification be
applied to the style of *Don Juan*:

> With Ariosto we jump backwards and forwards apparently at
> random through a bewildering array of episodes in which a love
> story is followed by a battle or some feat of magic, a tragical
> suicide, or by a farcical knockabout. But it is precisely through
> this striking kaleidoscope that a convincing pattern emerges.
> Ariosto sees life as a random succession of tragic and comic,
> serious and frivolous elements, and he blends his collection of
> tales and adventures so as to represent life as it appears to
> him.[13]

The organising principle of Byron's narrative is equally episodic,
and it is in keeping with Byron's own observation that Ariosto's
plan was in fact 'no plan at all'.

II

In the Russian episode Byron was indebted to William Tooke's *Life of Catherine II*[14] for some of the details concerning Catherine's physiognomy and amorous propensities, such as 'her blue eyes or grey', her passion for 'fair faced Lanskoi' and her reaction to 'mad Suwarrow's rhymes'. For other details about Catherine and her Court Byron turned to Masson's *Mémoires secrètes sur la Russie*[15] especially for the lavish way in which Catherine's former lovers were rewarded. In keeping with Byron's obsession with using actual facts his 'materials' were firmly grounded on contemporary historical surveys and biographical accounts. It was in this way that Byron gave a factual basis to his satirical vision. Indeed, he went so far as to support Gibbon's defence of Tasso's use of historical material:

> Gibbon makes it a merit in Tasso 'to have copied the minutest details of the *Siege of Jerusalem* from the Chronicles'. In *me* it may be a demerit, I presume; let it remain so.

This statement which appeared in the Appendix to the first edition of *The Two Foscari*[16] was an attempt to justify his borrowing of factual details for his version of the wreck of the 'Trinidada' from contemporary prose accounts and to give a literary precedent for the use of such material in the forthcoming Cantos of *Don Juan*.

It is highly probable that Byron's reading of Casti's satirical account of the young Tommaso's sojourn at the Court of Catherine in the first four Cantos of *Il Poema Tartaro* exerted a strong influence on his treatment of virtually the same subject matter in Canto IX of *Don Juan*. Although there are no instances of direct verbal borrowing, there are passages which seem to point to a thorough assimilation of Casti's satirical mode. Speaking of Catherine's amorousness Casti explains the Empress's disposition to love as an uncontrollable impulse stemming from a generous heart – 'Core sempre all'amor facile e prono'. By nature and by temperament Catherine is inclined to devote herself to the service of love. As Casti wryly remarks:

> Ma siccome per uso e per natura
> Nei servigi d'amor troppo esigea;

> Forzandosi essi di mostrar bravura,
> In pochissimo tempo gli rendea
> Grassi di borso e magri di figùra:
> Onde amanti cangiar spesso solea
> Senza ritegno di servil vergogna,
> Per supplir pienamente alla bisogna.
>
> (*PT*, ii, viii)

(But since by custom and by nature/ she was too exigent in the ritual of love;/ and since they sought to prove their worth,/ in a very short time their purses were fattened and their figures became thin:/ and therefore she frequently changed her lovers/ without the slightest shame/ in order to satisfy her need to the full.)

Byron makes a similar comment on Catherine's inordinate sexual passion:

> She could repay each amatory look you lent
> With interest, and in turn was wont with rigour
> To exact of Cupid's bills the full amount
> At sight, nor would permit you to discount
>
> (*DJ*, ix, lxii, 5–8)

> With her the latter though at times convenient,
> Was not so necessary; for they tell
> That she was handsome and though fierce look'd lenient,
> And always used her favourites too well
>
> (lxiii, 1–4)

More striking, perhaps, is the similarity between Casti's description of the reaction of the obsequious Russian Court to Catherine's latest favourite and Juan's impact on the Empress and her entourage at St Petersburg. Casti focuses the reader's attention on Tommaso's elegant appearance as a dashing beau:

> Candido farsettino indosso avea
> Con nastri di gentil roseo colore,
> Bianca fascia la fronte gli cingea,
> Un ciuffo in testa, e sopra il ciuffo un fiore;
> Polifemo istessimo parea,
> Ma Polifemo in abito d'amore;
>
> (*PT*, iv, vi)

(He wore a white waistcoat/ with fine rose ribbons/ a white
band encircled his forehead/ a forelock on his brow, and above
that a flower/ he looked like Polyphemus himself,/ but
Polyphemus wearing a garment of love.)

Byron's method shows a curious resemblance to that of the Italian
poet. The reader is asked to visualise the details of Juan's attire:

> Suppose him in a handsome uniform;
> A scarlet coat, black facings, a long plume,
> Waving like sails new shiver'd in a storm . . .
>
> > (*DJ*, ix, xliii, 1–3)

> Behold him placed as if upon a pillar! He
> Seems Love turn'd a lieutenant of artillery!
>
> > (ix, xliv, 7–8)

> His bandage slipp'd down into a cravat;
> His wings subdued to epaulettes; his quiver
> Shrunk to a scabbard, with his arrows at
> His side as a small sword, but sharp as ever . . .
>
> > (ix, xlv, 1–4)

This metamorphosis of the God of Love into a dashing young
officer who becomes the centre of attraction at St Petersburg is in
itself an instance of Byron's clever elaboration of a particularly
Castian vein of humour. In fact, Byron goes a step further in his
facetious delineation of the situation and attributes this wondrous
transformation to the amazing ingenuity of an army tailor:

> That great enchanter, at whose rod's command
> Beauty springs forth, and Nature's self turns paler
> Seeing how Art can make her work more grand
>
> > (*DJ*, ix, xliv, 3–5)

There is, however, an underlying seriousness of purpose beneath
these witticisms for Byron here surreptitiously stresses the preval-
ence of illusion over reality as a corrupting influence in the Court
of Catherine. The world of artifice as Casti had shown has its
subtle dangers, for the outer transformation of Juan implies a
deeper and more profound change within the hero himself. For all

Juan's self-conscious blushing there is, we are told, a gradual corroding inward change which betokens the insidious influence of the Court:

> There was something in his turn of limb,
> And still more in his eye, which seemed to express,
> That though he look'd one of the seraphim,
> There lurked a man beneath the spirit's dress
>
> (*DJ*, ix, xlvii, 3–6)

It is here that the sustained correspondence between appearance and essence breaks down. Juan's spirit falters under the pressures of the illusory world of which he himself now forms part. The hero's succumbing to this modern Semiramis is a foregone conclusion.

The influence of *Il Poema Tartaro* on *Don Juan* is also apparent in Byron's description of Juan's reception at St Petersburg. In the corresponding episode in Casti's poem, a feast is held in honour of Catherine's latest lover and the reaction of the guests is described in some detail. There is a mixture of awe and curiosity in their attitude to the handsome young stranger who has captivated the heart of their Empress. Casti's account seems to be given from an onlooker's point of view:

> Per desìo di veder l'Adon novello
> D'ogni banda ciascun tosto s'è mosso:
> Ov'è egli? ov'è egli? . . . eccolo là . . . si quello,
> Ah, ah quel bel zerbin del naso grosso:
> Oh che bel tocco d'uom! oh bello! oh bello!
> E ognun l'osserva e gli tien l'occhio addosso,
> E un all'altro chiedea la patria e il nome,
> E perchè venne, e d'onde, e quando, e come.
>
> (*PT*, iv, lxxxviii)

(In their craving to see this new Adonis/ they immediately gathered from all sides/ Where is he? where is he? . . . there he is . . . yes it's him/ Ah, it's that fop with the plump nose;/ Oh what a fine man! Oh beautiful, beautiful!/ And they all observe him and fix their eye on him/ and they asked each other his nationality and his name,/ and why he came, and whence, and when and how.)

Byron adopts much the same technique in recording Juan's impact on the Russian Court:

> The whole court melted into one wide whisper,
> And all lips were applied unto all ears!
> The elder ladies' wrinkles curl'd much crisper
> As they beheld; the younger cast some leers
> On one another, and each lovely lisper
> Smiled as she talked . . .
>
> (*DJ*, ix, lxxviii, 1–6)

> All the ambassadors of all the powers
> Inquired, who was this very young new man,
> Who promised to be great in some few hours?
>
> (*DJ*, ix, lxxix, 1–3)

Byron's version, it must be admitted, is a more elegant and refined paraphrase of his Italian model – the exclamations and the ejaculations of the bystanders are toned down and Byron introduces a distinct element of psychological insight into the feminine mind, for the women of the Court are caught in the act of vying with each other to attract the attention of this young and handsome stranger.

The scenes and circumstances of the episodes relating to Gulbeyaz and Catherine in *Don Juan* are no doubt influenced by Byron's wide reading of the Italian narrative poems as well as the burlesques they gave rise to. That Byron was extremely well versed in this tradition is evident from his many comments on Ariosto, Berni, Pulci and their precursors. Indeed, Byron considered himself very much an expert in this field as is evident in his letter to Murray (18 April 1822) acknowledging receipt of Lord Glenbervie's translation of Niccolo Forteguerri's *Ricciardetto* in which he expresses his considered opinion that the author was 'very amusing and able upon the topics he touches upon' but he was critical of Glenbervie's introductory survey of Italian burlesque poetry and found 'part of the preface pathetic'.[17]

In the course of this chapter I have endeavoured to demonstrate the influence of the Italian romantic and narrative poems, in particular Casti's burlesque poem *Il Poema Tartaro*, on the theme and structure of the middle Cantos of *Don Juan*. What transpires from a close analysis of these Cantos in relation to their indebtedness to the Italian romantic poems is a marked similarity in Byron's treatment of the motifs of the seduction of the young hero, the illusion created by the lavish splendour of the East which the hero mistakes for reality and the artificiality of the earthly Paradise which is no substitute for the loss of Eden. As Harry Levin points out:

> Those notorious gardens of their respective enchantresses – where Ruggiero is seduced by Alcina in the *Orlando Furioso* or where Rinaldo dallies with Armida in the *Gerusalemme Liberata* – are decadent and illusory versions of Eden.[18]

It would be interesting, I believe, to account for the appeal of the romance mode on a poet of Byron's temperament. A probable reason for this appeal was that romantic narrative verse as developed by Ariosto and Berni enabled the poet to steer a middle course between fiction and verisimilitude without his having to settle in any one consistent tone. The romance poets exploited the curious combination of the sensible and the unfamiliar to such an extent that they succeeded in achieving artistic harmony between elements which were essentially dichotomous. The Italian poets exemplified this paradox, for while they portrayed certain aspects of early Renaissance social life, the worlds they created were essentially unreal. Casti's burlesque of the chivalric romances, despite its obvious limitations, had served the purpose of showing Byron how the fantastic and bizarre world of the romances could be adapted *mutatis mutandis* to the contemporary scene. Following Casti, Byron applied the values of the romances, appropriate enough to an imaginary and artificial world, to a real world in which his hero is gradually corrupted by all that is false and spurious.

It is worth recalling here that earlier in 1813, Byron had come to see himself in the role of a Rinaldo seduced by the sorceress in the person of Jane Elizabeth Scott, Lady Oxford.[19] It was she who placed the painting of Armida and Rinaldo in Byron's bedroom, and Byron, who was all too willing to escape politics for a while, fancied himself enchanted. His extensive reading of the Italian epics and burlesques seemed to confirm his impression that in literature, and indeed in life, the young Juans of his day were often more seduced than seducing.

Like Casti, Byron expected his literate audience to follow the parallels with the Italian romances and to pick up the allusions. From as early as the first Canto of *Don Juan* Byron assumed in his audience an acquaintance with this type of poetry. Juan's seduction by Donna Julia is in fact described in terms of the romances:

> . . . but ne'er magician's wand
> Wrought change with all Armida's fairy art
> Like what this light touch left on Julia's heart
>
> (*DJ*, i, lxxi, 7–8)

The parallelism with the romances is indeed sustained throughout the middle Cantos of *Don Juan*.

Judging from the hostile reaction of some contemporary reviews, it is possible to conclude that even the more enlightened members of the reading public failed to comprehend the subtlety of Byron's mode in *Don Juan*. The parallel with the corresponding scenes in the narrative poetry of the Italians was entirely missed by the reviewers who accordingly thought it proper to censure the poet for writing 'poetry in which the deliberate purpose of the author is to corrupt by inflaming to seduce to the love of evil which he himself has chosen as his good'. This tendency to impute to Byron the perverse intention of corrupting his hero's character into that of 'a generous but ungovernable boy of 17 . . . artfully enveloped in a constant maze of temptation'[20] is a measure of the utter failure on the British reader's part to appreciate the tradition in which Byron's 'epic satire' was rooted.

6 Casti's *Animali Parlanti*, the Italian Epic and *Don Juan*: The Poetry of Politics

' "To be perfectly original" said Byron, "one should think much and read little, and this is impossible, as one must have read much more before one learns to think; for I have no faith in innate ideas whatever I may have of innate predispositions. But after one has laid in a tolerable stock of materials for thinking, I should think the best plan would be to give the mind time to digest it, and then turn it all well over by thought and reflection by which we make the knowledge acquired our own . . .".'[1]

This was Byron's somewhat evasive reply to the charge of plagiarism which Lady Blessington tactfully introduced in the course of her conversation with the poet. Indeed, despite the autobiographical elements, and apart from the poet's natural inclination to self-assertion, his major work abounds in literary reminiscences which had their origin in the poet's 'stock of materials for thinking'. Some of these reminiscences may be assumed to stem from Byron's self-consciousness in relation to his cultured audience – Murray's literary synod in particular, with brilliant dilettanti like John Hookham Frere and William Stewart Rose who would reasonably be expected to pick up and relish any allusion or echo, however remote. Other literary reverberations were probably the result of the poet's unconscious assimilation of ideas and attitudes which eventually percolated into his poetry. Yet other parallels and similarities may be attributed to temperamental affinities with the authors he had read which Tom Moore ascribed to 'those generic points of resemblance which it is so interesting to trace in the characters of men of genius'.[2]

A book which seems to have had a considerable impact on Byron's sensibility at the time of the composition of the middle Cantos of *Don Juan* was Giambattista Casti's *Animali Parlanti* which Byron, in his letter of thanks to Pryse Gordon for the latter's inspired gift of the *Novelle Galanti*,[3] claimed to have read. It is difficult to ascertain when exactly Byron had read the *Animali* or if he actually was acquainted with Da Ponte's annotated edition which was published in London in 1802. What is certain, however, is the fact that our *terminus ad quem* is 1815 and that therefore Byron must have read Casti's poem long before he settled in Venice.

The first edition of the *Animali Parlanti* appeared in Paris in 1802 and was immediately popular. Casti's 'epic history' which extended to twenty-six cantos in *sesta rima* was a long-winded allegory on the nature of man and his constant but ineffectual endeavour to establish some form of stable government. In writing this rather unique poem, Casti may have been influenced by Goethe's *Reineke Fuchs*, a versified fable and satire on social *mores* which first appeared in 1793, but the actual plot and ideas of Casti's *Animali* owe very little to Goethe. The theme of Casti's poem is an extended poetical commentary with numerous authorial digressions on the vicissitudes of the talking animals who attempt to govern themselves. Casti in effect deals with the following themes in turn: the election of the king, the deviousness and dishonesty of his ministers, the scandals and intrigues of the Court, the subversive attempts of the demagogic Fox who instigates the rebellion of the lower animals, the ferocious battle ending in the utter rout of the rebels, the attempt to achieve a lasting peace by means of a congress and the final catastrophic convulsions that shake the animal world to its very foundations. The animals, besides, are shown as taking part in political debates, they hold conferences and funeral orations, they are ruthless as well as magnanimous and, as is usually the case with beast fables, they are endowed with human virtues and vices. So much for the plot of the *Animali*, which, as we have seen, is remarkably straightforward. Unlike Goethe, however, Casti turned the beast fable into a useful vehicle for political satire.

In the Preface to the *Animali*, Casti took the opportunity to present his literary credentials to his aristocratic readers as the person best qualified by virtue of his wide experience to write a political allegory:

La molta lettura da me fatta su tale materia, la lunga esperienza che ho avuto tutto l'agio d'acquistare, le ripetute osservazioni,

che nel genere di vita da me tenuto ho avuto campo di fare in
tutte le parti dell'Europa, mi offrirono si gran copie d'idee, di
pensieri e di riflessioni che più difficile mi è stato di restringermi
nel componimento di quest' opera, che di dilatarmi.[4]

(My wide reading in the subject, the broad experience that I
have had the time to acquire, the repeated observations which
in the course of my life I have had the opportunity of making in
all parts of Europe, have given me such a flow of ideas, of
thoughts and reflections that it has been more difficult for me to
restrain myself in writing this work than to expand it.)

Besides being a declaration of intent, the Preface is also a graceful
apologia for the prolixity of an old poet whose mind is saturated
with ideas and experiences. The form of the poem suggested itself
to Casti partly because it allowed him sufficient scope for didactic
moralising and also because he was prudent enough to seek to
camouflage his allusions to the irascible potentates of his day.
Despite Casti's repeated denials that it was his intention to
satirise contemporary European rulers, the thinly veiled allusions
would seem to point to the fact that Casti did have particular
princes in mind during the actual composition of the poem. Van
den Bergh, for instance, in his commentary on the *Animali* goes so
far as to identify Ferdinand II of Naples and his court with the
court of King Lion.[5] Casti's portrayal of the Lioness was taken by
some of the poet's contemporaries to be a satirical portrait of
Catherine of Russia. Another reason for its success was that the
Animali was banned in France by edict of Napoleon himself.
Lorenzo Da Ponte who edited and annotated the London edition
of 1802, recalled in his memoirs that Casti's poem:

. . . sotto il velo della favola contiene delle pitture vivissime dei
primi personaggi d'Europa e la storia critica, per così dire, degli
eventi più importanti della rivoluzione: colla morte di quella e
colla fine della rivoluzione l'interesse di quel poema parve
scemare e non si legge così universalmente come solevasi . . .[6]

(. . . beneath the veil of fable it contains most vivid pictures of
the leading personages of Europe, and a critical history, so to
speak, of the most important events of the revolution; with the

death of the latter and the end of the revolution, the interest of
that poem seemed to fade and it is not as universally read as it
used to be . . .)

What emerges from this passage is that, despite Casti's claim that
he lashed the vice but spared the person 'ho avuto di mira . . . i vizi
e i difetti dei governi e non dei governanti',[7] the popularity of the
poem was mainly due to the fact that contemporary readers
equated the animals with the foremost rulers of the times and that
interest in the poem subsided once it was no longer felt to be
directly relevant.

The *Animali Parlanti* was introduced to the British public by
way of William Stewart Rose's verse adaptation entitled the *Court
of Beasts*, anonymously edited in 1816. Murray immediately sent
Byron a copy for his comment and Byron wrote back pronouncing
Rose's version 'excellent'.[8] Rose's *Court of Beasts*, it must be said, is
a free adaptation – at times more Rose than Casti – toning down
the vehemence of the original, 'boiling down three thick volumes
to one'.[9] Rose felt free to expurgate the original wherever
necessary and his version concentrates almost entirely on the plot
which, as far as Rose was concerned, assumed an importance
greater than its political import. As a consequence, Casti's
digressions on politics, the vanity and incompetence of politicians, the futility and injustice of wars, the travesty of justice,
the ineffectuality of democracy, the inevitability of violence and
aggression and the inadequacy of any form of government – all
these political and philosophical themes have been quietly
discarded by Rose. Indeed, one wonders whether Rose actually
appreciated the political import of Casti's fable, especially since
his criticism of Casti was based on the fact that he:

> . . . employs his beasts in things entirely foreign from their
> habits and attributes to them actions which are obviously
> impossible.[10]

In his admirable review-article occasioned by the increasing
interests of the British public in satiric-jocose poetry, Ugo Foscolo
branched off into a discussion of the *Animali Parlanti* for the benefit
of those readers who had read Rose's *Court of Beasts* and were
interested in forming a 'just idea of their Italian prototypes.'[11]
Foscolo's comments on the *Animali* were, on the whole, none too

flattering. He was exasperated by the poem's longwindedness and took Casti to task for his lack of 'variety of harmony in verse'. Like Rose, Foscolo objected to the poem's lack of allegorical consistency:

> The animals do not occupy themselves according to their real habits; they are introduced as actors in political scenes, and placed in situations nature never intended them . . . The fiction is destitute of probability.[12]

Significantly, he too disregarded the political content of the fable and focused on the poet's lack of art and his sprawling method of composition:

> Casti drawls, and he attempts to gain the semblance of vigour by the help of points and epigrams: but he resembles a withered beauty who flirts in the dance exciting sensations which are at once ludicrous and mournful.[13]

A classicist by training and a Romantic by temperament, Foscolo was out of patience with poets like Casti who subjected their art to the propagation of political ideas.

The *Animali Parlanti* has its roots in the Enlightenment culture of the late eighteenth century with its glorification of the faculty of intellect and reason as the only antidote to ignorance and prejudice. Casti was well read in Enlightenment literature and some passages in the *Animali* show a close reading of Voltaire's *Dictionnaire philosophique* from which he derived his contempt for all political systems and his convictions about the futility of wars. Casti's starting point in the *Animali* is the demystification of chivalric ideals 'le frivole . . . cavalleresche idee dell'età vecchia'[14] and his innate distrust of any philosophical system or metaphysical doctrine which, by confusing the issues, gives men a false sense of security:

> Poichè il filosofar sopra ogni tema
> Vaghe e dubbiose ognor rende l'idee.
>
> (*AP*, xvii, xxx)

(because philosophising on any subject/ renders the ideas vague and dubious.)

Casti's outlook is undoubtedly empirical and reductive: the true knowledge of things as they are can only be gained by experience of the world based on observation rather than intuition. Abstract systems of philosophy or metaphysics are, ludicrously inadequate, says the poet, and only serve to befog the minds of the rational man. Thus in the seventeenth Canto, Casti digresses to satirise the inconsequence of all metaphysical thinking:

> La troppo perigliosa esperienza,
> La ragion frale e i fallaci sensi,
> E l'ingannevolissima evidenza
> Non entran punto in ciò che credi e pensi,
> Ed impostura e ciarlataneria
> Tace a te avanti, e non si sa che sia.
>
> *(AP*, XVII, xx)

(One's very dangerous experience,/ one's frail reason and fallacious senses/ and the deceptive evidence/ have nothing whatsoever to do with what you believe and think/ and imposture and charlatanry/ are silent in your presence and you don't know what is what.)

This anti-metaphysical trait is a convenient device enabling the poet to touch on a subject without pursuing the matter at any uncomfortable depth or, rather, to give the semblance of an attempt at rational thought while avoiding thought itself. The excuse normally given is that of not wishing to bore the reader with unnecessary speculation.

The politics of the *Animali Parlanti* is deeply entrenched in the tradition of the Enlightenment with its insistence on truth and reason as a protective talisman against the threatening forces of superstition and ignorance. Indeed, there are in the poem constant appeals to man's rationality or to his power of right reasoning – referred to in the poem as Filosofia and Ragione – as the only hope for man to free himself from the restrictions of his own making. The twenty-sixth Canto ends with an invocation to Truth and Reason to help man regain his senses:

> Vieni, o santa Ragion, risplendi amico
> Raggio di Verità, risplendi, e sgombra

E l'ignoranza e il pregudizio antico che
I cuori umani e gli intelletti ingombra,
E Virtù teco facci a noi ritorno,
E fissi sulla terra il suo soggiorno.

(AP, xxvi, c)

(Come, O Holy Reason, let shine/ a friendly ray of Truth, shine
and clear away/ the ancient ignorance, and prejudice/ which
burdens the human heart and ignorance/ and bring Virtue to us
again/ and establish your realm on our earth.)

The *Animali* synthesises in popular form most of the ideas of the
Enlightenment *philosophes* especially those of Voltaire and Montesquieu whom Casti especially admired. Voltairian scepticism
and mockery of superstition and naïveté had pervaded most of the
Novelle Galanti. In the *Animali* Casti draws on Voltaire, in
particular, his *Dictionnaire philosophique*, for support in his indictment of war and its consequences and his probing into the
morality of *real-politik*. There are passages in the *Animali* where
Casti simply versifies a Voltairian idea while preserving the same
ironic flavour: the idea for instance that civilised man invokes his
God when he is about to exterminate his neighbour. In the section
on war, Voltaire argued:

le merveilleux de cette entreprise infernale c'est que chaque
chef des meurtriers fait bénir ses drapeaux et invoque Dieu
solennellement avant d'aller exterminer son prochain.[15]

Casti echoes this thought in:

E per tre di' con simulato zelo
Furo ordinate pubbliche preghiere,
L'alto favore ad implorar del cielo
Sopra le regie lionine schiere,
Onde far strage gloriose e belle
Sugl'inimici e sullo stuol ribelle.

(AP, xix, i)

(And for three days, with simulated zeal/ public prayers were
ordered/ in order to invoke the high favour of heaven/ over the
lion's regal troops/ so that they could effect glorious massacres/
on their enemies and on the rebellious crowd.)

The idea is further developed in Casti's contempt for the unscrupulous and ambitious rulers who lead their country into war on the most trivial of pretexts, but the real targets of his scorn are the unthinking masses who remain ignorant of the reasons and purpose of war. In an interesting aside Casti puts forward his case:

> Se a due potenti ambiziosi, altieri
> In capo vien di divenir nemici
> Si straziano fra lor popoli interi,
> Stati e regni divengono infelici,
> E la ragion, ciò che più bello è ancora,
> Non preme, non si esamina o si ignora.
>
> (*AP*, xxi, lv)

(If two ambitious and potent rulers/ decide to become enemies/ between them they tear apart entire nations,/ whole states and realms become miserable,/ and the funny thing is the reason is of no consequence/ it is not analysed but remains ignored.)

This again is versified Voltaire. In the section on war in the *Dictionnaire philosophique*, the French philosopher repeatedly exposed the crass ignorance of the masses about the reasons of state which had caused their destruction. As he says, 'Ces multitudes s'acharnent les unes contre les autres non seulment sans avoir aucun intérêt au procès, mais sans savoir même de quoi il s'agit.'[16] The notion occurs with the frequency of a refrain for Casti constantly deplored the passive acquiescence of the masses who allowed themselves to become victims of a tyrant's caprice – 'per servir sempre vincitor o vinti'. Following Voltaire, Casti shows ignorance and superstition to be none other than terrible weapons in the hands of an unscrupulous tyrant. Fanaticism of every kind is deplored because it leads to self-destruction:

> Abbiti pur per massima costante,
> E nel fondo del cor tientela teco,
> Che popolo fanatico, ignorante,
> Di superstizione ingombro e cieco
> Un'arma ella e terribil sempre in mano
> D'arbitrario despotico sovrano.
>
> (*AP*, xvi, xliv)

(Take this as a lasting maxim,/ and keep it close to your heart,/ that an ignorant and fanatic people/ burdened and blinded by superstition,/ is always a terrible weapon,/ in the hands of an arbitrary and despotic ruler.)

This is in keeping with Casti's constant expression of repugnance for absolute monarchy which usually takes the form of ironical compassion for those who are victims of their own 'inerzia e stupidezza' and who are willing to attribute to their monarch the qualities of a god. The monarchy itself is attacked on various scores: the faulty education of the coutier which aims at fostering a sense of hauteur and opportunism, the moral laxity which prevails in the court itself and the principle of heredity which is shown to be absurd.

Casti's cynicism, enforced by his first-hand observation of *real politik* as practised by the foremost rulers of Europe is apparent in his inability to see an abiding system of government. All forms of alliances between nations become the butt of the Italian poet's ridicule. Likewise Casti repeatedly sees through the speciousness of congresses in their bid to establish a lasting peace. Above all, the vehemence of Casti's satire is directed at the unthinking masses who are too willing to allow themselves to be exploited by unscrupulous tyrants. As Casti wryly remarks:

> Ma finchè al mondo vi sarà taluno
> Che vittime a migliaia e il sangue altrui
> Possa immolar senza suo rischio alcuno,
> E come e quando e quanto aggrada a lui,
> Non ti doler della barbarie sua,
> O schiava umanità, la colpa è tua.
>
> (*AP*, xxi, lvii)

(But so long as in this world there is someone/ who can sacrifice thousands of victims and the blood of others/ without any risk to himself/ and this how and when and as often as it pleases him/ do not grieve over his cruelty/ O slavish humanity, the fault is yours.)

The bitter irony of the third and fourth lines stresses the sheer callousness of the tyrant who sacrifices the lives of thousands at no risk to his own.

In spite of the poet's vast experience in the courts of Europe and his acquaintance with high-ranking diplomats there is, strangely enough, no coherent vision in the *Animali*. The poet's stance is one of puzzling ambivalence: on the one hand Casti seems to give his whole-hearted support to radical revolutionary movements in their attempt to oust the tyrant while, on the other hand, he treats the ignorant with unreserved contempt. This may be partly due to the excesses of the French Revolution which compelled Casti to see things in a different perspective and to realise that one form of tyranny was after all being replaced by another. It very probably endorsed the Italian poet's cynical cast of mind in his belief that so long as human nature was base nothing good could come out of it.

The overall theme of the *Animali* as a fable is the ineffectual efforts of the animals to preserve themselves from self-destruction and their uncontrollable urge to wage war against each other on the slightest provocation. In this 'rhymed dissertation' as Foscolo called it, the reader fails to see the poetry for the politics, since the poet, as we have seen, was mainly, though not exclusively, concerned with popularising some of the main trends of contemporary political thought. There is little doubt that Casti was at heart a pacifist and that he repeatedly denounced all wars of conquest. The description of the atrocities on the battlefield in which the rebels are ruthlessly massacred is evidence enough of this. Casti goes so far as to question the very notion of heroism on the battlefield and contrasts the savagery of the animals in the fable with the actions of 'heroic' soldiers in war. The comparison is admittedly facile and the rhetoric somewhat hollow but the satire is nonetheless trenchant:

> Voi valorosi eroi dei nostri tempi,
> Che grande avete in sen l'anima e il core,
> Non sentite infiammarvi a tali esempi,
> Di nobil generoso emulo ardore,
> La brutal gloria ad oscurar con belle
> Inclite gesta e anche maggior di quelle?
>
> (*AP*, xxii, ii)

(You valiant heroes of our times,/ who have great souls and great hearts,/ do you not feel aroused at such examples,/ with a generous and noble ardour,/ to obscure the brutal fact of war/ with great deeds and even greater ones?)

The point of the exclamation is to equate the natural ferocity of the animals with the 'inclite gesta' of contemporary heroes. This gives rise to the poet's frequent outbursts on Honour and Glory as the main causes of war and widespread misery, the cruel idols which exact their toll of human life – Honour is indeed the *ignis fatuus* which leads man to his destruction:

> Onore! onor! idol crudel, di cui
> Il culto costa a umanità cotanto!
> Tu il mondo acciechi coi prestigi tuoi
> Tu presti ai gran delitti il nome, e il manto,
> Qual Proteo ognor ti cangi, e agli occhi nostri
> Nel vero aspetto tuo raro ti mostri.
>
> (*AP*, xviii, lv)

(Honour! honour! cruel idol/ the cult of which is so costly to humanity! You blind the world with your fame/ you lend a name and a mantle to great crimes/ you are always changing like Proteus, and to our eyes/ you hardly show yourself in your true aspect.)

Thus, according to the poet, Honour is a protean figure which lends respectability to base crimes.

Casti's stance is one of incomprehension and mystification when faced with the irrationality of human behaviour:

> Nè per altra ragion sparger dovranno
> Fiumi di sangue i sudditi infelici,
> Che per cangiar e non cangiar tiranno?
> Che cal se amici sieno o sieno nemici
> Gli inumani guerrier? Forse miglior
> I difensori son degli aggressori?
>
> L'uom fiero più delle più fiere belve
> E di sua specie, disonor, vergogna.
> Pugnan color nelle natie lor selve
> In lor difesa e per la lor bisogna,
> L'un contro l'altro s'armano in lor danno
> Gli uomini folli e lo perchè non sanno.
>
> (*AP*, xiv, xliv, xlv)

(Nor is there any reason why the wretched subjects/ should bleed rivers of blood/ except that of whether to change or not to change a tyrant?/ What does it matter if the inhuman warriors/ be friends or whether they be enemies/ Are the defenders perhaps better than their aggressors?

Savage man is worse than the savage beasts/ and a dishonour and a shame to his species/ Those fight in their own dens/ and in their defence and because of their need/ but foolish men arm themselves to the destruction of each other/ and they do not know the reason why.)

The comparison with animal behaviour is to be expected in a beast fable where the analogy between men and animals is somewhat laboured. Casti, however, presses the analogy to his advantage by demonstrating that whereas animals fight each other in self-defence, human beings go to war against each other without knowing the reason why. This indictment of war was no doubt prompted by Casti's first-hand experience at the court of Joseph II of Austria where he became aware of the ruthlessness of princely ambition and rivalry, the cost of wars of conquest and the pointlessness of human sacrifice. Nor is this the sole object of Casti's satire: he lashes out against all social institutions with the skill of a demolition expert – his incisive and penetrating intellect cuts through the flimsy veil of human pomp and ceremony. As Giulio Sindonia aptly comments:

La satira, spesso amara ed atroce, gli sorge spontanea nell'animo indignato e commosso e gli crea nel pessimismo delle sue convinzioni, quasi il piacere di negare e di distruggere.[17]

(His satire, often bitter and fierce, arises spontaneously in his indignant and moved heart. This creates in the pessimism of his convictions almost a joy in denying and destroying.)

The quasi-perverse pleasure that the poet seems to derive from demolishing human institutions stems from deep-seated cynicism which is primarily the result of his wide experience in the courts of Europe. The *saeva indignatio* of the poem has its roots in what seems to be a genuine revulsion of feeling for unscrupulous despots as well as for the ignorant and servile masses. In a sense Casti has been misunderstood by those critics who seemed too willing to see him as a modern Thersites denouncing all human endeavour with venom and acerbity. The bitterness of the satire must not blind us to the sincerity of Casti's pacifist convictions.

Although Casti shares most of the views and tenets of the Enlightenment *philosophes*, his political outlook differs in one interesting aspect. Unlike Voltaire and Montesquieu, he is unable to posit the concept of a benevolent and enlightened monarch. In his *L'Esprit des lois*, Montesquieu had accepted the notion of the despotic monarchy founded on fear and servility as distinct from benevolent monarchy whose power was limited by an independent legislative body. The philosopher of Ferney, in turn, hailed Frederick the Great of Prussia as the Philosopher King and idolised Catherine of Russia as 'Notre Dame de Saint Petersbourg'. When it came to monarchs Casti had no illusions. His lifelong experience in the courts of Europe had taught him that they were at best untrustworthy. In one of his numerous digressions in the *Animali* he proclaims:

> Ma in monarchia la cosa è differente:
> Difettosa è in se stessa, e tal la rende
> Suo visio radical; naturalmente
> La monarchia al dispotismo tende
> Nè forse esiste autorità reale,
> Che dritto non si arroghi universale.
>
> (*AP*, IV, xcvi)

(But with the monarchy it's a different case:/ it is defective in itself, and its radical nature makes it so/ essentially, monarchy tends towards despotism./ Nor perhaps does a royal authority exist which does not abrogate to itself a universal right.)

Indeed, Casti's underlying purpose in *Il Poema Tartaro* was to show the corruptive effect of absolute power – 'la monarchia al despotismo tende' (the natural tendency of monarchy to despotism) – as a counterblast against the adulation of Catherine by the Encyclopaedists. Casti's main contention, and one which is somewhat laboured in the *Animali* is that potentates are ruthless enough to sacrifice a whole nation out of self-interest or personal rancour:

> Che se tormenta ed agita i potenti
> Ansia interesse, odio, rancor privato,
> Perché dai lor privati irritamenti
> La ruina seguir dee dello Stato?
> Perché immolar di vittime uno stuolo
> Alla feroce passion d'uno solo?
>
> (*AP*, xix, xxxv)

(Since what annoys and troubles the powerful/ is fear, personal interest, hatred and personal rancour/ why is it that from personal animosity/ the ruin of the state should follow?/ Why sacrifice a whole crowd of victims/ to the burning passion of only one?)

For all the rhetoric, these lines expressing the poet's incomprehension of man's blind obedience to an unscrupulous despot strike at the root of the matter. What puzzles the poet is the fact which he constantly reiterates, that supposedly rational human beings are prepared to go like cattle quietly to the slaughterhouse without ever bothering to know the reason why. As Casti despairingly says with epigrammatic bitterness:

> L'un contro l'altro s'armano in lor danno
> Gli uomini folli, e lo perchè non sanno
>
> (*AP*, xiv, xlv)

(They arm against each other to their detriment/ these foolish mortals, without knowing the reason why.)

The weakness of Casti's satire is precisely this tendency to pose the question without an attempt to pursue the matter in all its psychological complexity.

The middle Cantos of *Don Juan* (vi–ix), as Steffan and Pratt have shown, were finished as a sort of unit and sent off to England by the beginning of September 1822.[18] There is an obvious change of focus in Bryon's satire and a shift of scene from the harem to Ismael and its surroundings, from the blandishments of Gulbeyaz to the grim battle scene around Ismael. As Byron himself announced to Murray, the Cantos were meant to demonstrate the futility and inhumanity of all wars of conquest:

I have written three more cantos of *Don Juan* and am hovering on the brink of another (the ninth). The reason I want the stanzas again which I sent you is, that as these cantos contain a full detail . . . of the siege and the assault of Ismael, with much of sarcasm on those butchers in large businesses, your mercenary soldiery, it is a good opportunity of gracing the poem with these things and these fellows, it is necessary, in the present clash of philosophy and tyranny, to throw away the scabbard . . . the battle must be fought; and it will be eventually for the good of mankind . . .[19] *Don Juan* will be known by and by, for what it is intended – a Satire on abuses on the present state of Society, and not an eulogy of vice.[20]

The scope of the satire in these Cantos has been broadened to include the poet's ironical reflections on, and denunciation of, all forms of tyranny, but especially those despots like Catherine who, out of pride and vainglory, plunge the nation into a war of conquest in order to subjugate the neighbouring territories.

It is perhaps worthwhile to pause for a moment to consider the extent to which Byron's attitude to war and glory changed from the time he wrote the third and fourth Cantos of *Childe Harold* until he came to write the middle Cantos of *Don Juan*. Byron's notion of freedom and glory was somehow linked to the rise and fall of Napoleon – perhaps an attempt to come to terms with his disenchantment with his former hero and the mixed feelings produced by the realisation that the bane of kings and tyrants had become himself both 'conqueror and captive of the earth'. The restless spirit of his soul had urged Napoleon to soar above the narrow confines of its being – he had overreached himself by aspiring 'beyond the fitting medium of desire' (III, xlii) because of the fatal fever at the core which makes him incur the hate of those below. Napoleon, according to the poet, paid the price for attempting to rise above mediocrity and the restless spirit is doomed to eat into itself and 'rust ingloriously'.

Indeed, Napoleon has much in common with the Byronic hero whose spirit 'but once kindled, quenchless evermore,/ Preys upon high adventure . . .' (III, xlii). Byron, in these stanzas, is at pains to point the moral that such men deserve the fate that befalls the 'madmen who have made men mad/ by their contagion' (III, xliii). The conclusion is all too pat and unconvincing for the poet is obviously at a loss to equate Napoleon's achievement with his downfall. He can only exclaim:

> He who surpasses or subdues mankind
> Must look down on the hate of those below.
> Though high above the sun of glory glow,
> And far beneath the earth and ocean spread,
> Round him are icy rocks, and loudly blow
> Contending tempests on his naked head,
> And thus reward the toils which to those summits led.
>
> (*CH*, III, xlv)

Thus the poet evades the issue: it is the lot of those who soar beyond their confines to be forever contending with the tempests and these men are to be pitied rather than envied. Yet one must not lose sight of the context of these reflections, which in effect, epitomise the poet's meditations on France's defeat at Waterloo and form a sequel to Byron's imaginative evocation of the glorious heroism of the British soldier (*CH*, III, xxii–xxx). Standing on 'this place of skulls' the Childe has responded romantically to singing the praises of the fallen brave in 'Battle's magnificently stern array' (III, xxviii, 5). The subject demanded lofty treatment and the poet skilfully provided the accompanying rhetorical flourish:

> And there was mounting in hot haste: the steed,
> The mustering squadron, and the clattering car,
> Went pouring forward with impetuous speed,
> And swiftly forming in the ranks of war;
> And the deep thunderpeal on peal afar;
> And near, the beat of the alarming drum
> Roused up the soldier ere the morning star;
> While throng'd the citizens with terror dumb,
> Or whispering, with white lips – 'The foe! they come! they come!'
>
> (*CH*, III, xxv)

This was reality as the poet imaginatively conceived it for the benefit of the British reading public. But there was another side to the fame of Waterloo which was certainly less attractive and which in its own way disturbed the poet's composure. Byron, it appears, was struck by the bitter irony of an apparently insignificant detail which he recorded eight years later. I refer here to the case of the Young Captain Grose mentioned by name in *Don Juan* (VIII, xviii, 8), an acquaintance of the poet whose name appeared in the *London Gazette Extraordinary* (22 June 1815) as Captain Grove in the list of those killed. Byron's own comment is significant:

> I recollect remarking at the time to a friend: – 'There is fame! a man is killed, his name is Grose, and they print it Grove.'[21]

Yet though this remark on the irony of fame must have been deeply felt during the actual composition of the third Canto of *Childe Harold*, Byron excluded it because he presumably felt that it would not have been in keeping with the solemnity of the sentiments expressed on fame throughout the Canto. The purpose of the evocation of the Waterloo scenes was to glorify the common soldiers' heroic stand against the despot who trampled on Europe's vineyards. The formal structure of the stanzas with their rousing crescendo could hardly be expected to accommodate the poet's ironical reflection on the pointlessness of fame.

There is perhaps a reason why the *Animali Parlanti* may have appealed to him at that particular time. The abortive Neapolitan uprising of 1820, the re-establishing of absolute monarchy by the Austrians in Naples and Piedmont a year later, together with his own disenchantment with resistance movements made Byron aware of the woeful insufficiency of the common people to shake off the yoke of tyranny. He may well have come to realise for himself the deep truth underlying Casti's political maxims and truisms: indeed, the pragmatic doctrine of the *Animali* must have had a particular relevance at that time. Like Casti, Byron could foresee the end of the 'king-times' and with the Italian poet shared a lack of faith in human systems:

> It is still more difficult to say which form of Government is the *worst* – all are so bad. As for democracy, it is the worst of the whole; for what is (*in fact*) democracy? an Aristocracy of Blackguards.[22]

It is certainly highly probable that when it came to the treatment of the themes of glory and war in the middle Cantos of *Don Juan*, Byron's mind reverted to Casti's 'epic': the Italian poet's cynical reflections on virtually the same theme provided him with a model

on which to base his own sceptical observations on the 'nothing-
ness of life'. Not only did Byron delight in stripping off the tinsel of
sentiment – much to La Guiccioli's annoyance – but he also
proceeded in Castian fashion to debunk most of the illusions
entertained by his contemporaries on such topics as glory and
war. Like the Italian poet whom he admired, Byron was
determined to expose the lust for glory as one of the main evils
pervading contemporary society.

The reawakening of Byron's interest in the *Animali* at the time of
the composition of the middle cantos of *Don Juan* may well have
been due to his recent reading of Voltaire's works. Byron had in
fact purchased the works of Voltaire in a 92-volume set (the *kehl
duodecimo*) in 1817 and had come to appreciate the French writer's
sense of freedom and healthy respect for fact. In his comments on
the apothegms of Bacon, Byron referred to Voltaire as 'that great
and unequalled genius – the universal Voltaire' and in his Preface
to Cantos vi–viii he felt obliged to lean on Voltaire for support in
his attack on the over-refining of the language of the upper classes
as a gloss on the depravity of manners. ('Plus les moeurs sont
dépravées, plus les expressions deviennt mesurées; on croit
regagner en langage ce qu'on a perdu en vertu').[23] To Byron's
mind such linguistic refinement was a manifestation of the moral
and political cant which he vehemently detested mostly because it
was in effect none other than a respectable garb for villainy.
Hence his detestation of the 'impious alliance which insults the
world with the name of "Holy"!'[24] Byron must have found
corroboration of this attitude in Casti who, it will be recalled, had
enlarged upon this Voltairian idea in the *Animali* by demonstrating how the politicians had debased the language for the purpose
of veiling their misdeeds ('presta/ ai gran delitti il nome, il
manto'). As Casti put it:

> Perciò nomi inventar sonori e belli
> D'onor di dignatade e di decoro,
> E mille altri vocaboli novelle,
> Che versatile e vaga idea fra loro
> Prender solean, secondo l'interesse
> Di quei che farne applicazion volesse
>
> (*AP*, xviii, liii)

(Therefore they invent resonant and attractive names/ of

honour, dignity and decorum/ and a thousand other new words/ that assume vagueness and versatility, according to the interests/ of those who wish to apply them for their purpose.)

The Marquis Gabriel de Castelnau's *Essai sur l'histoire ancienne et moderne de la Nouvelle Russie* published in Paris in three volumes in 1820 provided, as Byron was quick to acknowledge in the Preface, the factual basis for the Ismael Cantos of *Don Juan*. It is evident from Coleridge's annotations and collations of the parallel passages that Byron echoed his source very closely, sometimes verbatim, especially in those passages which described the actual preparations made by the Russian invaders and the course of the siege. The main appeal of Castelnau's accounts as far as Byron was concerned was that it purported to be based on an eye-witness account of a Russian officer who fought there. The general drift of Castelnau's narrative, as Miss Boyd points out in her fine study of the literary background of *Don Juan*,[25] was to berate contemporary historians for sliding over the facts ('glisse sur des faits')[26] especially concerning the assault of Ismael which he considered to be 'un événement à noter entre les plus hardis de ce genre'.[27] In going on to extol the heroism of war and record his fascination with military glory, Castelnau advises the historian not to spare the readers any of the details:

> ... mais qu'il rende un compte exact d'une action liée a l'héroisme, c'est un devoir qu'il doit s'efforcer de bien remplir.[28]

Miss Boyd is undoubtedly right in claiming that the main purpose of the Ismael Cantos is a satiric attack on the wars of conquest as a direct reaction against Castelnau's glorification of the horrors of war.[29] Indeed, Byron went further and while versifying Castelnau's narrative he could step aside, as it were, and attack the mentality of people like Castelnau who were prepared to gloss over the atrocities committed in the name of heroism and glory.

An analysis of Byron's method of procedure is necessary, I think, in order to demonstrate the exact nature of his debt to Casti and especially the devices employed by the poet in breaking down the illusions of his contemporaries concerning military fame and glory. At its most obvious, Byron's method was to indulge occasionally in mock apostrophes and outbursts introducing some truism about the inescapable baseness of human nature.

The facile analogy with the animal species to the detriment of mankind is a clear instance of this. Byron's aside in the seventh Canto:

> Dogs, or men! – for I flatter you in saying
> That ye are dogs – your betters far – ye may
> Read or read not, what I am now essaying
> To show ye what ye are in every way.
>
> (vii, 1–4)

echoes Casti's comment on man's destruction of his own species:

> Crudelissime bestie! O bestie nate
> Per lo sterminio della vostra specie
>
> (*AP*, xviii, xxxiii, 1–2)

(Most cruel beasts! O beasts born/ to exterminate your own species!)

and the idea that mankind is more rapacious than the beasts of the jungle is a point which pervades Casti's allegory.[30] Casti's comment on the mercenaries in the Russian army engaged by Catherine against the rebels stresses the notion that for a small sum men are prepared to butcher their fellow men and perpetrate the most heinous of crimes:

> E pronta per meschin guadagni vili
> A qualunque atto opprobrioso infame;
> E a far, a prezzo di pochi danari
> I ruffiani, i carnefici e i sicari.
>
> (*PT*, vi, lxviii)

(And ready for a vile and wretched wage/ to perform any hateful and infamous act;/ and to become, for a few pence/ ruffians, butchers and assassins.)

The idea is taken up by Byron in his comment on the preparations made by the Russians before the siege of Ismael:

> Then there were foreigners of much renown,
> Of various nations, and all volunteers;

> Not fighting for their country or its crown
> But wishing to be one day brigadiers;
> Also to have the sacking of a town . . .
>
> (*DJ*, VII, xviii)

This throwing away of the scabbard when it came to surveying the European political scene is neither Horatian nor Juvenalian: it is an attitude firmly rooted in the Enlightenment philosophy which Casti's poem had popularised. The notion of the hero as murderer, and the battlefield the scene of butchery which somehow metamorphosed into glory, is a recurring theme in both the *Poema Tartaro* and the *Animali* and can be traced in Casti's work as far back as *La Divota*, one of Casti's early *novelle*.

One of the characters in this *novella* (the sixth) leaves his wife in order to fight honourably for his country. Casti's wry comment is worth quoting:

> Staccòsi Carlo dalla sposa amata
> Per ire a unirsi ai micidiali eroi,
> Ed appena che fu giunto all' armata,
> Senza che il come a raccontar v'annoi,
> Colpito da solenne archibusata
> Terminò glorioso i giorni suoi,
> Dall'immortal allor incoronato
> Che in sostanza vuol dir che fu ammazzato.
>
> (*LD*, VI, xix)

(Carlo departed from his beloved wife/ to join the homicidal heroes,/ and hardly had he joined the army/ – without boring you with the details – he was hit by a solemn outburst of arquebusade/ and gloriously ended his days/ and immortally crowned/ which in essence means he was killed.)

The irony here undercuts the reader's concept of what is truly noble and heroic. The soldiers are forthwith dismissed as 'micidiali eroi' – and the last line sardonically dispels the notion of glory by its abrupt statement of fact: for all that is said about immortal glory this young man was instantly deprived of both his life and his pretty young wife.

Ironic deflation and the insistence on telling the truth by stripping off the veil of illusion were Casti's manner of arousing his readers to an awareness of the brutal fact of war. In this respect the *Animali*, as Foscolo reluctantly admitted, abounded in point and popular wisdom especially in its delineation of the baseness underlying men's motives. Thus in *Il Poema Tartaro*, in dealing with the theme of valour, Casti shows a preference for the direct and crisp utterance rather than for subtle innuendo. With the righteousness of a sage he can stand aside and reveal the truth about human nature:

> Non è nobil coraggio e valor vero
> Con queste schiere e quello incontro mena
> Ma l'impunito di ladron mestiero
> Cui legge alcuna, alcun poter non frena.
>
> *(PT*, vi, xcviii)

(It is not noble courage or true valour/ which moves this flank against that/ but the unpunished trade of robbery/ which no law or power can stop.)

What should be particularly noticed at this stage is that in his poetry of politics Byron adopts very much the same attitude in his handling of the theme of heroism. Although there are a few mock-heroic passages in *Don Juan*, the stress in the Ismael Cantos is decidedly on the grim truth the poet discloses. Like Casti, Byron was disinclined to engage in 'metaphysical discussion'. Portraying things as they are rather than as people wish them to be, is the poet's 'grand desideratum' and the Homeric epic with its tendency to magnify human action is of its very nature too inadequate a medium to enable the poet to achieve this. The invocation to Homer in the seventh Canto is not simply a travesty of the epic *invocatio*. Rather, it is the poet's drawing attention to the difficulty of establishing the norm in a world of changing values, in which heroes turn out to be 'butchers in great business'.

> Oh, thou eternal Homer! I have now
> To paint a siege, wherein more men were slain,
> With deadlier engines and a speedier blow,
> ·Than in thy Greek gazette of that campaign;
>
> *(DJ*, vii, lxxx)

This may well be Byron's indirect reply to Murray and Foscolo who had urged him to undertake some 'great work' ('an Epic poem, I suppose, or some such pyramid'),[31] but it is also, in my view, a conscious echo of Casti's comment on the battle scenes he describes in the latter part of the *Animali* where the animals having established some kind of order in the state, set themselves to the task of exterminating their enemies:

> Quell'atroce conflitto, e furibondo
> Descrivir non potria coi carmi suoi
> Omero stesso, se tornasse al mondo,
> E quanti furon vati e prima e poi.
>
> (*AP*, xxii, xxxvii)

(That atrocious and fierce conflict/ could not be described in verse/ by Homer himself, if he were to return to the world/ nor by as many poets before or afterwards.)

Homer himself, Casti argues, would have been at a loss to describe the savagery of the battle scene. Byron makes very much the same point and elaborates on Casti's irony:

> . . . The work of glory still went on
> In preparations for a cannonade
> As terrible as that of Illion,
> If Homer had found mortars ready made;
> But now, instead of slaying Priam's son,
> We only can but talk of escalade,
> Bombs, drums, guns, bastions, batterier, bayonets, bullets;
> Hard words, which stick in the soft Muses' gullets.
>
> (*DJ*, vii, lxxix)

Contemporary military warfare with its cruel machines of destruction leaves no room for exploits of glory for the epic poet to extol in verse. The romantic narrative poet has no option but to allude to this 'sad reality' which has become something of an anachronism in the age of gunpowder. As Byron ironically admits:

> But now the town is going to be attacked
> Great deeds are doing – how shall I relate 'em?
>
> (*DJ*, vii, lxxxi, 5–6)

The concluding six stanzas of the seventh Canto assume an Ariosto-like flavour and it is possible to suggest that such ironical observations on warfare were directly inspired by Ariosto's outburst against gunpowder in the *Furioso*:

> Come trovasti, o scelerata e brutta
> invenzion, mai loco in uman core?
> Per te la militar gloria è distrutta,
> per te il mestier de l'arme è senza onore;
> per te è il valore e la virtù ridutta,
> che spesso par del buono il rio migliore;
> non più la gagliardia, non più l'ardire
> per te può in campo al paragon venire.
>
> (*OF*, xi, xxvi)

(O wicked and brutal invention/ how were you conceived in a human heart?/ Because of you military glory has been destroyed/ because of you the use of arms is without honour;/ because of you valour and virtue,/ which often seem to be the better stream of good have dwindled./ Because of you, no longer can boldness and bravery/ reach their peak on the battlefield.)

Following Ariosto, Byron shows the devastating effects of Friar Bacon's 'humane' discovery on the common soldier in search of glory who in the person of Juan stumbles aimlessly and ingloriously on the battlefield ('He knew not where he was, nor greatly cared,/ For he was dizzy, busy . . .') (viii, xxxiii). Ariosto's stance in the *Furioso* was to reduce and deflate the heroic dimensions of the action by adopting a morally ambiguous attitude to his material. As Thomas M. Greene rightly observes, this attitude:

> . . . wavers rather between a bourgeois impulse to moral judgement, and a wearier, more refined inclination to shrug the shoulders. The risk run by such a wavering lies with the poem's heroic ambitions; in the moral ebb and flow, they are likely to get lost.[32]

This same tension, I would argue, exists in Byron's versified adaptation of Castelnau's account of the siege of Ismael: on the one hand there is a Castian mockery of 'Medals, ranks, ribands, lace, embroidery, scarlet'[33] and all such 'things immortal to

immortal man' and an utter *reductio ad absurdum* of man's
aspiration to fame and glory. There is in fact a conscious imitation
of Casti's rhetoric in the seventh Canto in Byron's exclamation on
the theme of glory:

> Oh, foolish mortals! Always taught in vain!
> Oh, glorious laurel! since for one sole leaf
> Of thine imaginary deathless tree,
> Of blood and tears must flow the unebbing sea.
>
> (*DJ*, VII, lxviii, 4–8)

though the awkward inversion of the last line may be taken as an
indication that the Castian garb did not fit too comfortably on
Byron's shoulders. On the other hand Byron shows a grudging
admiration for military leaders like the shrewd and resourceful
Suwarrow, that 'Harlequin in uniform' who despite his bizarre
appearance rallied his troops and 'took the city'.

This admixture of admirable traits of character and downright
absurdity of behaviour is strongly reminiscent of Casti's burlesque technique and Byron may have learned from the Italian
poet the method of presenting a character who is at once likeable
and contemptible. In the *Poema Tartaro*, for instance, Potemkin is
described as a wily courtier who is nonetheless a buffoon, for he
does not hesitate to receive visitors in his night-shirt and night-
cap:

> Parlator franco e cortigian sagace,
> Colla maligna abilità buffona
> Che tutto il dì si disapprova e piace,
> Piacegli censurar ogni persona.
>
> (*PT*, II, xiii)

(A candid talker and a sagacious courtier/ with a malicious
comic talent/ for disapproving and pleasing/ and taking
pleasure in censuring every person.)

The remarkable thing about this Canto is that there is a strange
combination of Castian starkness and an Ariostean tendency to
shrug the shoulders which could be taken as evidence that the
poem gained in 'mobility' as it was being written, with Byron
refusing to settle in any comfortable stance.

In his survey, Ginguené[34] singled out this passage as a fine example of Tasso's narrative art and of his skill in arousing his audience and this was probably the reason for its appeal to the romantic side of Byron's nature. The mention by Castelnau of a sultan's sons who died fighting bravely beside their father must have struck Byron as a remarkable coincidence since Tasso had treated a surprisingly similar episode in his epic. Here for Byron was another instance where the airy fabric of poetry seemed to coalesce with down-to-earth fact. The remarkable thing about all this is that Byron departed from his primary source, which was after all a contemporary account of what actually took place at Ismael, and felt the need to derive inspiration from a 'poetical' version of a similar situation. But while Byron consciously imitated the scene in Tasso, he characteristically effected a significant shift in focus by reinterpreting the episode in terms of his sceptical outlook. There is, to be sure, the expected stress on the courage of the old man and his sons in the manner of Tasso; the Russian assailants are, in spite of themselves, 'Touch'd by the heroism of him they slew'. But within its larger context the passage must be seen not as an abrupt transference to the elegiac mode, as Jerome McGann argues,[35] but as inextricably linked with Byron's disquisition on the unpredictability of human nature and human behaviour.

As we have seen, Byron's purpose was to provide an ironic commentary on Castelnau's glorification of the art of war. The incompetence and inefficiency of the Russian engineers, the disorder and confusion of the soldiers scurrying under heavy fire, the wild and frantic shooting of the defenders, the dogged, almost bestial, determination of the assailants in their craving for plunder – all this comes in for satirical treatment by the poet. But what was perhaps more inherently puzzling as far as Byron was concerned was the mystery of human motivation. What impulse in the souls of men inspires them to 'fight like fiends for pay or politics'? The whole episode of the Tartar Khan and his sons is an attempt to fathom this mystery in artistic terms. By ironically focusing our attention on the paradox of human behaviour Byron refuses to allow the episode to speak for itself. A good example of this is his account of the death of the fifth son:

> The fifth, who, by a Christian mother nourished
> Had been neglected, ill-used, and what not,

Because deform'd, yet died all game and bottom
To save a sire, who blush'd that he begot him.

$$(DJ, \text{VIII, cx, 5–8})$$

This is a far cry from Tasso's lyrical and elegiac treatment of the same situation. Byron has subtly shifted the focus from the filial love and parental affection extolled in the Latinus episode to a deeper concern with the apparent irrationality and unpredictability of man's behaviour. This is also apparent in Byron's comment on the reaction of the Russian soldiers after the death of the Tartar Khan:

'Tis strange enough – the rough, tough soldiers who
Spared neither sex nor age in their career
Of carnage, when this old man was pierced through
And lay before them with his children near,
Touched by the heroism of him they slew,
Were melted for a moment; though no tear
Flow'd from their bloodshot eyes, all red with strife
They honoured such determined scorn of life.

$$(DJ, \text{VIII, cxix})$$

The whole nature of heroism becomes the subject of Byron's probing: the craving for fame or notoriety, the lust for plunder are motives in themselves, but the poet's analytical mind penetrates deeper into the mystery of that strange creature that is man:

Their reasons were uncertainty, or shame
At shrinking from a bullet or a bomb,
And that odd impulse, which in wars or creeds,
Makes men like cattle, follow him who leads.

$$(DJ, \text{VIII, xxxviii, 5–8})$$

The last couplet is distinctly Castian in tone – there is a similar questioning in *Il Poema Tartaro* of the motives that lead a soldier to confront death on the battlefield:

Nè per coraggio o per ragion non mica;
Ma per servile istinto e stupidezza
Va contro i strali dell'oste nemica;
Non conosce il periglio e non l'apprezza,

Mentre a perir l'ignaro e brutal duce
Le vilipese vittime conduce.

(*PT*, ii, lxxx)

(Not out of courage nor even for their rights/ but out of a servile instinct and stupidity/ does he go against the enemy host/ he does not perceive danger, nor does he weigh it/ and meanwhile the dastardly and brutal leader/ leads his abused victims to perdition.)

Castelnau's account had glossed over the carnage and atrocities of a siege, apologetically attributing these horrors to the soldiers' frenzied state of mind in the circumstances:

Détournons nos regards du spectacle affreux dont nous n'avons donné que l'idée; passons sous silence des actes de ferocité pires que la mort, tirons le rideau sur des excès degoûtants, et des crimes impossibles à empêcher quand la fureur du soldat ne peut être contenue.[36]

Unlike his 'author', Byron was temperamentally disinclined to draw the curtain on the grim realities of a war of conquest. If the soldiers are somehow to be exonerated, the blame must be laid squarely on those capricious tyrants who, by imposing their will on the people, plunged the nation into war thereby causing untold hardship and misery:

And whom for this at last must we condemn?
Their natures? or their sovereigns, who employ
All arts to teach their subjects to destroy?

(*DJ*, viii, xcii, 6–8)

Byron was probably influenced here by a similar comment in Casti's *Animali Parlanti* where the poet lashes out at the folly and wilfulness of those monarchs who are too willing to sacrifice their subjects to the god of war:

Perché immolar di vittime uno stuolo
alla feroce passion d'uno solo?

(*AP*, xix, xxxv)

(Why sacrifice a host of victims/ to the fierce passion of only one?)

In more ways than one, Catherine who ordered the taking of Ismael is the culpable 'teterrima causa belli'. As Bernard Blackstone puts it 'she swallows lovers as she swallows king-doms'[37] and following the drift of *Il Poema Tartaro* Byron quietly underlines the inter-relationship between Catherine's sexual propensities and her lust for conquest:

> Now back to thy great joys, Civilization!
> War, pestilence, the despot's desolation,
> The kingly scourge, the lust of notoriety
> The millions slain by soldiers for their ration
> The scenes like Catherine's boudoir at three-score
> With Ismael's storm to soften it the more.
>
> (*DJ*, VIII, lxviii, 2–8)

The siege of Ismael should be seen in its wider perspective as a sustained satire on the corruption of man by the civilised condition to which he inevitably aspires. The imposition of a despot's will in a civilised, humane society marks the beginning of a regression to barbarism – the second fall, in fact – the symptoms of which are unrestrained violence and senseless destruction which degrade man below the level of beasts. By comparison with fallen civilised man:

> The rudest brute that roams Siberia's wild
> Has feelings pure and polished as a gem –
> The bear is civilised, the wolf is mild:
>
> (*DJ*, VIII, xcii, 3–5)

The debt to Casti is here generic: the whole point of Casti's allegory was to show how ignorance, superstition and blind submission to the whims of a tyrant had reduced man to a worse than bestial state, and elsewhere in *Il Poema Tartaro* the soldiers in Catherine's army are vividly described as descending upon their enemies like mad dogs:

> Can rabbiosi venir ringhiando a'morsi
>
> (*PT*, VI, lxxvii)

(Angry dogs running, snarling and biting.)

For Byron, the sack of the city of Ismael had a profound significance which transcended the Castian notion of the bestial debasing of man: it epitomised for him the total loss of painfully acquired values which he associated with a second 'original' state. Jerome McGann is right in saying that:

> For Byron, what is 'Original' to man is not 'paradise' and then 'sin' but civilization and then barbarity.[38]

What the destruction of Ismael really meant to Byron, if we are to approach the poet on his own terms, is perhaps best expressed in George Steiner's eloquent account of the fall of Illium:

> At the core of the Homeric poems lies the remembrance of one of the greatest disasters that can befall man: the destruction of a city. A city is the outward sum of man's nobility in it, his condition is most thoroughly humanized. When a city is destroyed, man is compelled to wander the earth or dwell in the open fields in partial return to the manner of a beast. That is the central realization of the *Illiad*. Resounding through the epic, now in stifled allusion, now in strident lament, is the dread fact that an ancient and splendid city has perished by the edge of the sea.[39]

However, a qualification of this statement ought to be made. Whereas Homer is silent about the death of Troy, Byron devotes two entire Cantos of ironic commentary to the death throes of Ismael. One aspect must also be emphasised and this is that Ismael, as Byron acutely points out, is a pagan city 'sore beset/ by Christian soldiery' and eventually destroyed by order of the Christian Empress Catherine. It is possible to suggest that Byron took as his model Ariosto's account of the taking of Bizerta by the Christian army in the fortieth Canto of the *Furioso*. Indeed, this Canto must have been in Byron's mind when he wrote the Ismael Cantos, for there is a marked similarity in his treatment of basically the same theme. Admittedly, all sieges tend to follow a similar pattern but the tone with its modulations of solemnity and levity is unmistakably there. Thus, for instance, in the uncertain opening of the battle, Ariosto comments facetiously on the fact that the baptised heads suffered damage ('Molto patir le battez-zate teste').[40] Later in his description of the actual sack of the city, he subtly focuses on atrocities committed by the rapacious Christian army which Orlando and Astolfo knew of but were unable to prevent. Unlike Ariosto, however, Byron is not content to allow the scene to speak for itself but he increases the frequency and pitch of the Ariostean modulations of tone, interspersing the narrative with caustic comments in the manner of Casti. Indeed, the siege of Ismael based as it was on a contemporary account, served as a useful focal point for his reflections on the contempor-ary political scene, and some of these reflections originated in his reading of *Il Poema Tartaro* and the *Animali Parlanti*. In this context Tom Moore's evidence concerning the effect of Byron's reading on his method of composition is most revealing and is certainly worth citing:

> . . . it was, I am inclined to think, his practice, when engaged in the composition of any work, to excite thus his vein by the perusal of others, on the same subject or plan, from which the slightest hint caught by his imagination, as he read, was sufficient to kindle there such a train of thought as but for that spark, had never been awakened, and of which he himself soon forgot the source.[41]

Evidently Byron had absorbed much of Casti's spirit and intellectual vigour. Temperamentally, there seems to have been a marked affinity between them: both were very much men alive to the contemporary political scene and they were both libertines and men of the world. They were not original thinkers: Casti confined himself to versifying and popularising a great deal of the ideas and attitudes of the French *philosophes*, especially Montes-quieu and Voltaire whom he particularly admired. Byron, for his part, assumed no consistent philosophical outlook and his political opinions, as Lady Blessington shrewdly observed, were 'wholly governed by the feeling of the moment' and stemmed from 'no fixed principle of conduct or of thought'.[42] There is a ten-dency in both poets to be aloofly intransigent and relentless in their denunciation of tyranny in all its forms and this is coupled with a strong urge to expose the weaknesses of all political systems.

In the *Animali*, as we have seen, monarchism and republican-

ism are attacked with equal vigour but Casti's overall political
outlook is somewhat simplistic and his vision narrow:

> Me ne favellar, né agir mai fanno
> Odio, interesse, adulazion, stipendio;
> Amo il giusto governo, odio il tiranno
> Della dottrina mia questo è il compendio
>
> > (*AP*, xxiv, cxxxi)

(Hatred, personal interest, adulation and remuneration/ never
make me speak or act/ I like a just government, and hate the
tyrant/ this is the gist of my doctrine.)

Byron, who as early as 1814 had recorded that he had 'simplified
my politics into an utter detestation of all existing governments',[43]
must have found corroboration of this attitude in his reading of
Casti and, like the Italian poet, declined to embark on metaphysics but simplified his politics to an abhorrence of tyranny:

> Tyrants and sycophants have been and are.
> I know not who may conquer: if I could
> Have such a prescience, it should be no bar
> To this my plain, sworn downright detestation
> of every despotism in every nation.
>
> > (*DJ*, ix, xxiv, 4–8)

Here again Byron achieves a Castian poise and rigour in his
condemnation of contemporary European politics.

One other instance of probable Castian influence deserves
special attention. During his stay in Venice, Byron composed five
stanzas in *ottava rima* which he transcribed on to four blank fly
leaves of a volume of Italian poetry of the sixteenth century
entitled *Lirici Veneziani del Secolo* xvi. These were presumably
experimental verses written at the time of the composition of the
first Cantos of *Don Juan* but eventually discarded by the poet. The
first stanza containing Byron's cynical observations on the abuse
of power by those who wield it, is of particular interest here since
it has a distinct Castian ring about it. Byron's draft stanza reads:

> This thieving love in great men is ambition –
> The great and wisest only steal the surest –

And when they want more land – they send a mission
To say they'll take it – this way is the *purest* –
Instead of taking it before their wish on
The subject's known. Thus rich men to the poorest
Thus kings to kings – and lords to commoners –
Go on as far as mankind domineers.[44]

It is indeed likely that Byron may have rejected this stanza because he was only too aware of his debt to the Italian poet.

The many similarities between these two poets should not be allowed to obscure their significant differences. In both the *Poema Tartaro* and the *Animali Parlanti* political doctrine tended to flourish at the expense of art with the consequence that both these poems suffer inevitably from diffuseness and repetitiveness. Byron, on the other hand succeeds in keeping his 'politics' under control, maintaining a harmonious equipoise between downright political comment and whole-hearted involvement in the flow of the narrative. Where Casti is vague and generic in his rhetorical outbursts, Byron confines his rhetoric to forthright condemnation of the statesmen and generals of his own day whom he does not hesitate to name. Byron, in fact, applied Castian vigour to the targets of his scorn but unlike Casti he contained his politics within his terms of reference, thus giving his poem an urgency and immediacy which was lacking in his source.

7 'My Finest, Ferocious Caravaggio Style': Byron's Debt to Pulci

> And perhaps it was the same politic drift that the devil whipt St Jerome in a lenten dream, for reading Cicero; or else it was a phantasm bred by the fever which had then seized him. For had an angel been his discipliner, unless it were for dwelling too much upon Ciceronianisms, and had chastised the reading, not the vanity, it had been plainly partial, first to correct him for grave Cicero and not for scurril Plautus whom he confesses to have been reading not long before; next to correct him only, and let so many more ancient Fathers wax old in those pleasant and florid studies without the lash of such a tutoring apparition; insomuch that Basil teaches how some good use may be made of Margites a sportful poem, not now extant, writ by Homer; and why not then of Morgante an Italian romance much to the same purpose?[1]

John Milton had no hesitation whatsoever in classifying Pulci's *Morgante* among the books generally acknowledged as ludicrous if not 'scurril'. However, early nineteenth-century attitudes to Pulci were not as clear-cut, for dilettanti and scholars alike were uncertain as to the proper interpretation of Pulci's burlesque treatment of the romance of Orlando.

Byron's interest in Pulci may be traced as far back as 1817. Delighted with Frere's *Whistlecraft*, which was brought over to him by William Stewart Rose, Byron developed an interest in Frere's original and turned his attention to the account of the *Morgante Maggiore* given by Ginguené in his *Histoire littéraire d'Italie*.[2] Byron had also read John Herman Merivale's adaptation of the *Morgante* entitled *Orlando in Roncesvalles* which was published by Murray in

1814 and which may have occasioned what seems to be Byron's first attempt at *ottava rima* – a few experimental verses ridiculing Southey's rise to the Laureateship.[3] Byron thought highly of Merivale's version and he wrote to the author expressing his 'very great pleasure'.[4] This unqualified praise from Byron, however, calls for some comment. To begin with, Merivale in a short preface, had drawn the reader's attention to the difficulty of understanding and appreciating the Pulcian spirit. Merivale argued that:

> Even the critics most positive in favour of the ludicrous side of the question admit the grand tragic effect of much of the latter cantos: nor can they fairly do so much without also admitting a considerable portion of the earlier part of the poem to be equally serious. On the other hand, it is impossible to deny that, in the most serious passages the reader is often offended by the sudden interposition of low buffoonery or of the grossest profaneness; and the same debasing strain is often continued throughout several successive cantos.[5]

In view of this difficulty, it is not surprising that Merivale should have decided to solve the problem in his own way by eliminating those passages which seemed to him to be incongruous and by concentrating on what he considered to be the main Cantos of the poem. The overall result of such a procedure was to reduce Pulci's twenty-eight Cantos to five, dealing with the more serious episodes, and thus purging the poem of the offending passages containing the poet's irreverent humour. As a consequence, Merivale's version had a Miltonic ring about it which was at odds with the spirit of the original. What is indeed surprising is that Byron should have had such a high opinion of the *Orlando in Roncesvalles* especially when it so obviously distorted the spirit of Pulci. It is possible to suggest, however, that at the time Byron had not fully understood the Pulcian tone and that he merely confined his judgment to the five Cantos adapted by Merivale. Byron's letter to Merivale is particularly interesting because of his helpful criticism concerning a choice of two lines in the last Canto. The letter itself seems to have been written in haste and his remarks are not altogether clear. Byron, it seems, objected to a line describing Rinaldo's feelings on the very morning of the battle of Roncesvalles. The relevant passage reads as follows:

Oh who that sees it rise shall mark its ending?
Oh who shall live, in after years to say
What tides of precious blood, their channels bleeding,
What streams accurst and vile, have roll'd their way.[6]

The first two lines, Byron felt, suggested that the whole situation was predetermined and as such implied 'a doubt of Roland's power or inclination'.[7] Nonetheless, Byron went on to praise Merivale's handling of the measure which he thought was 'uncommonly well chosen & welded'.[8]

In *Whistlecraft*, on the other hand, Frere preserved the comic flavour of the original by concentrating on the ludicrous encounter between Sir Tristram and the troublesome giants to the entire exclusion of the serious religious elements. Thus, for instance, the important stanzas in the first Canto of Pulci's *Morgante* describing the conversion by Orlando of the giant Morgante are largely ignored by Frere who concentrates instead on the enlisting of Morgante's services by the Monks. Frere's focusing on the farcical siege of the monastery and the timorous apprehension of the Monks at the expense of the serious religious elements, leads one to suspect that he was deterred by the delicacy of the subject which involved Pulci's rather controversial disquisition on the nature of God's justice and mercy. In grafting Pulci's genial humour on to native stock, Frere adapted the poem to his own carefree and indolent disposition and tactfully avoided the danger of introducing seemingly incongruous elements. As R. D. Waller convincingly demonstrates,[9] Frere skilfully adapted most of Pulci's stylistic mannerisms including the use of vernacular terms, slang expressions, *doubles-entendres* and broken and imperfect rhymes for humorous effect. Although this transplanting of the Pulcian style was effectively carried out, Frere felt obliged to discontinue the work partly because he must have felt that the Pulcian levity of tone without its complementary seriousness was of its nature far too brittle to endure long. As Frere admitted, he had no inclination to 'persevere in a nonsensical work for the sake of good judges of nonsense'.[10] Whereas Merivale's version had bordered on Miltonic high-seriousness, Frere's adaptation never went beyond a dilettante's *jeu d'esprit*. Merivale was perhaps justified in pointing to the difficulty of capturing the essence of the Pulcian spirit which he believed 'remained among the unexplained and perhaps inexplicable phenomena of the human mind'.[11]

Byron's interest in Pulci was renewed after his reading of *Whistlecraft*. It is obvious from his letters to Murray on the subject that he was uncertain as to the actual role of Pulci in the development of Italian burlesque poetry. In the first instance, he drew Murray's attention to the fact that the style of *Whistlecraft* was ultimately derived from Berni, 'the original of all',[12] but contradicted himself two years later by maintaining that Pulci's *Morgante Maggiore* was the parent 'not only of *Whistlecraft* – but of all jocose Italian poetry'.[13] This contradiction has been plausibly explained by R. B. Ogle who argues that it stems from Byron's change of sources and his discarding of Sismondi in favour of Ginguené whom he began to read in earnest.[14] Indeed, that Byron came to have a high regard for Ginguené as a literary historian and that he considered the Frenchman as superior to either Muratori or Tiraboschi is evident from remarks made in his journal apropros of Baron Grimm.[15]

Byron's attitude to Pulci was a rather complex one and requires further examination since it cannot be simply explained as mere literary curiosity on Byron's part. To begin with, it should be noted that Byron became seriously interested in Pulci as late as January 1820, that is, more than two years after his reading of *Whistlecraft* and the subsequent publication of *Beppo*. This fact prompts the question: to what extent was Byron's translation of the *Morgante* undertaken as an exercise and why should he have translated the first Canto of the *Morgante* when he was occupied with the composition of the third and fourth Cantos of *Don Juan*? The answer is usually explained as a task which Byron set himself in order to stave off boredom at a difficult time in his relationship with Teresa Guiccioli in Ravenna. However, the task itself must have been a salutary exercise in self-discipline for Byron with his natural tendency to compose 'in red-hot earnest' and to dash off his verses impulsively. That he himself came to think of it as such can be gauged from his comments to Murray at the time. He repeatedly insisted to Murray that the translation was a painstaking piece of work and that he was busy 'servilely translating stanza for stanza and line for line two octaves every night'.[16] In another letter to Murray he suggested that the translation be printed side by side with the Italian original, 'because I wish the reader to judge of the fidelity',[17] and he went on to reiterate that the work was undertaken 'stanza for stanza and often line for line if not word for word'.[18] Nor was this all. Three weeks later Byron went to the trouble of sending Murray his own copy of Pulci 'in case in your country you should not readily lay hands on the Morgante Maggiore'.[19] He even went so far as to insist to Murray that he should ask William Stewart Rose the proper meaning of the word *usbergo* which he was about to translate as 'cuirass' but which he thought might mean 'helmet'.[20] In yet another letter he took Ginguené to task for his 'superficial decision' to gloss *usbergo* as *bonnet de fer* and again impressed on his publisher the difficulty of the task of translating Pulci:

> The Dictionary – the Italian woman – the Frenchman – there is no trusting to a word they say . . .[21]

Byron also let it be known that he had consulted the Italians themselves – La Guiccioli, Sgricci the *improvisatore* and the young bride of the Count Rasponi – but he still was not satisfied with their answers. Obviously the process of translation performed the function of compelling Byron to pay more attention to detail than he was accustomed and it was especially salutary in that it served to modify his distaste for revision and correction. Indeed, this fastidiousness with the translation of Pulci is out of keeping with the impression Byron generally sought to convey to Murray and his Synod that he composed his verses with the negligent ease of an aristocrat and could not be bothered with the tedious job of proof-reading. Perhaps he himself came to realise that the Pulcian style was not so easy to imitate after all, or indeed Murray may have communicated John Wilson Croker's advice to the poet on the first two Cantos of *Don Juan*. Croker's suggestion to Murray was that he should persuade Byron to revise the style of *Don Juan*:

> . . . experience shows that the Pulcian style is very easily written. Frere, Blackwood's Magaziners, Rose, Cornwall, all write it with ease and success; it therefore behoves Lord Byron to distinguish his use of the measure by superior and peculiar beauties. He should refine and polish; and by the *limae labor et mora*, attain the perfection of ease.[22]

Since criticism of Byron's translation of the *Morgante* has been largely generalised and often not too discriminating, it would be worthwhile, I believe, to consider Byron's attempt to capture the spirit of the original. The laborious process of undertaking a verse-for-verse translation was Byron's way of assimilating the spirit of Pulci by understanding the meaning and translating it into a new form. It was in this way that the Italian poet could become part of his own consciousness – a quality which Shelley thought belonged to the best of poets who:

> . . . are a very camaeleonic race: they take the colour not only of what they feed on, but of the very leaves under which they pass.[23]

But whereas Shelley seemed more concerned with the spirit – 'those delicate and evanescent hues of mind, which language delights and instructs us in precise proportion as it expresses'[24] – Byron turned to the very letter of the original text in an attempt to come to grips with his author. The actual translation no doubt had some therapeutic value in that it helped tide him over some awkward moments in his liaison with Teresa Guiccioli.[25] However, it also helped to stimulate his creative faculties at a period when he felt barren of inspiration, especially after the publication of the first two Cantos of *Don Juan*. He even confessed to Murray that he had his doubts about proceeding with the publication of new Cantos since he felt they lacked the spirit of the first:

> . . . the outcry has not frightened but it has *hurt* me and I have not written *con amore* this time.[26]

In his Advertisement to the translation of the *Morgante*, Byron called the reader's attention to the practical difficulties involved in the delicate task of capturing the essence of the original and particularly that of 'combining his interpretation of the one language with the not very easy task of reducing the same versification in the other'.[27] Another problem equally hazardous was that of conveying the full flavour of the antiquated dialect in which Pulci wrote, 'with its great mixture of Tuscan proverbs'.[28] In view of this Byron hoped that the reader would be disposed to be 'indulgent to the present attempt', and expressed his wish to present 'in an English dress a part at least of a poem never yet rendered into a northern language'.[29] The main reason for the choice of Pulci was that the *Morgante* 'has been the original of some of the most celebrated productions on this side of the Alps, as well as those recent experiments in England'.[30]

A closer look at the translation proper would, I think, throw some light on Byron's actual achievement. The first thing to be noticed is that there are no departures from the sense of the original, which is to be expected in a translation which purports to be faithful to the Italian original. Indeed, the text is closely followed with a pertinacity which is unusual in a poet of Byron's disposition. On the whole, there is a marked balance between Byron's need to preserve the literal meaning on the one hand and the strict necessity of satisfying metrical exigencies on the other. Only very occasionally is fluency of rhythm sacrificed because of strict adherence to the literal meaning of the text. An example of this occurs in:

> He gazed; Morgante's height he calculated,
> And more than once contemplated his size
>
> (*MM*, lvii, 1–2)

which is a close rendering of:

> E riguardava e squadrava Morgante,
> La sua grandezza ed una volta e due;[31]

At times however, the meaning of the original is slightly dislocated so as to accommodate the rhythmic flow of the *ottava rima*, such as:

> Morgante i moncherin mostrò per fede
> Come i giganti ciascun morto giace
>
> (*MM*, lvi, 5–6)

which Byron translates as:

> Morgante with the hands corroborated,
> A proof of both the giants' fate quite clear.
>
> (lvi)

Here the phrase 'with the hands corroborated' is an awkward rendering of 'mostro per fede'; but instances of this type are admittedly rare.

There are, too, quite a few instances where Byron's version fails to convey the full vigour of his original. For example, 'rechimi a memoria' (i, 7) becomes 'shall help ... my 'song' in Byron's translation. Again, 'faticarsi' (iv, 3) is rather feebly rendered as 'carry prose or rhyme'. There is also an instance where Byron mistranslates the sense of Pulci as in 'col senno, col tesoro' (vii, 8) which is rendered as 'with knightly courage, treasure' instead of 'with good sense'. Another obvious example is provided by Byron's rendering of:

> Ma la Fortuna attenta sta nascosta
> Per guastar sempre ciascun nostro effetto
> *(MM*, ix, 1–2)

which is translated as:

> But watchful Fortune, lurking, takes good heed
> Even some bar 'gainst our intents to bring.
> *(MM*, ix, 1–2)

where the sense of 'guastar' 'to waste' or to 'bring to nothing' is considerably toned down. But perhaps the most interesting example of Byron's mistranslations of his original is afforded by his curious rendering of 'mazzafrusti' (xxix, 2). The word actually means a whip of five or six wires with a piece of lead attached to each wire and, in popular tradition, it was a weapon much favoured by giants. The context corroborates this meaning since the Abbot does all he can to dissuade Orlando from undertaking his foolhardy enterprise against the giants. The Abbot's mention of the giants being armed with 'mazzafrusti' would have deterred a lesser man than Orlando. It is surprising, therefore, that for all Byron's obsession with accuracy he should have actually translated this word as 'ballast stones'.[32]

These occasional flaws in the translation should not, however, be allowed to obscure the excellence of the translation as a whole. What is most impressive about Byron's version is its closeness to the flavour of Pulci. Indeed, Byron succeeds in capturing that popular, proverbial idiom which was the essence of the Tuscan dialect and which Pulci so skilfully tapped for humorous effects. A fine example of this is provided by the rendering of:

E pensa che di ferro abbi la schiena
E forse non credeva schiacciar uova

(lxviii, 3–4)

which, in Byron's version, becomes:

Thinking that he a back of iron had
Or to skim eggs unbroke was light enough

There are no obvious signs of strain throughout. On the contrary, it is remarkable how effectively Byron succeeded in transplanting the Pulcian fluctuations of tone and tempo which have baffled so many of his readers. Some indication of the complexity of the Pulcian style is given by G. Fatini in his introduction to his edition of the *Morgante*. According to Fatini the Pulcian style is:

> . . . uno stile rapido e spassoso, ora asciutto ora colorito, che talora si fa duro e oscuro per amore di gergo furbesco, ricco di equivoci e di sottintesi spintosi; più spesso assume una andatura trasandata . . . Uno stile che si snoda liberamente in periodi incuranti delle norme sintattiche e morfologiche, nei quali trionfano gli anacoluthi, i rapidi cambiamenti di soggetto, le sconcordanze dei tempi nei verbi, il repentino passaggio da un tempo all'altro, gli idiotismi più pittoreschi, i costrutti populari . . .[33]

> (A deft and amusing style, at times dry and at times coloured, which occasionally becomes hard and obscure and, because of its cunning slang full of indelicate puns and *doubles entendres*, often becomes inelegant . . . It is a style which easily flows into sentences which defy syntactical and morphological norms and in which anacolutha dominate a style in which there are sudden changes of subject, verbs and tenses in discord, the sudden shift from one tense to another, the most colourful banalities in the popular idiom . . .)

This convergence of heterogeneous elements, the mingling of the serious and the frivolous, the abrupt changes of theme and mood, the juxtaposition of solemn biblical language and the coarse and vulgar idiom of the market place – all these stylistic elements must have contributed to the difficulty of translation. Yet in spite of the

complexity of the problem Byron succeeds admirably in conveying the freshness and effervescence of the original. It was with
some justification that he could claim that:

> . . . the *Pulci* I am proud of – it is superb – you have no such
> translation.[34]

It is precisely this convergence of disparate elements woven into
the texture of the *Morgante* which has led to the difficulty of
understanding the Pulcian tone. Ginguené himself came to the
conclusion that it was futile for the reader to make an effort to
come to terms with the spirit of Pulci and to try to determine
whether the *Morgante* was to be regarded as a serious poem or
not.[35] For all his acumen as a critic of Italian literature, Ginguené
eschewed the vexed question of Pulci's seemingly ambiguous tone
and ascribed Pulci's irreverent disposition to the grossness of the
times.

It was John Herman Merivale who first sought to draw the
attention of the British reading public to the fact that Pulci's work
had been seriously underestimated and in his *Critical Observations
on the 'Morgante Maggiore'* he argued that Pulci deserved 'a higher
rank in the poetical scale than late authors have been inclined to
give him'.[36] In attempting to defend Pulci against the grave
charge of irreverence and irreligion, Merivale tended to consider
the *Morgante* not only as written in the tradition of the chivalric
romance but also as an expression of the Renaissance spirit.
Merivale's case for a reappraisal of Pulci rested on the fact that the
Italian poet was only too conscious of writing in a tradition of
parody and burlesque which in its own peculiar way had become
a serious criticism of life. Merivale, in fact, rebutted the charge of
irresponsibility which was levelled at Pulci:

> . . . his frequent use of quotations from Scripture which (if his
> poem had been a burlesque, as is represented) would be
> unpardonable; but in another view we may readily excuse him.
> The manners of the times are his apology; the institutions of
> chivalry (not yet decayed) which blended the wildest notions of
> romance with the most enthusiastic devotion; which formed, in
> its original intentions, devout warriors, and religious lovers;
> and in its decline and corruption, produced superstitious
> ruffians and sanctified debauchees.[37]

However, it was Foscolo over a decade later who actually focused on the serious nature of some of the burlesque poems and who first put forward the view that though Pulci accommodated his poetry to the spirit of the age, the *Morgante* was to be regarded as a serious work. According to Foscolo, Pulci's bizarre humour had its origin in the:

> . . . contrast between the constant endeavours of the writers to adhere to the forms and subjects of the popular story-tellers, and the efforts made at the same time by the genius of these writers to render such materials interesting and sublime.[38]

The notion that the light-hearted jesting and buffoonery of some passages did not entirely counteract the poet's seriousness of purpose was the primary cause of mystification in most critics of Pulci. In his preface to the *Orlando in Roncesvalles* Merivale confessed his inability to come to terms with the spirit of the poem:

> What can be thought of a poem, so strange in its design and tendency, that, to the present moment, it remains undecided whether it was intended as a burlesque or as a serious composition?[39]

The later Cantos of the *Morgante* with their 'grand tragic effect' were commendable, but Merivale felt duty bound to warn the reader against the 'sudden interposition of low buffoonery or of the grossest profaneness'[40] even in those passages in the poem which were meant to be serious. J. N. Fazackerly's letter to Ugo Foscolo on the subject of the adaptation of Frere and Rose of the *ottava rima* is further evidence of the British public's failure to appreciate the tone of Italian burlesque poetry in general:

> There is nothing in the follies and negligencies of life at which these writers laugh, which deserves to be treated in any other manner: it is done with so much good humour that the objects of the ridicule might even join in the laugh. They have nothing in common with the caustic persiflage of Voltaire. I know nothing like Rose's style in our language, it is much more taken from the writers with whom he is so familiar – Pulci, Berni, Casti: and tho' one has no right to compare him to the second or perhaps even to the first, yet we should be indulgent to the first

imitation of their masterwork in a language new to that species of poetry . . .[41]

The whole question of the seriousness or otherwise of Italian burlesque poetry is taken up again by Byron in the Advertisement to his translation of the *Morgante*. Byron alerted the reader to the fact that:

The serious poems on Roncesvalles in the same language [English] and more particularly the excellent one of Mr Merivale are to be traced to the same source. It has never yet been decided entirely whether Pulci's intention was or was not to deride the religion which is one of his favourite topics. It appears to me, that such an intention would have been no less hazardous to the poet than to the priest, particularly in that age and country; and the permission to publish the poem, and its reception among the classes of Italy, prove that it neither was nor is so interpreted.[42]

An important point emerges from the Advertisement and from Byron's letters written at that time. The ostensible reason for the translation was that the poet decided to undertake an experiment out of his 'love for, and partial intercourse with, the Italian language'.[43] There was, however, a deeper motive underlying this experiment which immediately becomes apparent if we look at Byron's letters to Murray at the time. In order to impress the reader with the degree of accuracy attained, Byron insisted to his publisher that the translation was to be printed alongside the original. But it is also clear from a close reading of his letters that he had ulterior motives for this. The translation, it will be recalled, was undertaken after the composition of the first two Cantos of *Don Juan* at a time when he was particularly sensitive to the public's hostile reception. An anonymous reviewer berated the poet for:

. . . impiously railing against his God – madly and meanly disloyal to his Sovereign and to his country, and brutally outraging all the best feelings of female honour.[44]

What must have been more galling for Byron at the time was Hobhouse's communication to the poet of his conversation with the dandy Scrope Berdmore Davies on the first Cantos of *Don Juan* in which they both felt that 'the blasphemy, and bawdry and the domestic facts overpower even the great genius it displays'.[45] As far as Byron was concerned, the translation of Pulci could serve as an indirect form of self-justification for the improprieties of *Don Juan*. The translation therefore would serve the purpose of drawing the reader's attention to the fact that Byron was writing after a tradition of poetry in which an occasional laugh at things sacred was considered salutary. As a matter of fact, in recommending his translation of Pulci to Murray, Byron expressed the hope that:

> . . . you will see what was permitted in a Catholic country and a bigotted age to a Churchman on the score of religion; – and so tell those buffoons who accuse me of attacking the liturgy.[46]

This same note of indignation is struck a month later in his reply to Murray's assertion that Pulci in so far as the reading public was concerned was the sort of writer who 'went without clothes'. Murray's point was that public sensibility had, since Byron's departure from England, become more refined and somewhat intolerant of irreligious jesting. Byron's reply speaks for itself:

> You talk of *refinement*; – are you all *more* moral? are you all *so* moral? No such thing.[47]

The moral cant of the day was beginning to impose on the creative artist a concern with propriety which Byron found stultifying. The reason why he insisted to Murray that there were to be no alterations or mutilations was not so much that it spoiled the effect of the translation but that any omissions or alterations would emasculate Pulci:

> . . . the original has been ever free from such in Italy, the Capital of Christianity, and the translation may be so in England.[48]

Here again Byron felt the need to educate the reading public's sense of moral propriety by pointing to the fact that the same jesting spirit which was allowed to survive in Pulci's own day, in spite of the tyranny of the inquisition, was being gradually stifled by a straitlaced and hypocritical society in early nineteenth-century England. The translation therefore was primarily intended to demonstrate that a poet could be facetious about religious matters and still not incur the charge of blasphemy. The defence of Pulci in the Advertisement to the *Morgante* was Byron's indirect way of defending himself against the accusation of impiety levelled at the first two Cantos of *Don Juan*. Part of the Advertisement in fact echoes Byron's previous remonstrance to Murray:

> That he [Pulci] intended to ridicule the monastic life, and suffered his imagination to play with the simple dullness of the converted giant, seems evident enough, but surely it were unjust to accuse him of irreligion on this account, as to denounce Fielding for his parson Adams, Barnabas, Thwackum, Supple and the Ordinary in Jonathan Wild, – or Scott, for his exquisite use of his Covenanters in the 'Tales of my Landlord'.[49]

No doubt another reason why Byron chose to translate the first Canto rather than any other was because it best exemplified the many facets of the Pulcian style. The careful reader would be expected to notice how the heterogeneous elements of the poem were so extraordinarily blended together and how the total effect of the poem depended on the poet's constant modulations of tone. Thus, for example, the solemnity of the invocation to the Word and the Virgin in the opening stanzas gives way to a facetious description of the Court of Charlemagne which is in turn followed by the rollicking episode of the besieging of the monastery and the hilarious encounter of Orlando with the giants, the humorous conversion of Morgante and the abrupt transition to Orlando's sober disquisition on the quality of God's mercy and justice for the benefit of his loutish neophyte. All of this goes to show why the first Canto in particular with its rich variations of tone and mood appealed to Byron and why he applied himself to the task of translating it. The reader would be able to judge for himself that this kind of flippant impiety was tolerated in the 'capital of Christianity'.

Certainly some of the Pulcian flavour filtered into the first Cantos of *Don Juan*. The obvious instance of this normally cited by commentators of *Don Juan* is the passage in the third Canto in which Byron describes the revelry in honour of Haidée and Juan during the absence of Lambro.[50] The quickening tempo of the verse and the gusto with which the various dishes are described are rightly attributed to the influence of Pulci. There is another detail, however, hitherto unnoticed by the critics which Byron in all probability borrowed direct from the *Morgante*. The passage in question occurs in the account of the wreck of the *Trinidada* where the panic-stricken Pedrillo repents of his sins and vows to go on a pilgrimage to Salamanca. This episode is strongly reminiscent of the description of the storm at sea in the twentieth Canto of the *Morgante* where Pulci describes the plight of the despairing sailors:

> Che, se scampar potran sì crudel sorte,
> Ognun presto al Sepolcro ne fia andato;
> E stavano in cagnesco con la morte;
> Ma non valeva ancor prieghi nè voti
> Tanto il mar par che la nave percuoti.
>
> (xx, xxxviii, 4–8)

(that if they could escape such a cruel fate,/ each one would have gone quickly to the Holy Sepulchre/ for they were in the jaws of death itself;/ but neither prayers nor vows were of any avail,/ so hard did the sea strike the ship.)

The notion of exploiting the sailors' fear for humorous effects is a Pulcian trait which Byron adapted to the best advantage.[51]

Pulci's sense of the ridiculous occasionally takes the form of a spirited religious parody which would at first sight appear blasphemous to most of his readers. A good instance of his genial and irreverent wit is his clever parody of the *Credo* in the episode of Margutte. This vulgar gourmand is made to express his liking for food in terms of a Christian's solemn declaration of faith:

> Ma sopra tutto nel buon vino ho fede,
> E credo nella torta e nel tortello;
> L'una è madre e l'altro è l'suo figliolo,
> E il vero paternostro è il fegatello,
> E possono essere tre, due ed uno solo.
>
> (*MM*, xviii, cxvi)

(But above all I believe in a cake and little tart/ and one is the mother and the other the son/ and my true paternoster is the liver,/ which could be three, two or only one.)

The effect is, admittedly, bizarre but the poet's jovial humour tones down such blasphemous elements as may appear offensive. As a perceptive critic points out:

> . . . i misteri più cari al cuore di un cattolico, potrebbe apparire blasfema, ma blasfema non è, tanto è evidente il ridicolo di cui è impostata la suo grossolana natura.[52]

> (. . . the mysteries most dear to the heart of a Catholic might seem blasphemous, but this is not blasphemy because the ridiculous side of his coarse nature is so evident.)

Byron's parody of the ten commandments at the end of the first Canto of *Don Juan* has a distinctly Pulcian flavour with its subtle manner of compelling the reader to admire the wit while largely ignoring the profanity.

The influence of Pulci however, is not confined to the occasional borrowing of external details. In the course of this chapter I wish to consider the influence of Pulci on the tone and spirit of *The Vision of Judgment* – an influence which has been largely ignored by the critics who tend to regard Byron's satirical poem exclusively as a counterblast to Southey's occasional poem of the same name. The attitude generally adopted by most critics who consider *The Vision of Judgment* as Byron's finest work is that when Byron matured during his sojourn in Italy he somehow discarded the coarser features of his earlier satires, such as his tendency, in *English Bards and Scotch Reviewers*, to give vent to his splenetic outbursts directed at society at large or his inclination to indulge in frontal *ad hominem* attacks on the poets and critics he particularly disliked. Byron's sudden maturity is made to account for the purging of his many imperfections and the possibility of his coming into contact with fresh and invigorating foreign influence is conveniently discarded. Such an attitude is best exemplified in the study of Byron's satiric mode by the American scholar Richard Quintana.[53] Quintana's article was, admittedly, written over fifty years ago but modern scholars tend to adopt much the same approach. The reason for the difference in Byron's style in the period between the composition of *English Bards and Scotch*

Reviewers and the publication of *The Vision of Judgment* is attributed by Quintana to the fact that somehow in the intervening years Byron 'purged himself of the splenetic rancour and acquired an ironic and for the most part impersonal contemplation of the world'.[54] How this process of the purging of spleen actually came about or whether Byron may have been influenced by a single writer or writers with whom he came into contact, is unknown and the critic in question does not pursue the matter any further. To attribute the development of Byronic satire exclusively to forces inherent in the poet himself is to lose sight of an important dimension in a poet's artistic evolution. *The Vision of Judgment*, in my view, is compounded of various external literary reminiscences rather than being solely the product of the poet's mature personality.

The Vision of Judgment was begun just over a year after Byron forwarded to Murray his translation of the *Morgante*. Its *raison d'être* as Byron explained in the Preface was to attack 'the gross flattery, the dull impudence the *renegado* intolerance and impious cant' of Southey's pompous and portentous poem. The structure of Byron's poem is therefore determined in part by the form of Southey's poem since it was Byron's purpose to parody the poet laureate's verses on the entry of George III into Heaven. In his letter to Murray Byron disclosed his intention to counteract Southey's smug Toryism:

> . . . it is my intent to put the said George's Apotheosis in a Whig point of view, not forgetting the Poet Laureate for his preface and his other demerits.[55]

There were, however, other influences at work which contributed to the verve and vitality of Byron's spirited attack. Not only did the translation of the *Morgante* serve the purpose of enabling Byron to assimilate the Pulcian manner but it also helped to ignite his creative faculties. Nowhere is this more evident than in Byron's conception and development of the celestial and infernal scenes in *The Vision of Judgment*. It was, indeed, from the *Morgante Maggiore* that Byron derived the idea of the humorous treatment of infernal activity as a consequence of the carnage at Waterloo in the opening stanzas of *The Vision of Judgment*. In the twenty-sixth canto of the *Morgante* Pulci facetiously described the preparations made by the denizens of heaven and hell in their anticipation of the souls of the warriors after the bloody battle of Roncesvalles. It is in this Canto that Pulci deviates from his sources and from the traditional accounts of the battle by the *cantastorie* and gives full play to his bizarre fantasy. Here is his account of the scene near Roncesvalles while the actual encounter between Christian and pagan knights takes place:

> In Runcisvalle una certa chiesetta
> Era in quel tempo, ch'avea due campane;
> Quivi stetton coloro alla valetta
> Per ciuffar di quelle anime pagane,
> Come sparvier tra ramo e ramo aspetta,
> E bisogno che menassin le mane
> E che battessin tutto 'l giorno l'ali,
> A presentarle a' giudici infernali.
>
> (*Morgante*, xxvi, lxxxix)

(In Roncesvalles there was a certain little church/ in those days which had two bells;/ in which these lay in wait/ to catch the pagan souls/ as hawks that wait from branch to branch and they were compelled to use their hands/ and beat their wings all day/ to take them before the infernal judges.)

The devils are compared to sparrowhawks flitting about frantically in their zeal to seize the souls of the dead in mid-flight and carry them to the seat of infernal judgment. The bristling activity of the devils and the ensuing jubilation in the infernal regions form part of Pulci's phantasmagoric vision. The whole scene is described with great gusto and for a while the reader's attention is distracted from the plight of Rinaldo and the treachery of Gano. Pulci's eccentric personality momentarily takes over:

> Credo ch'egli era più bello a vedere
> Certo gli abissi, il dì, che Runcisvalle
> Ch'è saracin cadevano come pere,
> E Squarciaferro gli portava a balle;
> Tanto che tutte l'infernal bufere
> Occupan questi, ogni roccia, ogni calle,
> E la bolge e gli spaldi e le meschite,
> E tutta in festa é la citta di Dite
>
> (*Morgante*, xxvii, liii, 1–8)

(I think that it was certainly nicer to watch/ the abyss that day, rather than Roncesvalles/ because the Saracens fell like pears/ and Squarciaferro carried them like sacks/ and so many that the infernal wind/ and every rock and path was full/ as were the pits, projections and constructions/ and the city of Dis was all festive.)

It is clear from the passages cited above that Pulci exercised a powerful hold on Byron's imagination during the composition of *The Vision of Judgment*, particularly in the humorous treatment of the delicate theme of eternal judgment and damnation. Byron elaborates on the Pulcian comic notion of hectic activity in the infernal regions by dwelling on the contrast with the lackadaisical inactivity of the seraphs in heaven and by ascribing the infernal hustle and bustle to the 'crowning carnage' at the battle of Waterloo. Indeed, there is a parallel between Waterloo and Roncesvalles for both battles become the cause of great commotion in hell. In fact, Byron's 'besmeared with blood and dust' is strongly reminiscent of a verse in Merivale's adaptation of Pulci's account of Roncesvalles which reads 'Now half their fires are quench'd in dust and blood'.[56] Again, following Pulci, Byron develops the idea that Satan and his followers can hardly cope with the sudden influx of damned souls:

> . . . 'tis not mine to record
> What angels shrink from; even the very devil
> On this occasion his own work abhorr'd
> So surfeited with the infernal revel:
>
> (*VJ*, vi, 1–4)

But the most obvious instance of direct Pulcian influence occurs in Byron's humorous depiction of St Peter. In the *Morgante* Pulci burlesqued the custodian of heaven by presenting him as a timorous and somewhat garrulous old man who frets at the sight of an unexpected host of vociferous souls all chanting hosannas on the threshold of heaven:

> E così in ciel si faceva apparecchio
> D'ambrosia e nettar con celeste manna;
> E perchè Pietro alla porta è pur vecchio,
> Credo che molto quel giorno s'affanna

E converra ch' egli abbi buono orecchio,
Tanto gridavan quelle anime – Osanna –
Ch'eran portate dagli angeli in Cielo
Si che la barba gli sudava e 'l pelo.

(XXVI, xci)

(And so in heaven preparations were made/ with ambrosia and nectar and celestial manna/ and since Peter at the door was very old/ that day, I believe, he fretted a lot/ for he ought to have had a good ear/ with so many souls shouting Osanna – those who were carried to heaven by the angels/ so that even his beard and his hair sweated.)

This delightful touch of humour must have caught Byron's fancy and, though he alters the context, the debt to Pulci in the following verses is unmistakable:

He pottered with his keys at a great rate
And sweated through his apostolic skin.
Of course his perspiration was but ichor,
Or some such other spiritual liquor.

(*VJ*, xxv, 5–8)

It is also interesting to note how the original idea from Pulci was sifted through Byron's critical intelligence before it eventually filtered into his verse. There is a subtle change of context which makes St Peter's sudden fit of perspiration more plausible since the arrival of Satan is a greater cause for concern. Besides, Byron's enquiring mind elaborates on the notion as to whether a celestial body can actually perspire.

A less obvious but perhaps more profound influence on *The Vision of Judgment* can be detected in the delineation of the character of Satan and in the free spirit of tolerance which pervades the poem. The characterisation of Satan in *The Vision* is chiefly modelled, in my view, on that of the devil Astarotte in the *Morgante*. When Byron read the *Morgante* he must have realised that in the devil Astarotte who is summoned by Malagigi to assist the harassed Orlando, Pulci had created his finest and most original character. Indeed, a critic of the *Morgante* goes so far as to state that this fallen angel is 'la più originale rappresentazione del diavolo che sia mai fatto'[57] and he is probably justified in his claim. Astarotte's sombre aspect belies his tolerant and humane outlook on life. Pulci describes him as 'molto savio, terribil, molto fero' but in reality he is more of a theologian *manqué* who somehow ended up in hell. In his dealings with Malagigi and Orlando he is invariably dignified and polite. He constantly reminds Orlando that courtesy and good breeding are also to be found among the devils in hell.[58] While disdaining to complain of his own predicament he expatiates on the nature of sin and the possibility of man's redemption. Ginguené's comment on the eccentricity of this fallen angel is apposite:

> Il parle de la Vierge glorifiée dans le ciel, d'Emmanuel, du Verbe sainte, de l'ignorance invincible, et de l'ignorance voluntaire. En fin ce diable – ci est tout aussi savant que le serait un docteur de Sorbonne.[59]

Astarotte is in fact an abstraction of Pulci's sceptical and enquiring intellect given a local habitation and a name. The creed he expounds is a strange admixture of orthodoxy and heterodoxy: his catechism on God as the moving force of the universe is impeccable and yet almost in the same breath he will put forward the heretical view of universal redemption:

> Forse che il Vero, dopo lungo errore,
> Adorate tutti di Concordia,
> E troverete ogn'un misericordia.
>
> (*Morgante*, xxv, cciii, 6–8)

(Perhaps it is true that after persevering in error/ all of you will worship in harmony/ and each one of you will receive mercy.)

a doctrine which, as Merivale pointed out:

> . . . he insists upon with a zeal which we should more expect to meet with in a heresiarch of the early church than in a romance writer and buffoon of the fifteenth century.[60]

It is interesting to observe how this 'angel discreto' as Malagigi calls him influenced Byron in his conception of Satan and hell in *The Vision of Judgment*. As we shall see, Byron's Satan has close affinities with Astarotte. Following Pulci Byron uses very much the same *chiaroscuro* technique in presenting Satan as an angel of formidable aspect who inspires awe in the beholder and at the same time is both courteous and refined in his bearing. The spirit of genial tolerance which characterised Astarotte is also present in Byron's delineation of Lucifer:

> ... 'To me the matter is
> Indifferent, in a personal point of view;
> I can have fifty better souls than this
> With far less trouble than we have gone through'
>
> (*VJ*, lxiv, 1–4)

Byron here goes a step beyond Pulci by making the devil appear nonchalant. Undoubtedly, Byron must have identified sympathetically with Astarotte especially with the devil's predicament of having to accept his eternal punishment as a just decree of the Divine Will while at the same time envying the fortune of those repentant Christians who are given the opportunity to redeem themselves. Certainly his reading of Pulci must have had the effect of liberating Byron from his gloomy Calvinistic beliefs to which Lady Byron ascribed 'the mistery of his life'.[61] From the *Ravenna Journal* (1821) it is clear that Byron's thoughts were often engrossed in the metaphysics of hell. In fact, in an entry in this journal at the same time as the composition of *The Vision of Judgment*, Byron recorded that:

> A *material* resurrection seems strange, and even absurd, except for purposes of punishment; and all punishment which is to *revenge* rather than *correct*, must be *morally wrong*. And when the World *is at an end*, what moral or warning purpose *can* eternal tortures answer? Human passions have probably disfigured the divine doctrines here, but the whole thing is inscrutable. It is useless to tell me *not* to *reason*, but to *believe*. You might as well tell a man not to wake but *sleep*. And then to bully with torments! and all that! I cannot help thinking that the *menace* of Hell makes as many devils, as the severe penal codes of inhumanity make villains.[62]

It is perhaps because of his inability to come to terms with the orthodox notion of Divine Justice that he temporarily adhered to the heretical view of *misericordia dei* which Pulci put into the mouth of the devil. Indeed, Byron comes close to echoing Astarotte's very words to Orlando in 'I know one may be damned/ for hoping no one else may e'er be so', in giving poetic treatment to the 'absurdity' of material resurrection. This Pulcian blending of orthodoxy and heresy is an essential contribution to what Andrew Rutherford rightly calls Byron's 'blasphemous shock tactics'.[63] By adopting Astarotte's spirit of tolerance and by consciously putting forward the heretical view of universal redemption,[64] Byron counteracted Southey's presumptious arrogation of the divine office of sitting in judgment on his political adversaries.[65] Byron must have realised that the genial and urbane manner of Pulci's devil could be profitably assumed to deflate the sombre pomposity of Southey's tribute to George III.

There were then three main areas of interest which attracted Byron to Pulci's *Morgante*: the light-hearted handling of religious themes, the urbane treatment of the character of the devil and St Peter, and a genuine spirit of tolerance which Byron must have found to be a salutary antidote to the moral cant of his time. Another interesting example of the way in which Byron was influenced by the Pulcian manner is apparent in his deliberate use of a reminiscence from Dante. In the *Morgante*, Pulci made use of the atmosphere and cosmography of Dante's hell as a constant sphere of reference with which he expected his audience to be acquainted. As an Italian critic of Pulci aptly comments:

> Il mondo dei morti a cui si accenna qua e là è, nel Morgante, quasi sempre immaginato alla maniera dantesca.[66]

> (The world of the dead to which there are references in the Morgante is nearly always imagined in the Dantesque manner.)

Occasionally Pulci's allusions to the *Divina Commedia* serve the purpose of ironic effect. It seems likely that Byron may have borrowed the idea of inserting a Dantesque allusion as an underlying ironic comment. One example provides an interesting confirmation of how Pulci influenced Byron in this direction. In the forty-ninth stanza of *The Vision of Judgment* St Peter, indignant at the King's stubborn opposition to Catholic emancipation, denounces George III as 'Guelph' and refuses him entry to heaven. Critics have explained this sobriquet as a humorous but legitimate name for the royal family of German descent.[67] This explanation seems to me to be inadequate since it was historically the Ghibellines who were opposed to Papacy and supported the Emperor. One possible explanation is that Byron makes the irascible St Peter confuse the two factions in his sudden outburst of righteous indignation. However, it is most likely that Byron intended here an ironic comment by way of indirect allusion to Dante. Byron very probably had in mind St Peter's virulent denunciation of his unworthy successors, in particular Boniface VIII, for having been the cause of strife between people of the same creed.

> Non fu nostra intenzion ch'a destra mano
> dei nostri successor parte sedesse,
> parte dal l'altra del popolo Cristiano.[68]

(It was no intention of ours that on the right hand/ of our successors part/ of the Christian people should be set and part on the other.)

St Peter's indignation is directed at Boniface ('Lo principe de nuovi Farisei')[69] who in the interests of maintaining his temporal power separated the sheep (the Guelphs) from the goats (the Ghibellines). The point Dante makes here is that by assuming an uncompromising Guelph attitude he had become the cause of bitter dissension among his fellow Christians. Byron was quick to realise that there was a parallel situation in the case of George III who as the King of a Christian nation was obstinately opposed to Catholic emancipation ('The foe to Catholic participation/ In all the license of a Christian nation') and who was becoming the cause of a rift among his own subjects. Like Boniface, George III was uncompromisingly 'Guelph' and the result was that 'Five millions of the primitive' were being deprived of their rights by a Christian monarch. The sobriquet 'Guelph', therefore carries implications beyond its immediate context and is appropriately used by St Peter to berate George III for his narrow, partisan outlook.

The Vision of Judgment owes much of the richness of its texture to Byron's susceptibility to be inspired by books he was reading before the actual composition of a poem. His reading of Quevedo is yet another instance of how Byron's mind was stimulated by his perusal of foreign authors. Quevedo's *Sueños* with its bizarre account of the author's five dreams concerning the punishment meted out to the damned in hell was another book which seems to have had a strong impact on Byron at the time of the composition of *The Vision*. A feature of this strange book is that there is throughout a grotesque correlation between the sins committed by the damned in their former existence on earth and the punishment inflicted upon them in hell. One curious anecdote which seems to have taken Byron's fancy is that in which Quevedo describes the affliction of the mediocre poets in hell. In the Fourth Vision, Quevedo relates how he was struck by the sight of these poets, in particular 'the most miserable wretch of the whole company' whose fate was to read out his bad verses *adaeternum*. The passage in question reads:

> Ah! cried he, how heartily do I wish that the first innovator of rhymes and poetry were here in my place; and thus poetically made his moan:
>
>> 'Oh, this damned trade of versifying,
>> has brought us all to Hell for lying,
>> For writing what we do not think,
>> Merely to make our verses chink
>
> There cannot be a more ridiculous piece of madness, said I, than yours to be poetizing in hell . . . Nay, said the devil these versifiers are a strange generation of buffoons: the time that others spend in tears and groans for their sins and follies, these wretches employ in songs and madrigals . . .[70]

The novel idea of a poetaster in hell condemned to read out his verse to the consternation of the inmates appealed to Byron's sense of humour and the scene inspired him to include a splendid satirical passage on Southey declaiming his verse at the gates of heaven amidst the ensuing confusion. Here again is a good example of the way in which Byron was inspired by the authors he had read and of his extraordinary ability to remould his source to his own desire. Quevedo and Pulci certainly had much in common: they both revelled in the fantastic and the grotesque and both delighted in delineating the absurdity of human belief in life itself. But whereas Quevedo was merciless in his scourging of vice and depravity, Pulci's spirit of tolerance enabled him to present human nature in all its baffling complexity from the point of view of the artist whose essentially comic vision of life did not preclude an awareness of the seriousness of human existence. It was above all Pulci's serio-comic style – with its intricate blending of *chiaroscuro* effects on the canvas of life – that Byron found so congenial in his crusade against the moral cant of the day.

Abbreviated Titles

JOURNALS AND PERIODICALS

ELH	*A Journal of English Literary History*
FMLS	*Forum for Modern Language Studies*
JEGP	*Journal of English and Germanic Philology*
K–SJ	*Keats–Shelley Journal*
KSMB	*Keats Shelley Memorial Bulletin*
MLN	*Modern Language Notes*
MLR	*Modern Language Review*
MP	*Modern Philology*
N & Q	*Notes and Queries*
PMLA	*Publications of the Modern Language Association*
PQ	*Philological Quarterly*
SEL	*Studies in English Literature*
TLS	*Times Literary Supplement*
UTSE	*University of Texas Studies in English*

SHORT TITLES

AP	G. B. Casti, *Animali Parlanti: Poema Epico in Ventisei Canti* Amsterdam, 1804
Byron: Poetical Works	*Byron: Poetical Works*, ed., Frederick Page, revised and corrected by John Jump (Oxford University Press, 1970)
Hobhouse Recollections	*John Cam Hobhouse, Recollections of a Long Life*, ed., Lady Dorchester (London, 1911)
Marchand BLJ	Leslie A. Marchand (ed.), *Byron's Letters and Journals*, vols 1–7 (London: John Murray, 1973–77)
Medwin's Conversations	*Medwin's 'Conversations of Lord Byron'*, ed., Ernest J. Lovell Jr. (Princeton University Press, 1969)
Moore's *Life*	Thomas Moore, *Letters and Journals of Lord Byron, with Notices of his Life*, 2 vols (London: John Murray, 1830)
Moore *Works of Byron*	Thomas Moore, *The Works of Lord Byron with his Letters and Journals and his Life*, 17 vols (London, 1835)
PT	G. B. Casti, *Il Poema Tartaro*, ed., with notes by Lodovico Corio (Milan, 1887)

166

Prothero L&J	*The Works of Lord Byron: Letters and Journals*, ed., R. E. Prothero, 6 vols (London, 1898–1901)
Shelley Letters	*The Letters of Percy Bysshe Shelley* ed., F. L. Jones, 2 vols (Oxford, 1964)

Notes and References

Where a title is also cited in the bibliography with full details of publication only the date of publication will be given here.

PREFACE

1. C. M. Fuess, *Lord Byron as a Satirist in Verse* (1970) originally a doctoral dissertation presented at Columbia University in 1912.
2. C. P. Brand, *Italy and the English Romantics. The Italianate Fashion in Early Nineteenth Century England* (1957).
3. R. D. Waller (ed.), *The Monks and the Giants by John Hookham Frere* (1926).
4. George Ridenour, *The Style of 'Don Juan'* (1960).
5. Jerome McGann *'Don Juan'* in Context (London, 1976).
6. A. B. England, *Byron's 'Don Juan' and Eighteenth Century Literature* (1974).
7. Robert B. Ogle, *Byron and the Bernesque Satire*, doctoral dissertation, Illinois, 1952.

CHAPTER 1 BYRON'S EARLY ITALIAN INTEREST

1. *Marchand BLJ*, I, 94.
2. Ibid., III, 217. Journal entry for 23 November 1813.
3. Ibid., IV, 161. In his letter to Hobhouse from Athens (26 November 1810) Byron says 'I am now an Italoquist having been taught the tongue by necessity'.
4. *'Catalogue of a Collection of Books, late the Property of a Nobleman about to leave England . . . which will be sold by auction by Mr Evans, at his house,'* No 26 Pall Mall, on Friday, April 5. 1816. Copy in the British Library, Hereafter referred to as *Catalogue, 1816*.
5. *Marchand BLJ*, III, 133.
6. In his letter of 28 September 1812. *Marchand BLJ*, II, 217.
7. In her Memorandum 1812, Lady Byron copied extracts from *Il Pazzo* (Ariosto's *Orlando*) and inserted her own comments on the text. (Deposit Lovelace–Byron ff. 121–3 in the Bodleian Library.)
8. *Marchand BLJ*, IV, 161.
9. 'Oh Gioventù! Oh Primavera! Gioventù dell'anno/ O Gioventù Primavera della vita.' Journal entry for 1 December 1813. *Marchand BLJ*, III, 229.
10. Charles Du Bos, *Byron and the Need of Fatality*, trans. Ethel Colburn Mayne (1932) p. 146.
11. Leslie Marchand, *Byron: A Biography*, I (1957) p. 426.
12. *Marchand BLJ*, III, 253. Journal entry for 20 March 1814.
13. *Prothero L & J*, II, 405, f. 1.
14. *The Corsair*, I, ix, *Byron: Poetical Works*, p. 898. Byron actually quotes Sismondi's description of Ezzelin in vol. III of *History of the Italian Republics* in support of his contention that Conrad was not altogether a character 'out of nature'.
15. Edward Gibbon, *Miscellaneous Works*, III (London, 1796) p. 470.

16. Novella XLIV in *Novelle di Mateo Bandello*, ed. G. Ferrero (Turin, 1974).
17. Ibid., p. 364.
18. See his letter to Moore, 30 November 1813, *Marchand BLJ*, III, 184.
19. *Novelle di Bandello*, XLIV, p. 359.
20. Ibid., p. 360.
21. *Parisina*, ll. in *Byron: Poetical Works*, 307, 308.
22. *Novelle di Bandello*, p. 364.
23. Ibid., p. 363.
24. Ibid., p. 363.
25. *Marchand BLJ*, V, 22.
26. Cf. *Marmion*, stanzas xx–xxii, in *The Poetical Works of Sir Walter Scott*, ed. J. Logie Robertson (Oxford University Press, 1951) pp. 109–11.
27. *Giovanni Boccaccio: Il Decameron*, ed. A. Momigliano and E. Sanguineti, Giornata IV, Novella I (Turin, 1959) p. 147.
28. Ibid., p. 148.
29. Ibid., p. 150.
30. For a suggestive account of Shelley's influence on Byron in Switzerland see John Buxton, *Byron and Shelley: The History of a Friendship* (1968). See also Charles Robinson, *Shelley and Byron: the snake and the eagle wreathed in fight* (1977).
31. Translated by Thomas Moore in *The Works of Lord Byron*, IV (1835) pp. 322–3.
32. For a full account of the sources of *Manfred* see Samuel Chew, *The Dramas of Lord Byron: A Critical Study* (1915) pp. 60–6.
33. Letter dated 4 November 1792. *Epistolario di Vincenzo Monti*, ed. Alfonso Bertoldi, vol. I (Florence, 1928) p. 193.
34. Monti's debt to Goethe's *The Sorrows of the Young Werther* in this poem has been analysed by M. Kerbaker in his monograph *Shakespeare e Goethe nei Versi di Vincenzo Monti* (1897).
35. *Manfred*, Act I, Sc. ii, 24.
36. Vincenzo Monti, *A Don Sigismondo Chigi*, 194, *Opere di Vincenzo Monti*, ed. M. Valmigli and C. Muscetta (1953).
37. In her letter to Vincenzo Monti she refers to his 'poésies qui soutiennent encore l'honneur de la littérature moderne en Italie'. *Lettere inedite del Foscolo, del Giordani e della Signora de Staël a Vincenzo Monti*, eds G. and A. Monti (1876) p. 249.
38. Monti, *Aristodemo*, Act III, Sc. iii, *Opere di Vincenzo Monti*.
39. Cited by Charles Du Bos in *Byron and the Need of Fatality*, p. 126.
40. Madame de Staël, *Corinne or Italy*, 3 vols (printed for Samuel Tippner: London, 1807). The 1816 *Catalogue* lists this edition among Byron's collection of books. It is likely that Byron first read Madame de Staël's novel in this edition.
41. *Oeuvres de Madame de Staël. Corinne* (Paris, 1864) p. 66.
42. *Corinne*, p. 71.
43. Ibid., p. 12.
44. Sonnet no. 1 in Vincenzo da Filicaia, *Poesie toscane . . . con nuove aggiunte* (Florence, 1827).
45. *Historical View of the Literature of the South of Europe by Simonde de Sismondi*, ed. Thomas Roscoe, vol. I (London, 1850) p. 459.
46. Letter to Byron of 3 May 1820 (Box A22 in the Murray Archives).
47. '*Le Ultime Lettre di Jacopo Ortis*' *di Ugo Foscolo*, ed. Edoardo Sonzogno (Milan, 1887) p. 102. Foscolo's novel written in 1802 was published by Murray in 1817. Apropos of Medwin's remarks on Byron's literary borrowings Lady Byron remarked that Byron was usually candid in acknowledging his debt. 'He showed in the letters of J. Ortis the original idea of "burns the slow lamp" a line in the *Corsair*'. (*Medwin's Conversations*, p. 201, note 468.)
48. *Ultime Lettere di Jacopo Ortis*, p. 66.
49. E. R. Vincent, *Foscolo's 'Dei Sepolcri' The Commemoration of the Dead — an inaugural lecture* (1936) p. 48.

CHAPTER 2: BYRON, DANTE AND ITALY

1. Henry Boyd published the first translation of the *Divina Commedia* in 1802. Henry Cary's 'The Vision; or Hell' in *Purgatory and Paradise* (London, 1814) was in blank verse. The 1816 Catalogue lists an Italian text of Dante which Byron probably read alongside Boyd's translation: *Divina Commedia di Dante, illustrata di note dal Zotti* (London, 1808).

2. *The Letters of Percy Bysshe Shelley*, ed. F. L. Jones, vol. II, (1964) p. 112.

3. Byron actually read Hunt's *The Story of Rimini* (1816) in manuscript and inserted his pencilled comments. (BL, Ashley 906). For a detailed commentary see Clarice Short 'The Composition of Hunt's "The Story of Rimini"', K–SJ, 1973 p. 207. Byron also urged Murray to publish Hunt's poem.

4. *Marchand BLJ*, IV, 93.

5. Ibid., VI, 129.

6. Ibid., 121.

7. Leslie Marchand, *Byron: A Biography*, vol. II, (1957) p. 795.

8. Cf. the varied readings that Byron sent Murray (23 March 1820) in *Marchand BLJ*, VII, 58.

     Love, which the gentle heart soon apprehends,
     Seized him for the fair person, which in its
     Bloom was taen from me, yet the mode offends
   and
     Love which to none beloved to love remits
                    with mutual wish to please
     Seized me with wish of pleasing him so strong
   which, as Byron admits, are 'closer but rougher'.

9. Thomas Moore, *The Works of Lord Byron*, vol. II (1835) p. 309–11.

10. *Inferno*, XXXIII, 49.

11. *The Life of Percy Bysshe Shelley by Thomas Medwin*, ed. H. Buxton Forman (Oxford, 1913) p. 249.

12. Moore, *Works of Lord Byron*, vol. XI, p. 178.

13. This is Charles Du Bos's phrase in *Byron and the Need of Fatality* trans. Ethel Colburn Mayne (1932) p. 109.

14. Referred to by most Italian critics as 'la legge del contrapasso'. See Carlo Grabher's commentary on Canto V of the *Inferno* in his edition: *La Divina Commedia*, vol. I (Florence, 1934) p. 66, 'La bufera infernal transcina senza tregua gli spiriti con la forza rapace come – e nota il contrapasso – la bufera della passione li trascinò in vita'.

15. G. Hough, *Image and Experience* (1960) p. 138.

16. *Inferno*, V, 37–9.

17. Medwin records a conversation between Byron and Shelley on the topic of Dante's allegory. According to Medwin, Byron described the poem as a 'scientific treatise of some theological student, one moment treating of angels and the next of demons . . .', *Medwin's Conversations of Lord Byron*, ed. E. J. Lovell Jr. (1969) p. 161, note 378.

18. *Prothero LJ*, V, 193–4.

19. *Medwin's Conversations* p. 160.

20. Ibid.

21. Ibid., p. 158.

22. 'That fatal she', Dante is made to exclaim in Canto I, 172 of *The Prophecy of Dante*.

23. For a useful survey of this polemic see Cesare Cantù, *Vincenzo Monti e l'età che fu sua* (1879) and for a more detailed account see Guido Muoni, *Ludovico de Breme e le prime polemiche intorno a Madame de Staël e al romanticismo in Italia* (1902).

24. *Marchand BLJ*, VII, 151.

25. Giulio Perticari's *Dell'Amor Patrio di Dante* was printed privately in 1819.

26. *Dell'Amor Patrio di Dante: Apologia composta dal Conte Giulio Perticari* in *Opere del Conte Giulio Perticari*, vol. I (Bologna, 1838) p. 163.
27. Ibid., p. 187.
28. Ibid., p. 164.
29. Ibid., p. 349.
30. Ibid., p. 188.
31. *Versi di Albo Crisso*, vol. I (London, 1816) p. 265. As Byron records on the fly leaf of his copy (now in the British Library), the book was sent to him in Venice (June 1817) by 'some fair ladie on account of certain *poesie*'. This is, of course, a reference to Bossi's poem addressed to him.
32. Albo Crisso, *Versi*, p. 268.
33. Ibid., p. 269.
34. *Prothero LJ*, vol. v, 408.
35. *Prothero LJ*, vol. v, 152–3 Diary entry for 5 January 1821.
36. Alfieri's 'O gran Padre Alighier'; Sonnet LIII in *Rime di Vittorio Alfieri*, ed. F. Maggini (Florence, 1933).
37. 'La Vita di Vittorio Alfieri', ed. F. Maggini in *Opere di Vittorio Alfieri*, vol. IV (Florence, 1933) p. 235.
38. Ibid., p. 255.
39. Although Byron was at first impressed by Monti he soon grew disenchanted with Monti's turncoat politics. In the original draft of *The Prophecy*, Byron expressed his contempt for the Italian poet: 'The prostitution of his Muse and wife,/ Both beautiful and both by him debased/ Shall salt his bread and give him means of life'.
40. *Del Principe e delle Lettere*, pp. 133–4.
41. In a letter to Byron on the 14 September 1821, *Shelley Letters*, vol. II, p. 363. Shelley's judgment is confirmed by Byron's remark to Murray, '*The Prophecy of Dante* is the best thing I ever wrote, if it be not *unintelligible*'.
42. *Marchand BLJ*, VII, 77.
43. *Il Purgatorio*, Canto VIII. 'Era già l'ora che volge il disio ai naviganti, e 'ntenerisce il core/ lo dì c'han detto ai dolci amici addio;/ e che lo novo peregrin d' amore/ punge, se ode squilla di lontano/ che paia il giorno pianger che si more.'
44. *Medwin's Conversations*, p. 25.
45. Iris Origo, *The Last Attachment* (1971) p. 422.
46. Letter of 8 June 1820, *Marchand BLJ*, VII, 115.
47. Sonnet CCVIII in *Francesco Petrarca Canzioniere*, ed. Piero Cudini (Milan, 1974).
48. Leslie Marchand, 'Lord Byron and Count Alborghetti', *PMLA*, vol. LXIV (December, 1949) 976–1007.
49. Ibid., 978.

CHAPTER 3: THE LIBERTINE AS ARTIST

1. This was the full title of the first two Cantos of John Hookham Frere's burlesque poem published by John Murray in 1817. Byron refers to it as *Whistlecraft* after its supposed author.
2. Truman Guy Steffan, 'The Devil a Bit of Our *Beppo*' *Philological Quarterly*, vol. XXXII (April 1953) 154–71, gives an interesting analysis of Byron's original first draft of *Beppo* and his subsequent revisions.
3. *Marchand BLJ*, v, 267.
4. *Marchand BLJ*, VI, 24.
5. Frere's letter to Foscolo (8 May 1818) was written in reply to Foscolo's suggestion that *Whistlecraft* be translated into Italian. In the letter Frere points out that his immediate source was Pulci's *Morgante*. See Ugo Foscolo, *Epistolario*, ed. Mario Scotti, vol. VII (Florence, 1970) pp. 318–19.

6. In the anonymous 'Letter to the Right Honourable Lord Byron' now known to be by Lockhart, See *John Bull's Letter to Lord Byron*, ed. A. L. Strout (1947) pp. 80–2.

7. In R. D. Waller's introduction to his edition of *The Monks and the Giants* (1926) p. 51.

8. Hobhouse's diary entry of 29 August 1817 recorded in Leslie Marchand's *Byron: A Biography*, vol. II (1957) p. 708.

9. Ann Barton, 'Byron and the Mythology of Fact' *The Byron Foundation Lecture* (1968) p. 12 where the author sums up Professor G. Wilson Knight's views on Byron in his book *Lord Byron: Christian Virtues* (1952).

10. *Marchand BLJ*, v, 80.

11. Tom Moore's diary entry for 13 September 1819 records he 'looked over some of the *Novelle* of Casti, and found them much more licentious than expected'. *Memoirs, Journal and Correspondence of Thomas Moore*, ed. Lord John Russell, vol. III (1853) p. 10.

12. Giovanni Boccaccio, *Decameron*, ed. Cesare Segre (1966). The tales referred to are: v, 4; IV, 2; VIII, 8; IX, 10.

13. Foscolo's article translated by Francis Cohen first appeared in the *Quarterly Review*, vol. XXI (April 1819). His remarks on the poetry of Casti appear on p. 496.

14. Lady Morgan, *Italy* (1821) Appendix to vol. II, gives an extract from the *Index Librorum Prohibitorum* in which Casti's *Animali Parlanti* and *Novelle Galanti* are listed together with the works of Voltaire. A note in an unknown hand on the fly leaf preceding the title page of vol. I of an 1809 edition of Casti's 'Novelle' (Douce c. 40) reads as follows: 'Somebody said of Casti's work that everybody had read it but that no one acknowledged to have read it.'

15. B. Croce, *La Litteratura Italiana del Settecento* (1949) p. 314.

16. Ibid., p. 316.

17. *Marchand BLJ*, v, 80.

18. Casti's 'Novelle' XXVIII and XXXVI are, in fact, the only two set in Venice.

19. This is T. S. Eliot's criticism in his essay on Byron in *On Poetry and Poets* (London, 1957) pp. 195–6.

20. Vittorio Alfieri became for most Italians the symbol of patriotism. His dignified sonnets to Italy were mostly an attempt to arouse in his countrymen a feeling for liberty. Byron, as he himself recorded in his *Detached Thoughts* (15 October 1821), felt an affinity with the Italian nobleman who was outspoken against the tyranny of the foreigner. The sonnets referred to above are nos. XL, CIVIII, CLXIV, CLXXIII, CLXXX in *Opere di Vittorio Alfieri, Rime*, ed. Francesco Maggini (1933).

21. Leslie Marchand, *Byron: A Portrait* (1971) p. 270.

22. Andrew Rutherford, *Byron: A Critical Study* (1965) p. 97.

23. Ibid., p. 98.

24. Extract from a letter by Gifford to Byron in the Lovelace-Byron papers deposited in the Bodleian Library, Oxford, fols. 39–41.

25. *Marchand BLJ*, v, 186.

26. *Marchand BLJ*, II, 75.

27. See Moore's comment on Byron's poor taste in this passage '. . . to interrupt thus a prolonged tone of solemnity by any descent into the ludicrous . . .'. See the *Works of Lord Byron: with Letters and Journals and his life by Thomas Moore Esq.*, vol. VIII (1835) p. 48.

28. *Marchand BLJ*, v, 218.

29. *Byron: Poetical Works*, ed. J. Jump, p. 226.

30. *Marchand BLJ*, v, 147.

31. Ibid., v, 165.

32. The account of this anecdote, recorded by Emmanuele Cicogna in his diary, is quoted by Nazzareno Meneghetti in his book *Lord Byron a Venezia* (1910) p. 96, and varies only in some minor details from Hobhouse's account. In both versions, however, the woman was *married* to the owner of the *Regina d'Ungheria* inn.

33. Pietro Buratti, a contemporary Venetian poet, in a note to one of his satires, *Poesie e Satire* (Amsterdam, 1823) p. 184, refers to him as 'Il Conte Francesco Rizzo Patarol, amico intimo di Milord Byron non che del console'.

34. Boccaccio's fourth *novella* narrated on the fifth day (in the *Decameron*) tells about the ruse of the young lovers Caterina and Ricciardo to outwit the girl's strict father. Casti borrowed the details of *Il Rosignuolo* from this *novella*.
35. Alaric Watts, 'Lord Byron's Plagiarisms', *The Literary Gazette* (24 February 1821) p. 121. See also *The Literary Gazette* of 3, 10, 17 March for further attempts by Watts to demonstrate that Byron plagiarised from contemporary authors. Alaric Watts, however, does not mention Casti.
36. Anne Barton, 'Byron and the Mythology of Fact', *The Byron Foundation Lecture* (1968) p. 18.
37. G. B. Casti, 'Relazione di un Viaggio a Costantinopoli', *Opere Tutte di Casti*, vol. I (Turin, 1849) pp. 461–2. Casti's observation that the Pasha's favourite courtier was called Baba appears to corroborate the fact that Byron had read this work since he used this name for the eunuch of the seraglio in Canto V.
38. *Medwin's Conversations of Lord Byron*, ed. E. J. Lovell Jr. (1969) pp. 140–1. Medwin also refers to Byron's use of Casti's *La Diavolessa* in his *Life of Shelley* (London, 1847) pp. 335–6.
39. *Lady Blessington's Conversations of Lord Byron*, ed. E. J. Lovell Jr. (1969) p. 206.

CHAPTER 4: 'THE STYLE OF VOLUBILITY'

1. *The Letters of Percy Bysshe Shelley*, ed. F. L. Jones, vol. II (1964) p. 42.
2. Ibid.
3. *Marchand BLJ*, VI, 67.
4. T. G. Steffan, 'The Token–Web, The Sea Sodom, and Canto I of *Don Juan*', *UTSE* (1947) 108–68.
5. Ibid., 112.
6. Ibid., 131.
7. Lady Blessington's *Conversations of Lord Byron*, ed. E. J. Lovell (Princeton University Press, 1969) pp. 81–2.
8. *Marchand BLJ*, VI, 96.
9. Hobhouse, *Recollections of a Long Life*, vol. II, p. 86.
10. Despite Stendhal's claim that the Venetian satirist Pietro Buratti influenced Byron's style in *Beppo* and the early Cantos of *Don Juan*, the poet's actual debt to Buratti seems to me, on closer examination, to be negligible.
11. Letter to Murray, 2 January 1817. *Marchand BLJ*, V, p. 157.
12. Letter to Byron, 7 July 1818. Samuel Smiles, *Memoirs and Correspondence of the Late John Murray*, 1, 395–6.
13. Appendices B, C, D in T. G. Steffan's *Byron's 'Don Juan': The Making of a Masterpiece*, vol. I (Austin, Texas, 1957).
14. *Marchand BLJ*, VI, 59.
15. Letter to Hobhouse, 17 May 1819. *Marchand BLJ*, VI, 131.
16. *Novella* XXXIII in vol. IV of the *Novelle di Giambattista Casti*, *Romano* (Paris, 1809).
17. G. B. Casti, *I Tre Giuli: Sonetti di Niceste Abideno, sopra l'importunità d'un Creditor di Tre Giuli* (Rome, 1762) which was published pseudonymously.
18. Introduction to *The 'Tre Giuli' translated from the Italian of G. B. Casti* with a memoir of the author (Anon.) (London, 1826).
19. Prefatory letter to Abate Luciani, p. xi.
20. Ibid., p. xii.
21. Casti, *I Tre Giuli*, p. 99.
22. *Novella* XXXVIII, in vol. V of the *Novelle di G. B. Casti*.
23. *Opere di Agnolo Firenzuola*, ed. Delmo Maestri (Turin, 1977) pp. 421–2.
24. *Novella* V *Novelle di Mateo Bandello*, ed. G. Ferrero (Turin, 1974).
25. Ibid., p. 141.

26. Ibid., p. 142.
27. Ibid., p. 142.
28. Ibid., pp. 142–3.

CHAPTER 5: *DON JUAN, IL POEMA TARTARO* AND THE ITALIAN BURLESQUE TRADITION

1. Claude Fuess, *Lord Byron as a Satirist in Verse* (Columbia, 1912).
2. Letter from Geneva, June 1816. *Marchand BLJ*, v, 80.
3. Gabriele Muresu, 'Le Occasioni di Un Libertino (G. B. Casti)', *Biblioteca di Cultura Contemporanea*, vol. cix (Messina, 1973).
4. Herman Van den Bergh, *Giambattista Casti: l'homme et l'oeuvre* (1951) p. 143.
5. Francesco De Sanctis, *Storia della Letteratura Italiana*, ed. B. Croce, vol. i (Bari, 1949) p. 423.
6. T. G. Steffan, *Byron's 'Don Juan': The Making of a Masterpiece*, vol. i (Austin, Texas, 1957) p. 214.
7. Ibid., p. 209.
8. G. Melchiori, 'Byron and Italy', *Byron Foundation Lecture* (1958).
9. Robert F. Gleckner, *Byron and the Ruins of Paradise* (1967) p. 341.
10. George Ridenour, 'The Style of *Don Juan*', *Yale Studies in English*, vol. 144 (1960) pp. 33ff.
11. William Sotheby, *Oberon, a poem: from the German of Wieland* (London, 1798).
12. Elizabeth Boyd, *Byron's 'Don Juan': A Critical Study* (New York: The Humanities Press, 1958) pp. 125–6.
13. C. P. Brand, 'Ludovico Ariosto, Poet and Poem in the Italian Renaissance', *FMLS*, vol. iv (January 1968) 99.
14. William Tooke, *Life of Catherine II, Empress of Russia*, 3 vols (1800).
15. C. Masson, *Mémoires secrètes sur la Russie*, 2 vols (1800).
16. Published 19 December 1821.
17. *Prothero LJ*, vi, 50.
18. In Appendix A of Harry Levin's *The Myth of the Golden Age in the Renaissance* (1970) p. 182.
19. For an account of his relationship with Lady Oxford see David Erdman, 'Lord Byron as Rinaldo', *PLMA*, lvii (March 1942) 189–231.
20. 'Review of *Don Juan* vi–viii', *The British Critic*, xx (August 1823).

CHAPTER 6: CASTI'S *ANIMALI PARLANTI*, THE ITALIAN EPIC AND *DON JUAN*: THE POETRY OF POLITICS

1. *Lady Blessington's Conversations of Lord Byron*, ed. E. J. Lovell (Princeton University Press, 1969) p. 207.
2. Thomas Moore, *Memoirs, Journal and Correspondence*, ed. Lord John Russell (1858) vol. ii, p. 541.
3. *Marchand, BLJ*, v, 80.
4. Preface to G. B. Casti's *Animali Parlanti* (Amsterdam, 1804).
5. Herman Van den Bergh, *Giambattista Casti: l'homme et l'oeuvre* (1951) p. 176.
6. L. Da Ponte, *Memorie*, ed. G. Gamberin and Fausto Nicolini (1918) pp. 266–7.
7. Letter to L. Da Ponte cited in F. Bernini, *Storia degli 'Animali Parlanti'* (1901) p. 111.
8. *Marchand BLJ*, vi, 24.

9. W. S. Rose, *The Court and Parliament of Beasts: A Poem in Seven Cantos* (1819) p. 1.
10. W. S. Rose, *Thoughts and Recollections by one of the Last Century* (1825) p. 225.
11. Ugo Foscolo, 'Narrative and Romantic Poems of the Italians', trans. Francis Cohen, *Quarterly Review*, vol. xxi (April 1819) 486–556.
12. Ibid., p. 492.
13. Ibid., p. 494.
14. Casti, *Animali Parlanti*, 1, 77.
15. Voltaire, *Dictionnaire Philosophique*, ed. Garnier (1964) p. 218.
16. Ibid.
17. Giulio Sindonia, *Il Casti e il suo pensiero Politico negli 'Animali Parlanti'* (1925) p. 104.
18. *Byron's 'Don Juan', The Making of a Masterpiece*, ed. T. G. Steffan and W. Pratt, 2 edn, vol. 1 (Texas, 1971) pp. 222–44.
19. *Prothero L & J*, vi, 101.
20. Ibid., p. 155.
21. *Byron's 'Don Juan', Notes on the Variorum Edition*, ed. T. G. Steffan and W. Pratt, vol. iv (1957) p. 171.
22. See his diary entry for 13 January 1821.
23. Quoted by Byron in the Preface to Canto vi.
24. Quoted by Byron in the Preface to Canto vi.
25. Elizabeth Boyd, *Byron's Don Juan: A Critical Study* (1958).
26. Gabriel de Castelnau, *Essai sur l'historie ancienne et Moderne de la Nouvelle Russie* (1820) vol. ii, p. 207.
27. Ibid., p. 206.
28. Ibid., p. 207.
29. Boyd, *Byron's 'Don Juan'*, pp. 148–9.
30. The line 'All countries have their lions' (*DJ*, xii, xxiv, 7) is obviously an oblique reference to Casti's *Animali* and is further evidence that Byron had this poem in mind at the time.
31. *Marchand BLJ*, vi, 105.
32. Thomas M. Greene, *The Descent from Heaven: A Study in Epic Continuity* (1963) pp. 137–8.
33. *Don Juan*, vii, lxxxiv, 1–2.
34. P. L. Ginguené, *Histoire littéraire d'Italie*, vol. v (1824) pp. 447–50.
35. Jerome McGann, *'Don Juan' in Context*, p. 147.
36. Castelnau, *Essai sur l'histoire ancienne . . . de la Nouvelle Russie*, vol. ii, p. 207.
37. Bernard Blackstone, *Byron: A Survey* (1975) p. 332.
38. McGann, *'Don Juan' in Context*, p. 147.
39. George Steiner, *Language and Silence* (1967) p. 212.
40. Ludovico Ariosto, *Orlando Furioso*, ed. Lanfranco Caretti (Milan, 1954) Canto xl, xix, 6.
41. Thomas Moore, *Letters and Journals of Lord Byron* (1830) vol. ii, p. 541.
42. *Lady Blessington's Conversations of Lord Byron*, ed. E. J. Lovell Jr. (1969) p. 240.
43. Journal entry for 16 January 1814, *Marchand BLJ*, iii, 242.
44. See Leslie Marchand, 'An unpublished Byron Poem', *The Griffon*, Gennadius Library no. 6 (Summer 1970) 17–19.

CHAPTER 7: 'MY FINEST, FEROCIOUS CARAVAGGIO STYLE': BYRON'S DEBT TO PULCI

1. John Milton, *Areopagitica. For the Liberty of unlicensed Printing*, ed. K. M. Lea (Oxford 1973) pp. 12–13.
2. In vol. iv of P. L. Ginguené's *Histoire littéraire d'Italie* (1824).

3. Fragments of these verses are preserved in the John Murray Archives, London.
4. *Marchand BLJ*, IV, 12.
5. J. H. Merivale, Preface to *Orlando in Roncesvalles: A Poem* (1814) pp. xv–xvi.
6. Merivale, *Orlando in Roncesvalles*, p. 90.
7. *Marchand BLJ*, IV, 12.
8. Ibid.
9. In the introduction to R. D. Waller's edition of *The Monks and the Giants* (1926).
10. S. Smiles, *A Publisher and His Friends: Memoirs and Correspondence of the Late John Murray*, vol. I (1891) p. 170.
11. Merivale, Preface to *Orlando in Roncesvalles: A Poem*, p. xvi.
12. *Marchand BLJ*, VI, 24.
13. Ibid., VII, 42.
14. Robert B. Ogle, 'A Byron Contradiction: Some Light on his Italian Study', *Studies in Romanticism*, vol. XXII (Winter 1973) 436–42.
15. *Prothero L & J*, V, 197.
16. *Marchand BLJ*, VII, 39.
17. Ibid., VII, 42.
18. Ibid.
19. Ibid., VII, 54. This was the Naples edition in Quarto 1732.
20. Ibid.
21. Ibid.
22. Smiles, *Memoirs of John Murray*, vol. I, p. 416.
23. *The Letters of Percy Bysshe Shelley*, ed. F. L. Jones, vol. II (1964) p. 308.
24. Ibid., vol. II, p. 289.
25. Leslie Marchand, *Byron: A Biography*, vol. II (1957).
26. *Marchand BLJ*, VII, 35.
27. *Byron: Poetical Works*, p. 379.
28. Ibid.
29. Ibid.
30. Ibid.
31. All citations from Pulci throughout this chapter are from Franca Ageno's edition of the *Morgante* (Milan, 1955).
32. The *Vocabolario della Crusca* defines *mazzafrusti* as 'sorte di frusta fatta di cinque o sei cordicelle ofili di ferro . . . con palline di piombo in cima'.
33. '*Il Morgante' di Luigi Pulci*, ed. G. Fatini (Turin, 1947) p. 15.
34. *Marchand BLJ*, VII, 182.
35. Ginguené, *Histoire*, vol. V, p. 143.
36. J. H. Merivale, 'Critical Observations on the '*Morgante Maggiore*', *Monthly Magazine*, no. 142 (May 1806) 305.
37. Ibid., 308.
38. Ugo Foscolo, 'Narrative and Romantic Poems of the Italians', trans. Francis Cohen, *Quarterly Review*, vol. XXI (April 1819) 521.
39. Merivale, Preface to *Orlando in Roncesvalles*, p. xv.
40. Ibid., p. vvi.
41. Letter by J. N. Fazackerly to Ugo Foscolo dated January 1818 in *Ugo Foscolo: Epistolario*, ed. Mario Scotti, vol. VII (Florence, 1970) p. 277.
42. *Byron: Poetical Works*, p. 379.
43. Ibid.
44. 'Remarks on "Don Juan"', *Blackwood's Magazine*, vol. V (August 1819) 514.
45. John Hobhouse, *Recollections of a Long Life*, vol. II, p. 109.
46. *Marchand BLJ*, VII, 35.
47. Ibid., 61.
48. Ibid., 97.
49. *Byron: Poetical Works*, p. 379.

50. *Don Juan*, III, lxii–lxix.
51. The contemporary reader's inability to appreciate this brand of humour is best exemplified in Richard Belgrave Hoppner's remark to Byron '. . . forgive me if I do not like your shipwreck it is too serious a subject to be treated lightly' (Letter dated 25 October 1823 in the Murray Archives).
52. Umberto Biscottini, *L'arte e l'anima del 'Morgante'* (1932) p. 50.
53. R. B. Quintana, 'The Satiric Mood in Byron', *Washington University Studies*, Humanities Series, vol. IX (April 1922) 211–31.
54. Ibid., 215.
55. *Prothero L & J*, v, 385.
56. Merivale, *Orlando in Roncesvalles* Canto III, xxvi, 8.
57. C. Pellegrini, 'Luigi Pulci: L'uomo e l'artista', *Annali della R. Scuola Normale Superiore di Pisa*, vol. xxv (1913) p. 146.
58. 'E nell' inferno ti credo che sia
    Gentilezza, amicizia e cortesia.'
    (*Morgante*, xxvi, lxxxiv, 7–8)
59. Ginguené, *Histoire*, vol. IV, p. 240.
60. Merivale, *Orlando in Roncesvalles* p. 99.
61. In her letter to Henry Crabb Robinson (5 March 1855) in *The Diary, Reminiscences and Correspondence of Henry Crabb Robinson*, ed. T. Sadler, vol. II (1872) p. 353. She also refers to Byron's Calvinism as 'the Creed which made him see God as an Avenger not a father'.
62. *Prothero L & J*, v, 457.
63. Andrew Rutherford, *Byron: The Critical Heritage Series* (1970) p. 9.
64. Byron's momentarily identifies with the devil in '. . . God help me too! I am,/ God knows, as helpless as the devil can wish,/ And not a whit more difficult to damn' (*VJ*, xv, 1–3).
65. Byron actually gave vent to his feelings of indignation in the Appendix to the first edition of *The Two Foscari* (11 December 1821). 'There is something at once ludicrous and blasphemous in the arrogant scribbler of all works sitting down to deal damnation and destruction upon his fellow-creatures.'
66. G. Volpi, *'La Divina Commedia* nel *Morgante* di Luigi Pulci', *Giornale Dantesco*, XI (1903) 170.
67. See Edmund Miller, 'Byron's *The Vision of Judgment*, stanzas xlviii–li', *Explicator*, no. 33 (September 1974) item 4.
68. Dante, *Paradiso*, Canto XXVII, 46–8.
69. Dante, *Inferno*, XXVII, 85.
70. *Quevedo's 'Sueños'*, trans. Sir Roger L'Estrange, ed. J. M. Cohen (London, 1963) p. 107. Byron, it will be recalled, used the pseudonym 'Quevedo Redivivus'.

Select Bibliography

BIOGRAPHY AND CRITICISM

Azzolina, L., *Il Mondo Cavalleresco in Boiardo, Ariosto Berni* (Palermo, 1912).

Ball, Albert, 'Byron and Charles Churchill: Further Parallels', *N & Q*, ccv (March 1960) 105–7.

Ball, Patricia M., *Childe Harold's Pilgrimage, Cantos II & IV, and The Vision of Judgment* (Oxford: Blackwell, 1968).

——, *The Central Self: A Study in Romantic and Victorian Imagination* (Oxford University Press, 1969).

Bartlett Giamatti, A., *The Earthly Paradise and the Renaissance Epic* (Princeton, 1966).

Barton, Ann, 'Byron and the Mythology of Fact', *Byron Foundation Lecture* (University of Nottingham, 1968).

Beaty, Frederick L., 'Byron and the Story of Francesca da Rimini', *PMLA*, lxxv (September, 1960) 395–401.

——, 'Byron's Concept of Ideal Love', *K–SJ*, xii (Winter 1963) 37–54.

——, 'Harlequin *Don Juan*', *JEGP*, lxvii, no. 3 (1968) 395–405.

Benedetti, Anna, *'L'Orlando Furioso' nella vita intelletuale del popolo inglese* (Florence, 1914).

Bernardi, Jacopo, *Lord Byron a Venezia e alcune memorie a suo riguardo tratto dai diarii 1818–1819 del Generale Angelo Mengaldo* (Venice, 1881).

Bernini, Francesco, *'Il Ricciardetto' di Niccolo Forteguerri: Forma e Contenenza* (Bari, 1900).

——, *Storia degli 'Animali Parlanti'* (Bologna, 1901).

Berry, C. L., 'Byron in Venice, 1819', *N&Q*, cci (September 1956) 396–7.

Bewley, Marius, 'The Colloquial Mode of Byron', *Scrutiny*, xvi (March 1949) 8–23.

Bisconttini, Umberto, *L'arte e l'anima del 'Morgante'* (Leghorn, 1932).

Blackstone, Bernard, *Byron: A Survey* (London: Longman, 1975).

Blennerhasset, Lady, *Madame de Staël: Her Friends and Her Influence in Politics and Literature*, trans. J. E. Gordon Cumming, 3 vols (London, 1889).

Blessington, Lady, *'Conversations of Lord Byron'*, ed. Ernest J. Lovell Jr. (Princeton, Princeton University Press, 1969).

Bloom, Harold, 'George Gordon, Lord Byron', *The Visionary Company: A Reading of English Romantic Poetry* (New York: Doubleday, 1961) pp. 232–74.

——, *The Anxiety of Influence* (Oxford University Press, 1973).

Bosco, Umberto, 'Byronismo Italiano', *La Cultura*, iii (Rome: April 1924).

Bostetter, Edward E., 'Byron and the Politics of Paradise', *PMLA*, lxxv (December 1960) 571–6.

——, *The Romantic Ventriloquists* (Seattle: University of Washington Press, 1963).

———, *Twentieth Century Interpretations of 'Don Juan'* (New Jersey, 1969).

Bottrall, Ronald, 'Byron and the Colloquial Tradition in English Poetry', *Criterion*, XVIII (January 1939) 204–24.

Bowra, Maurice, 'Don Juan', *The Romantic Imagination* (Harvard University Press, 1949) pp. 149–73.

Boyd, Elizabeth, *Byron's 'Don Juan': A Critical Study* (London: Routledge & Kegan Paul, 1958).

Brand, C. P., *Italy and the English Romantics. The Italianate Fashion in Early Nineteenth Century England* (Cambridge University Press, 1957).

———, *Torquato Tasso: A Study of the Poet and His Contribution to English Literature* (Cambridge University Press, 1965).

———, 'Ludovico Ariosto, Poet and Poem in the Italian Renaissance', *Forum for Modern Language Studies*, IV (January 1968) 99–112.

———, 'Byron and the Italians', *Byron Journal* I (1973) 14–21,

Bredvold, Louis, *Lord Byron, Don Juan and other Satirical Poems*, Doubleday Doran Series in Literature, ed. Robert Schafer (New York: Doubleday, 1935).

Brilli, Attilio, *Il Gioco del 'Don Juan'* (Ravenna, 1971).

Brinton, Clarence C., *The Political Ideas of the English Romantics* (Oxford University Press, 1926).

Broughton, John Cam Hobhouse, Lord, *Italy: Remarks Made in Several Visits from the Year 1816 to 1854*, 2 vols (London: John Murray, 1859).

———, *Recollections of a Long Life*, ed. Lady Dorchester, 6 vols (London: John Murray, 1909–11).

Bruce, J. Douglas, 'Lord Byron's "Stanzas to the Po" ', *MLN*, XXIV (December 1909) 258–9.

Brydges, Sir Egerton, *An Impartial Portrait of Lord Byron, as a Poet and a Man, Compared with all the Evidences and Writings Regarding Him, up to 1825* (Paris: Galignani, 1825).

Bussi, Illidio, *Il Romanzo Cavalleresco in Luigi Pulci* (Turin, 1933).

Butler, Eliza M., 'Byron and Goethe', *Byron Foundation Lecture* (University of Nottingham Press, 1950).

Buxton, John, *Byron and Shelley: The History of a Friendship* (London: Macmillan, 1968).

———, 'The Poetry of Lord Byron', *Proceedings of the British Academy*, 56 (1970) 77–92.

Calvert, William J., *Byron: Romantic Paradox* (Chapel Hill: The University of North Carolina Press, 1935).

Cameron, Kenneth Neill, *Romantic Rebels: Essays on Shelley and His Circle* (Harvard University Press, 1973).

Cantù, Cesare, *Vincenzo Monti e l'età che fu sua* (Milan, 1879).

Capograssi, A., *Gl'inglesi in Italia durante le campagne Napoleoniche* (Bari, 1949).

Caretti, Lanfranco, 'A Cast of Casti, by Lord Byron', *New Anti-Jacobin* (April 1833) 30–53.

———, *Ariosto e Tasso* (Turin, 1970).

Castelnau, Gabriel de, *Essai sur l'histoire ancienne et moderne de la Nouvelle Russie*, 3 vols (Paris, 1820).

Catalogue of a Collection of Books, late the Property of a Nobleman about to leave England . . . which will be sold by auction, by Mr. Egans, at his house, No. 26, Pall Mall, on Friday, April 5 . . . 1816. The British Library.

Catalogue of the Books and Manuscripts at the Keats–Shelley Memorial House in Rome (Boston, 1969).

Catalogue of the Roe–Byron Collection Newstead Abbey (Nottingham, 1937).

Ceserani, R., 'L'Allegra fantasia di Luigi Pulci e il rifacimento dell' Orlando', *Giornale Storico*, cxxxv (1958) 171–214.

Chew Samuel, C., *The Dramas of Lord Byron: A Critical Study* (Baltimore, The Johns Hopkins Press, 1915).

———, *Byron in England: His Fame and After Fame* (London: Murray, 1924).

Poetical Works of Charles Churchill, ed. with notes by Douglas Grant (Oxford University Press, 1956).

Churchill, K. G., 'Byron and Italy', *Literary Half-Yearly*, xv (July 1974) 67–86.

Clearman, Mary, 'A Blueprint for English Bards and Scotch Reviewers: The First Satire of Juvenal', *K–SJ*, xix (1970) 87–99.

Cline, C. L., 'Unpublished Notes on the Romantic Poets by Isaac D'Israeli', *University of Texas Studies in English* (1941) 148–56.

———, *Byron, Shelley and their Pisan Circle* (London: John Murray, 1952).

Clubbe, John, 'Byron and Scott', *Texas Studies in Language and Literature*, xv (Spring 1973) 67–91.

———, 'The New Prometheus of New Men': Byron's 1816 Poems and Manfred', *Nineteenth Century Literary Perspectives. Essays in Honour of Lionel Stevenson*, ed. Clyde de L. Ryals *et al.* (Duke University Press, 1974).

Collins, John Churton, *Studies in Poetry and Criticism* (London: Bell & Co., 1905).

Cooke, Michael G., 'The Limits of Skepticism: The Byronic Affirmation', *K–SJ*, xvii (1968) 97–111.

———, *The Blind Man Traces the Circle: On the Patterns and Philosophy of Byron's Poetry* (Princeton University Press, 1969).

———, 'Byron's *Don Juan*: The Obsession and Self-Discipline of Spontaneity', *Studies in Romanticism*, no. 1 (1975) 285–302.

Cornwall, Barry, *A Sicilian Story and other Poems* (London, 1820).

Corrigan, Beatrice, 'The Byron–Hobhouse translation of Pellico's *Francesca*', *Italica*, xxxv (December 1958) 235–41.

Croce, Benedetto, *La Letteratura Italiana del Settecento* (Bari, 1949).

Culkin, Peter, 'Byron's Plagiarisms', *N&Q*, iii (January 1863) 55–6.

Dallas, R. C., *Recollections of the Life of Lord Byron, from the Year 1808 to the End of 1814; his early character and Opinions, Detailing the Progress of his Literary Career and including Various Unpublished Passages of His Works. Taken from Authentic Documents, in the Possession of the Author* (London, 1824).

Da Ponte, Lorenzo, *Memorie*, ed. G. Gambarin and Fausto Nicolini (Bari, 1918).

Dejob, Charles, *Madame de Staël et L'Italie, avec une bibliographie de l'influence française en Italie de 1796 à 1814* (Paris, 1890).

de Pange, Thomas, 'Madame de Staël and her English Correspondents', doctoral dissertation (Oxford, 1956).

De Sanctis, Francesco, 'La Poesia Cavalleresca', *Scritti vari inediti o rari*, ed. B. Croce (Naples, 1898).

———, *Storia della Letterature Italiana* ed. Benedetto Croce, 2 vols (Bari, 1949).

Doane, G. (ed.), *Catalogue of the Library of the Late Lord Byron . . . 6 July 1827*, privately printed, 1929.

Dobree, Bonamy, 'Byron's Dramas', *Byron Foundation Lecture* (University of Nottingham Press, 1962).

Doughty, Oswald, 'Dante and the English Romantic Poets', *English Miscellany*, II (1951) 125–69.

Du Bos, Charles, *Byron and the Need of Fatality*, trans. Ethel Colburn Mayne (London: Putnam, 1932).

Dyce, Alexander, 'Plagiarisms of Lord Byron', *The Gentleman's Magazine*, LXXXVIII (February 1818) 121 and 389.

Eichler, A., *John Hookham Frere: Sein Einfluss auf Lord Byron*, Wiener Beiträge zur Englishen Philologie, XX (Vienna, 1905).

Einstein, L., 'Luigi Pulci and the *Morgante Maggiore*', *Litterarhistorische Forschrungen*, 22 (Berlin, 1922).

Elledge, W. Paul, *Byron and the Dynamics of Metaphor* (Vanderbilt University Press, 1968).

——, 'Byron's Hungry Sinner: The Quest Motif in Don Juan', *JEGP*, LXLX (January 1970) 1–13.

Elledge, W. Paul and Richard L. Hoffman (eds), *Romantic and Victorian: Studies in Memory of William H. Marshall* (new Jersey, 1971).

Elliott, G. R., 'Byron and the Comic Spirit', *PMLA*, XXXIX (December 1924) 897–909.

Elton, Oliver, *A Survey of English Literature 1780–1880* (London: Arnold, 1912).

Elze, Karl, *Lord Byron: A Biography. With a Critical Essay on His Place in Literature* (London: John Murray, 1872).

England, A. B., *Byron's 'Don Juan' and Eighteenth Century Literature* (Associated University Press, 1974).

Erdman, David V., 'Lord Byron and the Genteel Reformers', *PLMA*, LVI (December 1941) 1065–94.

——, 'Lord Byron as Rinaldo', *PMLA*, LVII (March 1942) 189–231.

——, 'Byron and Revolt in England', *Science and Society*, XI (Summer 1947) 234–48.

——, 'Byron and "the New Force of the People" ', *K–SJ*, XI (Winter 1962) 47–64.

Ernle, Rowland E. Prothero, Lord, *The Ravenna Journal* (London: The First Edition Club, 1928).

Escarpit, Robert, *Lord Byron: Un tempérament littéraire*, 2 vols (Paris, 1957).

Evans, Bertrand, 'Manfred's Remorse and Dramatic Tradition', *PMLA*, LXII (September 1947) 752–73.

Festing, G., *John Hookham Frere and his Friends* (London, 1899).

Filicaia, Vincenzo da, *Poesie toscane . . . con nuove aggiunte* (Florence, 1827).

Foa, Giovanna, *Lord Byron, Poeta e Carbonaro* (Florence, 1935).

Foscolo, Ugo, 'Narrative and Romantic Poems of the Italians', *Quarterly Review*, XXI (April 1819) 496–556.

Frank, Frederick S., 'The Demon and the Thunderstorm: Byron and Madame de Staël, *Revue de littérature comparée*, XLIII (1969) 320–43.

Frere, John Hookham, *The Works of John Hookham Frere with a Memoir by the Rt. Hon. Sir Bartle Frere*, 3 vols (London, 1874).

Friederich, Werner Paul, 'Dante and English Romanticism', *Dante's Fame Abroad* (Chapel Hill: University of North Carolina, 1950) pp. 229–95.

Fuess, C. M., *Lord Byron as a Satirist in Verse* (Columbia, 1912).

Galt, John, *The Life of Lord Byron* (London: Bentley, 1830).

Gay, P., *Voltaire's Politics: The Poet as Realist* (Princeton, 1959).

Gennari, G., *Le Premier Voyage de Madame de Staël en Italie et la Genese de 'Corinne'*. Études de littérature étrangère et comparée (Paris, 1947).

Ginguené, P. L., *Histoire littéraire d'Italie*, 2nd ed., 14 vols (Paris, 1824).

Gleckner, Robert F., *Byron and the Ruins of Paradise* (Baltimore: The Johns Hopkins University Press, 1967).

Gordon, Pryse Lockhart, *Personal Memoirs; or Reminiscences of Men and Manners at Home and Abroad, During the Last Half Century*, 2 vols (London, 1830).

Grant, Douglas, 'Byron: The Pilgrim and Don Juan', *The Morality of Art: Essays Presented to G. Wilson Knight by his Colleagues and Friends*, ed. D. W. Jefferson (New York: Barnes & Noble, 1969) pp. 175–84.

Greene, Thomas M., *The Descent from Heaven: A Study in Epic Continuity* (New Haven: Yale University Press, 1963).

Gregor, D. B., 'Plagiarism or Parallelism?', *N&Q*, CXCI (July 1946) 24–5.

Grierson, H. C., 'Byron and English Society', *The Background of English Literature* (London, 1925).

Guiccioli, Teresa, Countess, *My Recollections of Lord Byron, and Those of Eyewitnesses of His Life*, trans. Hubert E. Jerningham (London: Bentley, 1869).

Guidi, A., 'Byron e i classici italiani', *Annali Triestini*, XXIII (1953) 215–26.

Hirsch, E. D., 'Byron and the Terrestrial Paradise', *From Sensibility to Romanticism: Essays Presented to Frederick A. Pottle*, eds F. W. Hilles and H. Bloom (Oxford University Press, 1965).

Hobhouse, John Cam, *A Journey through Albania and Other Provinces of Turkey* (London, 1813).

———, *Historical Illustrations to the Fourth Canto of Childe Harold: Containing Dissertations on the Ruins of Rome and an Essay on Italian Literature* (London: Murray, 1818).

Horn, Andras, *Byron's 'Don Juan' and the Eighteenth Century Novel*, Schweizer Anglistische Arbeiten, no. 51 (Bern: Praneke Verlag, 1962).

Hough, Graham, 'Byron', *The Romantic Poets* (London: Longman, 1953) pp. 97–121.

———, *Image and Experience* (London, 1960).

Hume, Robert D., 'The Non-Augustan Nature of Byron's Early Satires', *Revue des Langues Vivantes*, XXXIV, no. 5 (1968) 495–503.

Hunt, Leigh, *Lord Byron and Some of His Contemporaries, with Recollections of the Author's Life and His Visit to Italy* (London: Henry Colburn, 1828).

———, *Stories from the Italian Poets*, 2 vols (London, 1846).

James, D. G., 'Byron and Shelley', *Byron Foundation Lecture* (University of Nottingham Press, 1951).

Johnson, E. D. H., '*Don Juan* in England', *ELH*, XI (June 1944) 135–53.

Jones, Frederick L. (ed.), *The Letters of Percy Bysshe Shelley*, 2 vols (Oxford, 1964).

Joseph, M. K., *Byron the Poet* (London: Gollancz, 1964).

Jump, John D., '*Byron's "Don Juan": Poem or Hold-all?*' The W. D. Thomas Memorial Lecture (University College of Swansea, 1968).

———, 'Byron's *The Vision of Judgment*', *Bulletin of the John Rylands University Library of Manchester*, LI (1968) 122–36.

———, *Byron*, Routledge Author Guides (London: Routledge & Kegan Paul, 1972).

———, *Byron: 'Childe Harold's Pilgrimage' and 'Don Juan: A Casebook'*, (London: Macmillan, 1973).

——, *Byron: A Symposium* (London, 1975).

——, 'Lord Byron and William Gifford', *Bulletin of the John Rylands University Library of Manchester* LVIII (1975) 190–206.

Kennedy, James, *Conversations on Religion with Lord Byron and Others. Held in Cephalonia, a Short Time Previous to His Lordship's Death* (London: John Murray, 1830).

Kerbaker, M., *Shakespeare e Goethe nei Versi di Vincenzo Monti* (Florence, 1897).

Kernan, Alvin B., 'Don Juan', *The Plot of Satire* (New Haven: Yale University Press, 1965).

King, R. W., 'Italian Influence on English Scholarship and Literature during the Romantic Revival', *MLR*, xx (July 1925) 295–304.

Kirchner, Jane, *The Function of the Persona in the Poetry of Byron*, Salzburg Studies in English Literature: Romantic Reassessment, no. 15 (Austria: University of Salzburg, 1973).

Kitchin, George, *A Survey of Burlesque and Parody in English* (Edinburgh: Oliver & Boyd, 1931).

Klapper, M. Roxana, *The German Literary Influence on Byron*, Salzburg Studies in English Literature: Romantic Reassessment, no. 42 (Austria: University of Salzburg, 1974).

Knight, G. Wilson, 'Byron's Dramatic Prose'. *Byron Foundation Lecture* (University of Nottingham Press, 1953).

——, *Lord Byron: Christian Virtues* (London: Routledge & Kegan Paul, 1952).

Kroeber, Karl, 'Byron: The Adventurous Narrative', *Romantic Narrative Art* (University of Wisconsin, 1960) pp. 135–67.

Kuhns, Oscar, *Dante and the English Poets from Chaucer to Tennyson* (New York: Holt & Co., 1904).

Leavis, Frank Raymond, 'Byron's Satire', *Revaluation: Tradition and Development in English Poetry* (London: Chatto & Windus, 1936) pp. 148–53.

Levi, Eugenia, 'Byron and Petrarch', *The Athenaeum*, 20 July 1901, 95–6.

——, 'Foscolo e Hobhouse, e Lord Byron e di Breme e Monti e Pindemonte', *Rassegna Bibliografica della Letteratura Italiana*, xvii, nos. 10–12 (1909) 301–6.

Levin, Harry, *The Myth of the Golden Age in the Renaissance* (London: Faber, 1970).

Lovell, Ernest, J. Jr., *Byron: The Record of a Quest. Studies in a Poet's Concept and Treatment of Nature* (University of Texas Press, 1949).

——, *His Very Self and Voice: Collected Conversations of Lord Byron* (New York: Macmillan, 1954).

——, 'Irony and Image in Byron's *Don Juan*', *The Major English Romantic Poets: A Symposium in Reappraisal*, eds Clarence D. Thorpe *et al.* (Illinois, 1957) pp. 129–48.

——, 'Byron, Mary Shelley and Madame de Staël, *K–SJ*, xiv (Winter 1965) 13.

McGann, Jerome J., 'Byron's First Tale: An Unpublished Fragment', *KSMB*, xix (1968) 18–23.

——, *'Don Juan' in Context* (London, 1976).

——, *Fiery Dust: Byron's Poetic Development* (University of Chicago Press, 1968).

——, 'Milton and Byron', *KSMB*, xxv (1974) 9–25.

McMahan, Anna, *With Byron in Italy: Being a Selection of the Poems and Letters of Lord Byron Which Have to Do With His Life in Italy from 1816 to 1823* (Chicago, 1906).

Marcabruni, Mario, *Madame de Staël: La Connaissance de l'Italie d'après' Corinne'*, doctoral dissertation (Montpellier, 1910).

Marchand, Leslie A., 'Byron's *Beppo*', *Spectator*, CLXXX (April 1948) 468.

——, 'Lord Byron and Count Alborghetti', *PMLA*, LXIV (December 1949) 976–1007.

——, *Byron: A Biography*, 3 vols (New York, 1957).

——, *Byron: A Portrait* (1971).

——, 'Byron and the Modern Spirit', *The Major English Romantic Poets: A symposium in Reappraisal*, eds Clarence D. Thorpe *et al.* (Illinois, 1957) pp. 162–6.

——, *Byron's Poetry* (Cambridge, Mass.: Harvard University Press, 1968).

——, 'An Unpublished Byron Poem' *The Griffon*, Gennadius Library, no. 6 (Summer 1970) 17–19.

——, 'Narrator and Narration in Don Juan', *K–SJ*, XXV (1976) 26–42.

Marjarum, Edward Wayne, *Byron as Sceptic and Believer* (Princeton University Press, 1938).

Marshall, Roderick, *Italy in English Literature, 1755–1815* (New York: Columbia University Press, 1934).

Marshall, William H., *Byron, Shelley Hunt and 'Liberal'* (Oxford University Press, 1960).

——, 'A Reading of Byron's *Mazeppa*', *MLN*, LXXVI (February 1961) 120–4.

——, *The Structure of Byron's Major Poems* (Philadelphia: University of Pennsylvania Press, 1962).

Marti, M., *Cultura e stile nei poeti giocosi del tempo di Dante* (Pisa, 1953).

Masson, C., *Mémoires Secrets sur la Russie*, 2 vols (London, 1800).

Mayne, Ethel C., *Byron* (London, 1924).

Mead, W. E., 'Italy in English Poetry', *PMLA*, XXIII (1908) 421–70.

Medwin, Thomas, *Medwin's 'Conversations of Lord Byron'*, ed. Ernest J. Lovell Jr. (Princeton University Press, 1969).

Melchiori, Giorgio, 'Byron and Italy', *Byron Foundation Lecture* (University of Nottingham Press, 1958).

Meneghetti, Nazzareno, *Lord Byron a Venezia* (Venice, 1910).

Merivale, John Herman, 'Critical Observations on the Morgante Maggiore', *The Monthly Magazine or British Register* (May 1806) 304–8.

——, 'Remarks on the *Morgante Maggiore* of Luigi Pulci', *The Monthly Magazine or British Register* (July 1807) 439–2.

——, *Orlando in Roncesvalles: A Poem* (London, 1814).

——, *Poems Original and Translated* (London, 1844).

Miller, Barnett, *Leigh Hunt's Relations with Byron, Shelley and Keats* (London: Folcroft Library Editions, 1969).

Miller Edmund, 'Byron's *The Vision of Judgment*, Stanzas xlviii–li', *Explicator*, XXXIII (September 1974) item 4.

Monti, G. and A. (eds), *Lettere inedite del Foscolo, del Giordani e della Signora de Staël a Vincenzo Monti* (Leghorn, 1876).

Moore, Doris Langley, *The Late Lord Byron* (Philadelphia, 1961).

Moore, Thomas, *Letters and Journals of Lord Byron, with Notices of His Life*, 2 vols (London: John Murray, 1830).

——, *The Works of Lord Byron with his Letters and Journals and his Life*, 17 vols (London: John Murray, 1835).

———, *Memoirs, Journal and Correspondence of Thomas Moore*, ed. Lord John Russel, 8 vols (Boston, 1853–56).

———, *France*, 4th edn (London, 1818).

Morgan, Sidney Owenson, Lady, *France*, 4th ed. (London, 1818).

———, *Italy*, 3 vols (London: Henry Colburn, 1821).

Morpurgo, J. E. (ed.), *The Autobiography of Leigh Hunt* (London: Cresset Press, 1949).

Muoni, Guido, *Ludovico de Breme e le prime polemiche intorno a Madame de Staël e al romanticismo in Italia* (Milan, 1902).

Muresu, G., '*L'Orlando Furioso* nella storia della poesia melodrammatica di G. B. Casti', *Rassegna della Letteratura Italiana*, VII (1968) 8–64.

Murray, John (ed.), *Lord Byron's Correspondence, Chiefly with Lady Melbourne, Mr. Hobhouse, The Hon Douglas Kinnaird, and P. B. Shelley*, with Portraits, 2 vols (London: John Murray, 1922).

Natali, Giulio, *Ludovico Ariosto* (Florence, 1966).

Newman, F. H., *The Francesca da Rimini episode in English Literature* (Cambridge, Mass.: Harvard University Press, 1942).

Ogle, Robert B., 'A Byron Contradiction: Some Light on his Italian Study', *Studies in Romanticism*, XII (Winter 1973) 436–42.

Orel, Harold, 'Lord Byron's Debt to the Enlightenment', *Studies in Voltaire and the Eighteenth Century*, ed. Theodore Bestermann, XXVI (1963) 1275–90.

Origo, Iris, *The Last Attachment: The Story of Byron and Teresa Guiccioli as Told in Their Unpublished Letters and Other Family Papers* (London: Murray, 1971).

Palacio, Jean de, 'Byron traducteur et les influences Italiennes', *Rivista di Letterature Moderne e Comparate*, XI (December 1958) 209–30.

Panizzi, Antonio, '*Orlando Innamorato' di Bojardo: 'Orlando Furioso' di Ariosto: With an essay on the Romantic Narrative Poetry of the Italians. Memoirs and Notes by Antonio Panizzi*, 2 vols (London, 1830).

Paolucci, Anne, 'Dante's Satan and Milton's "Byronic Hero" ', *Italica*, XLI (June 1964) 139–49.

Paston George and Peter Quennell (eds), *'To Lord Byron': Feminine Profiles. Based Upon Unpublished Letters, 1807–24* (London: Murray, 1939).

Pellegrini, C., 'Luigi Pulci: L'uomo e l'artista' *Annali della R. Scuola Normale Superiore di Pisa*, XXV (Pisa, 1913).

Polidori, J. W., *The Diary of Dr. John William Polidori 1816, Relating to Byron, Shelley, etc.*, ed. William Michael Rossetti (London, 1911).

Pratt, Willis, *An Italian Pocket Notebook of Lord Byron*, University of Texas Studies in English, XXVII (1949) 195–212.

———, 'Byron and Some current Patterns of Thought, *The Major English Romantic Poets: A Symposium in Reappraisal*, eds Clarence D. Thorpe *et al.* (Illinois, 1957) pp. 149–61.

———, *Lord Byron and His Circle. A Calendar of MSS in the University of Texas Library* (New York, 1965).

Praz, Mario, *La Fortuna di Byron in Inghilterra* (Florence, 1925).

———, *The Romantic Agony* (Oxford University Press, 1933).

———, 'Tasso in Inghilterra', *Comitato per le celebrazioni di Torquato Tasso* (Ferrara, 1954).

———, 'Dante in England', *Forum for Modern Language Studies*, I, no. 2 (1965) 99–116.

————, 'Byron and Foscolo', *Renaissance and Modern Essays, Presented to Vivian de Sola Pinto in Celebration of His Seventieth Birthday*, ed. with the assistance of George Panichas and Allan Rodway (London: Routledge & Kegan Paul, 1966) pp. 101–18.

Pudbres, Anna, 'Lord Byron: The Admirer and Imitator of Alfieri', *Englische Studien*, XXXIII (1903) 40–83.

Quennell, Peter (ed.), *Byron: A Self-Portrait. Letters and Diaries, 1798–1824, with Hitherto Unpublished Letters*, 2 vols (London: John Murray, 1950).

————, 'Byron in Venice', *Horizon*, II (December 1940) 300–17.

Quintana, Ricardo B., 'The Satiric Mood in Byron', *Washington University Studies*, Humanities Series, IX (April 1922) 211–31.

Rajna, P., 'La Rotta di Roncesvalles nella letteratura cavalleresca italiana', *Propugnatore*, IV (1871) 57–8.

Redfern, Joan, 'A Precursor of Byron', *TLS*, 25 July 1936, 620.

Redpath, Theodore, *The Young Romantics and Critical Opinion, 1807–24* (London: Harrap, 1973).

Reiman, Donald H., *The Romantics Reviewed: Contemporary Reviews of British Romantic Writers*, 9 vols (New York: Garland Publishing Co., 1972).

Rice-Oxley, L., *The Poetry of the Anti-Jacobin* (Oxford University Press, 1924).

Ridenour, George M., 'The Style of *Don Juan*', *Yale Studies in English*, 144 (New Haven: Yale university Press, 1960).

————, 'The Mode of Byron's *Don Juan*', *PMLA*, LXXXIX (September 1964) 442–6.

————, 'Byron in 1816: Four Poems from Diodati', *From Sensibility to Romanticism: Essays Presented to Frederick A. Pottle*, eds F. W. Hilles and Harold Bloom (Oxford University Press, 1965).

Rizzo, T. L., *La Poesia Sepolcrale in Italia* (Naples, 1927).

Robinson, Charles E., *Shelley and Byron: the snake and the eagle wreathed in fight* (Baltimore: Johns Hopkins University Press, 1977).

Robinson, Henry Crabb, *Diary, Reminiscences and Correspondence*, ed. Thomas Sadler, 3 vols (London: Macmillan, 1869).

The Correspondence of Henry Crabb Robinson with the Wordsworth Circle (1808–1886), ed. Edith J. Morley, 2 vols (Oxford: The Clarendon Press, 1927).

Robinson, W. W., 'Byron as Poet', *Proceedings of the British Academy*, XLIII (1957) 251–62.

Rogers, Samuel, *Recollections of the Table–Talk of Samuel Rogers*, ed. A. Dyce (London, 1887).

Ross, Janet, 'Byron at Pisa' *The Nineteenth Century*, ed. James Knowles (1891) 753–63.

Rose, William Stewart, *The Court and Parliament of Beasts: A Poem in Seven Cantos, freely translated from the Animali Parlanti of Giambattista Casti* (London: John Murray, 1819).

————, *Thoughts and Recollections by One of the Last Century* (London: Murray, 1825).

Rotondi, G., 'Rileggendo il *Morgante*, *Convivium* (July–August 1936) 381–424.

Rudman, H. W., *Italian Nationalism and English Letters* (Edinburgh, 1940).

Russell, Bertrand, 'Byron', *History of Western Philosophy* (London, 1946).

Russo, Luigi, 'La dissoluzione del mondo cavalleresco: *Il Morgante* di Luigi Pulci', *Belfagor*, I (1952) 36–54.

Rutherford, Andrew, *Byron: A Critical Study* (Edinburgh: Oliver & Boyd, 1965).

————, *Byron: The Critical Heritage Series* (London: Routledge, 1970).

————, 'Byron: A Pilgrim's Progress', *Byron Journal*, II (1974) 6–26.

Sangiorgi, R. B., 'Giambattista Casti's *Novelle Galanti* and Lord Byron's *Beppo*', *Italica*, XXVIII (December 1951) 261–9.

The Poetical Works of Sir Walter Scott, ed. J. Logie Robertson (Oxford University Press, 1951).

Schenk, H. G., *The Mind of the European Romantics: An Essay in Cultural History* (New York, 1966).

Sheppard, L. A. 'Per una edizione londinense degli *Animali Parlanti*', *Giornale Storico della Letteratura Italiana*, XCII (1928) 212.

Short, Clarice, 'The Composition of Hunt's *The Story of Rimini*', *K–SJ*, XXI (1973) 207–18.

Signorini, Alberto, *Individualità e Libertà in Vittorio Alfieri* (Milan, 1972).

Sindonia, Giulio, *Il Casti e il suo pensiero politico negl' 'Animali Parlanti'* (Messina, 1925).

Sismondi, Sismonde de, *Historical View of the Literature of the South of Europe, translated from the original with notes and a life of the author by Thomas Roscoe* (London, 1846).

Smiles, Samuel, *A Publisher and His Friends: Memoirs and Correspondence of the Late John Murray*, 2 vols (London: Murray, 1891).

Smith, Earl C., 'Byron and the Countess Guiccioli', *PMLA*, XLVI (December 1931) 1221–7.

Steffan, Truman G., 'Byron at Work on Canto I of *Don Juan*', *MP*, XLIV (February 1947) 141–64.

————, 'The Token-Web, the Sea-Sodom and Canto I of *Don Juan*', *UTSE* (1947) 108–68.

————, 'The Devil a Bit of Our *Beppo*', *PQ*, XXXII (April 1953) 154–71.

Steffan, Truman G. and W. Pratt (eds), *Byron's 'Don Juan' A Variorum Edition*, 4 vols (University of Texas Press, 1957).

Steiner, George, *Language and Silence* (London, 1967).

Stendhal, Count de (pseud. for Henry Beyle), *Rome, Naples, and Florence in 1817. English translation. Sketches of the Present State of Society, Manners, Arts, Literature, etc.* (London: Henry Colburn, 1818).

Strout, Alan (ed.), *John Bull's Letter to Lord Byron* (University of Oklahoma Press, 1947).

Sutherland, James, *English Satire* (Cambridge University Press, 1958).

Symonds, Arthur, *The Romantic Movement in English Poetry* (London: Constable & Co., 1909).

Tennant, W., '*Anster Fair' and other Poems* (Edinburgh, 1838).

Thorpe, Clarence C., Carlos Baker and Bennett Weaver (eds), *The Major English Romantic Poets: A Symposium in Reappraisal* (Illinois University Press, 1957).

Thorslev, Peter L., *The Byronic Hero: Types and Prototypes* (Minneapolis: University of Minnesota Press, 1962).

————, 'The Romantic Mind is Its Own Place', *Comparative Literature*, XV (Summer 1963) 250–68.

Tooke, William, *Life of Catherine II, Empress of Russia*, 3 vols (London, 1800).

Toynbee, Paget, *Dante in English Literature from Chaucer to Carey*, 2 vols (London: Methuen, 1909).

Tribolati, Felice, 'Lord Byron a Pisa', *Nuova Antologia*, XXII (1874) 631–55.

Trueblood, Paul Graham, *The Flowering of Byron's Genius; Studies in Byron's 'Don Juan'* (California: Stanford University Press, 1945).

Van den Bergh, Herman, *Giambattista Casti: L'homme et l'oeuvre* (Amsterdam, 1951).

Van der Beets, Richard, 'A note on Dramatic Necessity and the Incest Motif in Manfred', *N&Q*, ccix (January 1964) 26–8.

Viglione, F., *L'Italia nel pensiero degli scrittori inglesi* (Milan, 1946).

Vigo, Pietro, 'L'Abate Casti e un' Edizione Clandestina del *Poema Tartaro*', *Rassegna Bibliografica*, xv (1907) 184–6.

Vincent, E. R., *Foscolo's 'Dei Sepolcri': The Commemoration of the Dead*: an inaugural lecture (Cambridge University Press, 1936).

———, *Byron, Hobhouse and Foscolo* (New York: Macmillan, 1949).

———, *Ugo Foscolo: An Italian in Regency England* (Cambridge University Press, 1953).

———, *The Commemoration of the Dead in Foscolo's 'Dei Sepoleri'*: an inaugural lecture (Cambridge University Press, 1936).

Volpi, G., *'La Divina Commedia nel Morgante* di L. Pulci', *Giornale Dantesco*, xi (1903) 170–5.

Voltaire, *Dictionnarie philosophique*, ed. Garnier (Paris, 1964).

Walker, Hugh, *English Satire and Satirists* (London: Dent, 1925).

Waller, R. D., *The Monks and the Giants by John Hookham Frere* (Manchester: The University Press, 1926).

Walton, Francis R., 'Byron's Lines on John William Rizzo Hoppner', *K–SJ*, xxi–xxii (1972–3) 40–2.

Watson, George, 'The Accuracy of Lord Byron', *Critical Quarterly*, xvii (Summer 1975) 135–48.

Watts, Alaric, 'Lord Byron's Plagiarisms!', *Literary Gazette*, no. 214 (24 February 1821) 121–4.

Weinstein, Leo, *The Metamorphoses of Don Juan*, Stanford Studies in Language and Literature, no. 18 (Stanford University Press, 1959).

West, Paul (ed.), *Byron and the Spoiler's Art* (London: Chatto & Windus, 1960).

———, 'Byronic Romance and Nature's Frailty', *Dalhousie Review*, xxxix (Summer 1959) 219–29.

———, 'Byron and the World of Things: An Ingenious Disregard', *KSMB* xi (1960) 21–32.

———, *Byron: A Collection of Critical Essays* (New Jersey, 1963).

Wiel, Taddeo, 'Lord Byron e il suo soggiorno a Venezia', *L'Ateneo Veneto* (Venice, 1905) 275–328.

Wiener, Harold S., 'Literary Sources of Byron's "Turkish Tales"', *Nineteenth Century Studies* (Cornell University Press, 1940).

Wilkie, Brian, 'Byron and the Epic of Negation', *Romantic Poets and Epic Tradition* (The University of Wisconsin Press, 1965).

Woodring, Carl, *Politics in English Romantic Poetry* (Cambridge, Mass., 1970).

Zaboklicki, Krzysztof, 'La Russia Cateriniana nel poema Tartaro di G. B. Casti', *Giornale Storico della Letteratura Italiana*, cxlix (1972) 363–86.

———, *La Poesia narrativa di G. B. Casti* (University of Warsaw, 1974).

Zacchetti, Corrado, *Lord Byron e l'Italia* (Palermo, 1919).

Zanco, A., 'L'Alfierismo di Byron', *Shakespeare in Russia* (Turin, 1945) pp. 143–64.

Index

References contained in notes have not been indexed.